THE *DO NO HARM* DOG TRAINING®
AND BEHAVIOR HANDBOOK

Featuring the Hierarchy of Dog Needs®

Linda Michaels

Front Cover: ©[cynoclub]/Adobe Stock
Back Cover: Linda Michaels with Ambassador Journey Wolfdog, Courtesy of Julie
All Other Images: Images ©/Adobe Stock

FIRST EDITION

Publisher's Cataloging-in-Publication data

Names: Michaels, Linda, author.
Title: The do no harm dog training and behavior handbook : featuring the hierarchy of dog needs / Linda Michaels, M.A., Psychology.
Description: Includes bibliographical references and index. | San Diego, CA: Do No Harm Dog Training, 2022.
Identifiers: LCCN: 2021922892 | ISBN: 978-1-7322537-0-4 (print) | 978-1-7322537-1-1 (ebook)
Subjects: LCSH Dogs--Training. | Dogs--Psychology. | BISAC PETS / Dogs / Training
Classification: LCC QL785 .M53 2022 | DDC 636.7/08/3--dc23

Library of Congress Control Number: 2021922892

Publishing Company
Do No Harm Dog Training

ABOUT THE AUTHOR

Linda Michaels, MA, Psychology, creator of the Hierarchy of Dog Needs® is rated one of the top ten dog trainers in the United States by *Top Ten Magazine* and other acclaimed reviewers. Linda holds a master's degree in Experimental Psychology (with Honors) and conducted laboratory research in behavioral neurobiology, earning the merit-based University Scholar Award from the Psychology Department of San Diego State University. Her unique combination of scientific training and hands-on experience with dogs, wolfdogs, and foxes, creates a bridge between the worlds of research, dog trainers and pet parents, as demonstrated in her presentation at the Pet Professional Guild (PPG) inaugural summit: "Understanding Research: Making the Case for Force-free Training" (Michaels, 2015a).

Linda is a staunch advocate for force-free, dog-friendly dog training. She worked with some of the most difficult behavior cases at the progressive San Diego Humane Society and SPCA for five years. Before becoming a private practitioner and pioneer for positive force-free training and non-aversive collars, Linda was the behavioral consultant and lead trainer for an upscale pet store in Del Mar, California. She was the first professional behavioral advisor for the *Wolf Education Project* in Julian, California, and has helped train some of the famed Russian Belyaev foxes at the *Judith A. Bassett Canid Education and Conservation Center* in Santa Ysabel, California. Working with aggressive domesticated dogs and typically people-shy wolfdogs convinced Linda that using punitive behavior modification methods are outdated and counterproductive to treating aggression with potentially dangerous animals. Linda is an outspoken animal welfare advocate opposing dominance-based dog training methods and aversive "training" collars that have been shown to be principally ineffective, unsafe, and inhumane. Collar devices designed to cause pain and harsh training methods are often a cause, not a cure of aggression.

The carefully crafted *Hierarchy of Dog Needs* (HDN)—*Standards of Care and Best Force-free Practices*, targeting wellness and force-free emotional and behavioral modification guidance, catapulted Linda into a leadership role in the dog training field. The HDN closes the door on the perceived need and advisability of using punitive or aversive methods to train our dogs, offering clear, easy-to-use, and *Do No Harm*/force-free guidance. The Hierarchy of Dog Needs has been translated into ten languages. Linda pioneered her emotional and behavioral modification *Do No Harm* practice onto social media platforms by grounding The Hierarchy of Dog Needs as the ethical and progressive standard in dog care and training.

Linda is a sought-after speaker, certified veterinary assistant and served as the flagship Southern California Victoria Stilwell Positively Dog Training (VSPDT) licensed behavior consultant. She is published in *BARKS from the Guild,* the Pet Professional Guild (PPG) international trade magazine, and has authored numerous articles and behavior columns which are included in *The Do No Harm Dog Training® and Behavior Handbook.* Linda appears as a featured expert on Huffington Post Live, Wolf Dog Radio (Michaels, 2015b), and as a special guest on the Pet Professional Guild World Services podcast. She served on the advisory board for the Art for Barks charity, in Rancho Santa Fe, California. As founder and head administrator of the wildly popular *Do No Harm Dog Training* social media group, force-free advocates from around the world gather to share resources, solve dog behavior problems, and promote animal welfare. She is an affiliate expert of the International School of Canine Psychology (ISCP). Linda is a certified fear, aggression, and reactivity consultant with FAR Beyond Dog Training, focusing on both the behavioral and psychological aspects of dog behavior that often mirror human psychological conditions, such as fear, separation/attachment disorders, and aggression. She is also a Pet Professional Guild Certified Professional Canine Trainer—Accredited (PCT-A). Her private practice serves select clients in Southern California from La Jolla to Beverly Hills helping dogs learn, recover, and thrive.

Linda is currently planning speaking events and international tours based upon the *Do No Harm Dog Training and Behavior Handbook.*

Author, Speaker, Creator of The Hierarchy of Dog Needs®
www.DoNoHarmDogTraining.com

PRAISE FOR THE
DO NO HARM DOG TRAINING®
AND BEHAVIOR HANDBOOK

This book is a champion for the ethical and respectful care all dogs deserve. Whether just curious, or a professional, if your life touches a dog's life, this book provides comprehensive and essential information to ensure the needs of dogs are met, backed up by the latest scientific knowledge. From diet to behaviour problems, and everything in-between, this is an excellent resource, in fact it should be compulsory reading! Those of us on the front line, dealing directly with clients and their dogs, spend a lot of energy dispelling training myths and rectifying the harm that certain techniques can cause to dog-human relationships. To have this resource, which applies psychology that is not harmful to the individual dog's mental or physical well-being, is extremely useful.

- Katrina Ward, DVM, Member of the Australia and New Zealand College of Veterinary Scientists (veterinary behavior)

Linda has created an amazingly comprehensive, scientifically accurate, ethical and compassionate gift to the world of dogs and the humans who love them. The *Do No Harm* contribution to the unregulated dog training profession will give much-needed support to the training and behavior professionals who already practice force-free protocols, invaluable guidance to dog owners who want the best relationships possible with their dogs, and, hopefully, a hefty leg up to those animal care professionals who are still on the path to dog-friendly handling, care and training methods.

- Pat Miller, Training Editor for *The Whole Dog Journal,* author of seven force free dog training and behavior books, earned a Lifetime Achievement Award from The Association of Professional Dog Trainers, named "One of the People Who Have Changed the Dog World" by *Dog Fancy Magazine*

The dedication at the beginning of this book speaks to its entire content and relevance to the world of pets and the progression we must strive for. This book has an abundance of knowledge to support any and all who want to journey into the practice of force-free pet training and care. Set with realistic boundaries and easy to follow guidelines it is a fabulous resource for anyone that interacts with dogs. Whether you are a pet professional, pet owner or one who works in or around the pet owner community, this book provides the much-needed tools and resources to help you and your canine community thrive together.

~ Niki Tudge, MBA, PCBC-A, CDBC, CDT, Founder and president of The Pet Professional Guild, principal author of *A Model for Raising the Bar to Protect Professionals,* Founder and president of DogSmith and DogNostics Career Center

Linda Michaels' *Hierarchy of Dog Needs,* adapted from Abraham Maslow's *Hierarchy of Needs,* is the single most important modern guide to ensuring that every aspect of our dogs' lives is the best it can be. This ground-breaking book describes in detail how to meet all needs, how to teach dogs using force-free, science-based methods, and how to deal with any behavior issues that may arise. *Do No Harm* is a must-read for every dog caregiver.

~ Lisa Tenzin-Dolma, Founder and Director of The International School for Canine Psychology & Behaviour Ltd. (ISCP)

It's not just that we love our dogs, but that our dogs Need our love. Combining compassion and science, Linda Michaels offers a roadmap into our dogs' fundamental needs. This book is a how-to choose, care, and train your dog with respect and love. Get ready to be enlightened by this thoughtful read.

~ Jennifer Cattet, PhD, Psychology, Author of *Selecting and Training Your Service Dog,* specializing in Animal Behavior (Ethology), research contributor to ongoing studies in the field of medical detection of diabetes, seizures, and cancer in dogs.

Complimenting the gold standards in animal welfare, the Freedoms, Five Domains and Five Needs, the *Do No Harm* ethic precedent, adapted from Maslow's work, adds freedom from abuse in dog training. In this breakthrough volume, an easy-to-follow training roadmap demonstrates how to fill our dogs' essential needs while ensuring mental well-being and positive experience. Bravo!

~ Denise O'Moore, Adip CBM, Chair of the Association of INTODogs, Certified Animal and Canine Behaviourist, Director of *Mighty Dog Graphics*

The Do No Harm Dog Training and Behaviour Handbook by Linda Michaels, MA, Psychology, covers some of the most important Five Needs with regard to the Welfare of Canines as outlined in the United Kingdom's "Codes of Practice for the Welfare of Dogs." It is a pleasure to see both force-free training and the welfare needs of a dog combined in one book.

~ *Jan E. Eachus,* Royal Society for the Prevention of Cruelty to Animals (RSPCA, UK) Chief Inspector (Retired)

Linda Michaels' new book provides a comprehensive science-backed guide to meeting your dog's needs from nutrition to training. Linda draws on her education in psychology and expertise in training dogs and wolfdogs to help you prevent behavior problems or solve existing issues using effective and humane methods. A great read for any dog lover.

~ *Rebekah Hudson, MPH, Public Health Biostatistics,* Founder of Canine Research Studies and cofounder of *Force Free Oregon*

DEDICATION

To our passionate and unfailingly devoted force-free dog trainers, pet professionals, and pet parents who have worked so hard to meet the challenge of the day to make this a better world for our dogs.

We tried to look away but couldn't. We saw the frightened, emotionally abandoned dogs who had been shocked, choked, pronged, and beaten down . . . some by cruelty and some with domination in the name of training. And in their eyes we saw bewilderment, fear, and an unspeakable sadness. We felt a deep sense of helplessness and cried out to the universe, "God, why don't you do something?" And god responded reminding us, "I did do something. I sent you . . . and you . . . and you."

~ Linda Michaels, MA, Psychology

TABLE OF CONTENTS

About the Author iii

Praise for *The Do No Harm Dog Training® and Behavior Handbook*. v

Dedication ix

Table of Contents xi

Foreword by Marc Bekoff, PhD xix

Preface. xxi

Acknowledgements xxv

Introduction—How This Handbook is Organized xxvii

PART 1
THE HIERARCHY OF DOG NEEDS® 1

The Hierarchy of Dog Needs [Pyramid Graphic]. 2

Standards of Care and Best Force-free Practices 3

    i. The Do No Harm Ethical Codes 5

    ii. Behavioral Models. 8

    iii. Maslow's Hierarchy of Needs—The Third Force in Behavior 10

For the Pet Professional. 12

    How to Use the Do No Harm Dog Training and Behavior Handbook in
Practice and Business. 12

    Examples for the Pet Professional 14

    Future Directions in Research, Law, and the Role of Celebrities 16

Chapter 1
Biological Needs 19

    Proper Nutrition 20

        Feeding a Biologically Appropriate, Nutritionally Balanced Diet 20

    Fresh Water 24

Sufficient Exercise 25
   Types of Exercise for Life Stages 26
Sufficient Air 29
   Airway Injuries from Choke and Prong Collars 30
   Brachycephalic Obstructive Airway Syndrome (BOAS) 31
Sufficient Sleep 32
   Dog vs. Human Sleep Patterns 34
Indoor Shelter 36
   Outdoor Emotional and Behavioral Risks 37
   Parasites, Insects and Wildlife 37
   Snake Aversion Training Using Shock 39
Safety 40
   Poisons, Toxins, and Household Hazards 41
   Swimming Practice and Drowning 42
Temperature Control 44
   Hyperthermia, Also Known as Heatstroke 44
   Hypothermia 46
Gentle Grooming 47
   Health Benefits of Grooming 48
   Nail Trims Are a Must 48
   Outdated and Dangerous Grooming Standards 49
Gentle Veterinary Care 51
   Benefits of Regular Veterinary Care 52
   Veterinarians and Behavior 53
   AAHA Guidelines for Canine Behavior Management 54
   Integrative Veterinary Care 57
   Dental Care 59
In Memory of Dr. Sophia Yin, DVM, MS 60

Chapter 2
Emotional Needs 62
Security 64
   Attachment and Abandonment 64
Love 65
   Oxytocin, fMRI's, and Genetics 65
Trust 68
   Stress and Distress 69
Consistency 70
   Predictability and Routines 70
Benevolent Leadership 70
   Dogs Have the Brain of a Toddler 70

Chapter 3

Social Needs. 72

  Bonding with People. 73

    Best of Friends?. 74

  Bonding with Dogs—Dog-Dog Bonding 75

    Critical Periods of Learning from Others During Development 75

  Play. 76

    Fair Play 77

Chapter 4

Cognitive Needs—Mental Events Are Causal. 79

  Choice. 81

    Consent. 82

  Novelty. 83

    Types of Enrichment. 83

  Problem-solving 84

    Intelligence 86

Chapter 5

Force-free Training Needs—*Do No Harm* **Management and Learning**. 87

Best Force-Free Practices from the Hierarchy of Dog Needs 87

  Defining Force-free Dog Training 88

  Choose Any or All Methods 89

    Management. 92

      Preventing Undesirable Behavior. 92

    Antecedent Modification. 93

      Modifying Stimuli That Precede a Trigger 93

    Positive Reinforcement (+R) 94

      Increasing Frequency Using Rewards. 94

    Differential Reinforcement (DR) of DRI, DRA, DRO, DRL 96

      Redirecting Undesirable Behavior 96

      Incompatible, Alternate, Other and Lower Rate Reinforcement . . 96

    Classical and Counterconditioning 98

      Creating Positive Associations and Modifying

      Negative Associations 98

    Desensitization 100

      Systematic Graduated Exposure. 100

    Premack Principle 102

      Preferred Behavior Can Reinforce Less Preferred Behavior. 102

    Social Learning—Also Known as Observational Learning

    (Bandura, 1965) 103

      Imitation, Emulation, Social Facilitation and

      Emotional Contagion 103

PART 2
SETTING YOUR DOG UP FOR SUCCESS

.... 105

Chapter 6
How to Find a Dog That Fits Your Lifestyle *Before* You Fall in Love....... 107
    Adopting a Dog or Puppy.................................. 109
    Avoiding Puppy Mills.................................... 110
    Selecting a Good Breeder and a Healthy Puppy.............. 111
    Preparing Your Home for Your New Dog.................... 113

Chapter 7
How to Find a Good Dog Trainer—Buyer Be Wary............. 114
    Harnesses and Leashes................................... 116
    Using Food as a Reward.................................. 117

Chapter 8
How to Find a Good Veterinarian and Groomer................ 119
    Gentle Veterinary Care................................... 120
        Vaccinations and Socialization Go Together............ 120
        How to Choose a Veterinarian...................... 121
        Home Practice.................................... 122
        Your First Veterinary Appointment.................. 124
    Gentle Grooming Care.................................... 125
        How to Choose a Groomer and Salon................. 126
        Home Practice.................................... 127
        Your First Grooming Appointment................... 129

Chapter 9
Socialization.. 131
    Avoiding Problems and Heartache.......................... 131
    Dog-Dog Play Rules and Manners......................... 133
    Dog Park and Dog Beach Safety Tips...................... 134

Chapter 10
Enrichment and Grazing Games™........................... 137
    "Living in a Human World".............................. 138
    Scavenging Changes Emotions and Behavior................ 139
    The Sensory Garden..................................... 141

Chapter 11
Dog Body Language—Observe and "Listen" First............. 142
    Flooding and Tonic Immobility........................... 144

PART 3
GOOD MANNERS AND BASIC TRAINING

. . . . 147

Chapter 12
Housetraining 151
   Using a Plan Your Dog Can Easily Understand 152
   The Top 10 Do's and Don'ts for Successful Housetraining. 152

Chapter 13
No Bite! and Chewing 157
   Puppy and Adult Dog Mouthing—Teaching "Kiss-Kiss" 157
   Chew This, Not That! 159

Chapter 14
Training Techniques 162
   Important Concepts in Training 163
   Capturing Behavior. 164
   Luring Behavior with Food 165
   Shaping Behavior 166
   The Premack Principle 167

Chapter 15
Trainer "Secrets" 169
   Real-life Reward Reinforcement 169
   Removing the Lure 171
   Linking Behaviors 171
   Alternate Reward Reinforcement. 171
   Random Reward Reinforcement 171
   Clicker Training Option 172

Chapter 16
Basic Skills 175
   Greetings and Jumping 175
      Greeting You and Visitors 175
      No Jump. 176
   Sit. 178
   Down and Settle Down. 179
   Wait/Stay 182
   Come 183
      Name Response. 184
      Lightning Recall aka "Come" Long Distance. 184
      Whistle Training Lightning Recall. 187

Leash-Walking. 187
    Leash-Walking Equipment 188
    Leash-Walking Skills 189

PART 4
WHEN THINGS GO WRONG
. . . . 193

Chapter 17
Aggression Prevention, Assessment, and Treatment
. . . . 195
    Greeting Protocols. 197
    Introducing a New Dog into Your Home 198
    Assessment 199
    Red Flags. 200
    What Behavior Consultants Should Provide in Aggression Cases. 202
        Assessment Intake Questionnaire for Behavior Consultations 203
        Functional Analysis. 214
        Liability Contract Template for Behavior Consultants. 216
        Veterinary Behavioral Report for Behavior Consultants. 218
    Management of Triggers at Home, At the Veterinarian,
    and At the Groomer 218
    Desensitization and Counterconditioning Techniques. 220
    Frustration Reactivity 222
    Realistic Expectations 222
    Human Aggression Treatment. 223
        The "Red Zone" Dog Myth 224
        DO NOT list for Family, Friends, and Visitors 224
    Dog-Dog Aggression Treatment 225
        Walks—Working Below the Threshold of Reactivity. 226
        How to Break Up a Dogfight 227
        Bites 229
    Sibling Rivalry—Multi-dog Household Aggression Treatment 229
        Prevention and Management. 230
        The No Jealousy Game 231
        Open Bar/Closed Bar 231
    Resource Guarding 232
        Handfeeding. 234
        Food Bowls 234
        Trade Up, and Drop 235
        Dog Property Laws 235

Chapter 18
Allergies 237
   Environmental Allergens 238
   Fleas 239
   Diet 239
   Preventing Infection 240

Chapter 19
Barking, Barking, Barking 241
   Why Dogs Bark 242
   How to Decrease Barking 242
   What *Not* to Do 244

Chapter 20
Dogs and Babies 245
   When You Become Pregnant 247
   Bringing Baby Home 249

Chapter 21
Fear 251
   What Drives Fear? 252
   Treatment 254

Chapter 22
Separation Anxiety 255
   Assessment 258
   Separation Anxiety Treatment 261
      Doggy Enrichment Land™ Containment—
      The Enhanced Environment 262
      Providing Comfort Items 263
      Separation Trials 265
      Using Food in Treatment 266
      Predeparture Desensitization and Counterconditioning Triggers 267
      Changing Your Routines—Arrivals and Departures 269

References 271
Online Resources 289
Photo Credits 291
Index 293

FOREWORD

by Marc Bekoff, PhD

Written from a passionate and compassionate point of view, this compelling teaching tool shows readers how to use force-free training to lovingly teach the heartbeats at our feet. The author's notable background in academia and research, and her practice in the area of emotional and behavioral modification, shaped by her years of experience in the shelter world that fueled her drive, provide the platform for a distinctive contribution to our field to improve the welfare of our beloved dogs.

Seizing the moment to embed the professional *Do No Harm* ethic into dog training makes this book uniquely important in helping us to meet the physical and the emotional needs of dogs. My extensive studying and writing about animal emotions, both in my books and for *Psychology Today* where I interviewed the author, hint at our mutual understanding of how imperative it is to fully recognize and respect the emotional lives of dogs. One of the powerful messages of this book is how similar we are across species, yet how dogs are separate and singularly rare unto themselves. Each dog must be viewed and treated as the unique individual they are. This training compendium supports *The Hierarchy of Dog Needs* with scientific evidence highlighting standards of care and best force-free practices and includes actionable steps for teaching our four-legged companions. As an ethologist devoted to the better understanding and treatment of dogs, I was more than happy to add my name and endorsement to *The Hierarchy of Dog Needs* and to this accompanying handbook.

In an unregulated dog training industry, this volume provides a timely and much needed alternative to existing teaching paradigms. It is written for all dog lovers. It may be used to train and solve problems with your own dog at home, or as a framework of principles and practices to present to pet professionals. This is how our dogs would choose to interact with us, and what most dog lovers would choose to practice . . . if they only knew how.

Learning to understand dogs through their body language fosters a style of communication that gives rise to and honors the human-animal bond. As more and more animal lovers have become aware, to truly thrive dogs not only need to have their biological requirements and primary needs fully met, but they also need to feel safe and secure in our relationships with them.

The Do No Harm Dog Training and Behavior Handbook belongs in the library of every dog lover, on the top shelf, thumb-worn from regular use. It shows us how to easily nurture and enrich our dog's lives, returning the love and acceptance our dogs so readily provide to us. The author fascinates the reader with many little-known facts about our dogs that serve to enhance the bond we all seek with our beloved, yet mysterious family companions. It engenders trust and love with those who speak to us through these pages.

Marc Bekoff, PhD
marcbekoff.com

Dr. Marc Bekoff is Professor Emeritus of Ecology and Evolutionary Biology at the University of Colorado, Boulder. He is also the co-founder with Jane Goodall of the *Ethologists for the Ethical Treatment of Animals*. In 2000 he was awarded the Exemplar Award from the Animal Behavior Society for major long-term contributions to the field of animal behavior. Dr. Bekoff is the author of more than 1000 scientific and popular essays and 30 books about many different aspects of animal behavior, behavioral ecology, cognitive ethology (the study of animal minds), and compassionate conservation. His two latest books are *Canine Confidential: Why Dogs Do What They Do* and *Unleashing Your Dog: A Field Guide to Giving Your Canine Companion the Best Life Possible*, Marc Bekoff and Jessica Pierce.

PREFACE

This book is written for our dogs, who cannot speak for themselves and for the people who love them. My passion for moving the dog training field forward in the face of difficult obstacles inspired me to create a wellness and training guide embedded with the *Do No Harm* ethical code. A straightforward, force-free, *Do No Harm* alternative to the traditional teaching model is needed in the unregulated dog training industry.

As an ardent animal lover, canine behavior modification professional, and animal welfare advocate, I felt compelled to write *The Do No Harm Dog Training® and Behavior Handbook* to support The Hierarchy of Dog Needs® (HDN) guide. Given the strong movement toward human-animal bonding, there is a societal imperative to develop a more dog-friendly, dog-needs based model of care and training. Too often, basic needs are either not met or are under met. The *Do No Harm* approach make dogs lives better because it is truly dog-friendly, safer, has longer lasting results; moreover, it is more effective when compared to punitive training.

The Hierarchy of Dog Needs concept as a wholistic system of care had been brewing within me for many years. I dreamt about it a lot. I was in a rather unique position of responsibility that spurred me to speak out on behalf of the dogs. My disappointment and frustration with the dog training field's direction toward shock, prong, choke collar devices, and other punitive methods inspired me to sit down and find a way to get my ideas into an easily understood visual form. My academic background in experimental psychology and learning, graduate training and research in behavioral neurobiology, plus hands-on experience training dogs and wolfdogs, prepared me to create a one-page teaching tool in the form of a handout that is easy-to-understand and easy-to-use. The development of The Hierarchy of Dog Needs came to life through considerable trial and tribulation and some tears. The *Do No Harm* ethic grows naturally from The Hierarchy of Dog Needs and expresses the ideology and practices within this book.

After decades of wading through the ocean of materials available on dog training, I decided to write my own manual where specific items of interest are easy to find for both pet parents and instructors. In this volume, The Hierarchy of Dog Needs combines training with a practical behavior and care handbook intended for educators, trainers, and pet parents. *The Do No Harm Dog Training and Behavior Handbook* looks at training not only from the trainer's perspective but also from the dog's point of view springing from my deep love of dogs. Focusing on our dogs' needs and non-punitive training methods, my mission is to enhance the well-being of our dogs through pet parent education and by providing pet professionals with teaching tools they can easily access and explain to their students.

For an interview in *Psychology Today* magazine entitled, "A Hierarchy of Dog Needs, Abraham Maslow Meet the Mutts," Dr. Mark Bekoff reached out to me to learn more about the development and application of the hierarchy, wherein the foundations for this book began to take form. The teaching tools in this handbook encourage force-free professionals to refer to and support other force-free professionals by supporting them in seeking direction from experts guided by the science of animal behavior. Animal Behavior PhD, Marc Bekoff, and canid research scientist, Simon Gadbois, PhD were some of the earliest endorsers of The Hierarchy of Dog Needs.

The *Do No Harm Dog Training and Behavior Handbook* was originally designed as my personal guide for teaching basic manners classes and later as the template for my own customized private behavior consultations problem-solving. The manual then evolved into a trainer's guide. For dog services-related professionals, this handbook provides an inside look at dog behavior and emotional and behavioral modification. This handbook is a practical guide for *any* dog-related professional seeking force-free solutions for specific problems. The interest from pet parents is so great that it became a handbook for anyone interested in learning about what makes our dogs "tick" and how we can learn to communicate with our dogs in a dog-friendly language our dogs can understand. This handbook also includes some of my updated and revised published articles.

The Hierarchy of Dog Needs, making no apologies for embracing protective ethics concerning our beloved dogs, was first unveiled in my presentation at the inaugural summit of the Pet Professional Guild, "Understanding Research: Making the Case for Force-free Dog Training," where it was enthusiastically received.

As a wolfdog trainer and an aggression specialist, I became further convinced that there is no justification for using collar devices designed to punish and cause pain; nor for using dominance, fear-inducing methods to train animals. Barring neurological damage or deficits, I have yet to see a case in my behavioral consulting practice that could not be effectively treated using non-aversive methods. Indeed, so-called *red zone* dogs are frequently ultra-sensitive to punitive training and become worse, not better, when the drive to aggress is not lessened but suppressed.

Together, we seek to move forward with sensible standardization of the dog training industry including theoretical and skill competency requirements, consumer transparency in advertising, professional accountability based squarely on humane treatment, and strengthening of the animal welfare laws in the United States and across the world.

My goal with this handbook is to shed light on some of the mysteries of dog behavior while providing practical step-by-step protocols with explanations and applications on topics that trainers need and want to explore. My hope is that The Hierarchy of Dog Needs and this handbook speaks in some way to every dog, every pet-related professional, and every pet parent. It was written with great love for our most true and best friends.

ACKNOWLEDGEMENTS

There are so many educators, researchers, animal welfare advocates, and colleagues to thank, without whom this work would not be possible. I stand on the shoulders of many classic and contemporary greats. My sincere thanks to the trainers, veterinarians and other professionals in dog-related fields worldwide who have endorsed and pioneered The Hierarchy of Dog Needs.

I would like to give special thanks to: Philip Langlais, PhD, Dean of the College of Sciences and well-published principal investigator at the Neurobiology Laboratory where I conducted research at San Diego State University for his brilliant guidance and great patience as my research mentor; Marc Bekoff, PhD, for being the first scientist to fully endorse the Hierarchy of Dog Needs and for the interview in *Psychology Today* magazine, helping to give me the confidence to publish; to Simon Gadbois, PhD, canid researcher, for his early and ongoing support and feedback for the project; to Sunny Elmore and April Bove-Rothwell for their research assistance gathering evidence to help make the new paradigm in dog training a reality; to Jen Bergren for editing, graphics and her multi-tasking genius; to Denise O'Moore for volunteering to administrate the *Do No Harm Dog Training®* group at a critical period helping to make it a success and important resource; to Francine Miller for encouraging me again and again to get into action to share my written work and for personal support during trying times; to Noelle Bahnmiller, Dr. Marnie Elam, and Lynn Tepper-Kelley for steadfastly being there, as only true friends will be; to my beloved mother for all she has done to support me in trying times, to Katherine Porter, Jeanine Kunkel-Jones, Rebekah Hudson, Laurie Delgatto-Whitten, and Diane Garrod for copy editing and feedback; to all of the *Do No Harm Dog Training* administrators, moderators and members past and present who had faith in the *Do No Harm* projects and who work worked tirelessly to help change the world for the better for our dogs; and to the Pet Professional Guild for giving the force-free community an organization we can count upon, and giving me the opportunity to unveil The Hierarchy of Dog Needs at the inaugural PPG summit. We sincerely thank our international friends and partners and every pet professional who helped with translations of The Hierarchy of Dog

Needs. Each translation has been a labor of love. I thank you with all of my heart. Each of you has had a profound impact on the trajectory of my life's work and this book. Truly, without you, sharing this message with dog lovers everywhere would not have been possible.

INTRODUCTION

A worldwide sea change in dog training that speaks for those who cannot speak for themselves is long overdue. The voices taking a clear stand against pain-based collar devices and aversive control methods masquerading as dog training grow louder.

The Hierarchy of Dog Needs defines *Standards of Care and Best Practices* in force-free training. Attending to animal welfare needs *and* exclusively force-free methods are setting the gold standard in emotional and behavioral modification and training. The ethical code embedded within *The Do No Harm Dog Training® and Behavior Handbook* and the *Hierarchy of Dog Needs®* (HDN) is grounded in animal welfare principles and dog-friendly dog training. By virtue of providing ethical standards and practices guidelines in the dog training field and industry, we hope to help lead the way, making life easier and more joyful for our dogs and the people who love them.

In developing a new force-free model of best practices, we no longer leave the door open for aversive/punitive measures in dog training. The extant training models focus largely on quadrants in learning theory yet sadly, have too often been misused as a rationale and justification for the application of punitive methods in training. The ubiquitous misapplication of methods in an unregulated industry is the problem. Doing psychological or physical harm to a captive dog points to a lack of skill and competence on the part of the trainer. There is no justification for harsh treatment or training with dogs, or any animal for that matter, unless one's life or safety is in immediate danger. The methods detailed in the HDN may be used in any order without risk to the dog: *Do No Harm* methods never asks or directs the pet parent to hurt their dog psychologically or physically. We seek to "do no harm" physically or psychologically to dogs under our care and training at all times.

Shock collar training is a serious animal welfare concern in the United States and across the globe. Frequently, animal abuse masquerades as dog training. How can the average pet parent be expected to make a well-informed decision with regard to behavior modification tools when so many dog trainers, misinformed professionals, and manufacturers of shock products misrepresent the true nature of their effects?

There is simply no place for shock, prong, choke, or other aversive devices in companion animal training.

In "Why Shock is Not Behavior Modification," principal investigator Dr. Karen Overall (2013), editor of the Journal of Veterinary Behavior states, "The use of shock is not treatment for pets with behavioral concerns" (p. 111). The popular myth that shock "saves lives" has no evidence to support it. Indeed, nothing could be further from the truth. A hypothetical fallacy with the alternative of either shocking a dog or euthanizing a dog is a patently false dichotomy commonly posed by shock proponents. Dr. Overall states unequivocally, "The use of shock does not bring dogs back from the brink of euthanasia; instead, it may send them there" (p. 111). Using punitive methods or devices in training can cause an increase in anxiety that often leads to further behavioral problems, resulting in pet parents relinquishing their animals to overflowing shelters. If progressive zoos are successful in changing the behavior of the animals in their care using force-free training methods alone, behavioral consultants, trainers and other professionals, ought to do the same for our pet dogs.

In addition, dog bites are an increasingly grave public safety issue, making dog-training methods a public health concern. Bite incidents resulting from the administration of shock are not uncommon—it is well documented in scientific literature that inflicting pain is a cause of aggressive behavior.

The Hierarchy of Dog Needs has received a very positive and warm response from the dog loving community. It is in use by veterinary behaviorists, integrative and holistic veterinarians, gentle groomers, dog walkers, pet sitters and service dog organizations, trainers, and pet parents. It is designed for dog trainers teaching classes and those conducting private consultations. The infographic is particularly helpful to shelters, rescues, foster pet parents, and animal welfare advocates. It is in use as a teaching guide in colleges, on websites, on television, and by a growing, international base of pet parents interested in the *Do No Harm* ideology and practice of dog training.

Dr. Katrina Ward, DVM, remarking on her presentation of the HDN to the Australian Veterinary Association conference said, "The Hierarchy of Dog Needs was very well received and hopefully will be taken up as a routine method of assessing needs and applying humane behavior modification" (as cited in Michaels, 2015/2020). Dr. Lynn Honeckman, DVM and behavior specialist in Orlando, Florida, uses the HDN to teach pre-vet students in her veterinary clinic presentations. Everyone from national crisis response human and dog trainers to working dog trainers are using it. In a television morning show featuring the Hierarchy of Dog Needs Maarja Tali, guest lecturer at Tallin University in Estonia says,

After the basic needs are met, dogs need to feel safe and loved. Relationships are as important to dogs [as they are to humans]. So, before we start drilling or shaping or teaching or training, it is much more important that we have a good trust-based relationship with

our dog. One of the most important messages here is that before we even get to training, we need to understand whether the dog is ready to learn. (Tali, 2019)

How This Handbook is Organized

Part 1. The Hierarchy of Dog Needs Standards of Care and Best Force-free Practices provides the theoretical foundations that support the Hierarchy of Dog Needs for each level of the pyramid and elaborates on each method of *Force-free Training*. Part 1 includes fully referenced, scientific citations for professionals and readers assuring scientific rigor. The citations enable force-free practitioners and supporters to empirically defend their stance on animal welfare needs, providing the evidence to do so at their fingertips. Part 1 is also designed for speakers, researchers, and instructors as the platform for teaching cutting edge, informative presentations based upon dog-centered needs and the *Hierarchy of Dog Needs/Do No Harm* paradigm. The For the Pet Professional section offers various ways that pet professionals can use The Hierarchy of Dog Needs and the *Do No Harm* handbook to teach others. Pet professionals will find information on creating presentations, how to use the handbook in private consultations, how to create coursework for class curricula and ideas for using the HDN and the handbook in social media with examples that both carry the *Do No Harm*/force-free message and enhance and support business goals.

Chapter 1 discusses *Biological Needs*, including proper nutrition, the need for fresh water, sufficient and appropriate exercise, sufficient air with a focus on brachycephalic breeds, sufficient sleep, avoiding outdoor hazards with indoor shelter, and proper temperature control avoiding hyperthermia and hypothermia. Chapter 1 also illustrates the critical need for gentle grooming and gentle veterinary care. Chapter 2 address the *Emotional Needs* for security which fosters secure attachment, love, trust, consistency, and benevolent leadership. Chapter 3, *Social Needs*, explores bonding with people and dogs, and the purpose of play. *Cognitive Needs* detailing the relevance of choice, novelty and problem-solving activities are examined in Chapter 4.

Chapter 5, *Force-free Training Needs* defines force-free dog training and thoroughly describes the best practices listed in the Hierarchy of Dog Needs guide: Management, antecedent modification, positive reinforcement, the types of differential reinforcement, classical and counterconditioning, desensitization, the Premack Principle, and social learning are all defined and illustrated with straightforward, clear, dog-centered examples of each method.

Part 2. Setting Your Dog Up for Success is useful for pet professionals and pet-parents, as it lays the groundwork for success in raising a dog: Chapter 6 explores why success begins with choosing a puppy or dog that is likely to fit your lifestyle. In chapters 7–8, specific criteria are outlined to help pet parents find a competent and kind dog trainer, and to select a dog-friendly veterinarian and groomer, some of the most determinative decisions one will make in a dog's lifetime. Chapter 9 explains how to socialize a puppy or dog safely and carefully and how to avoid the common pitfalls of flooding puppies and rescue dogs with stimuli that can cause well-intended plans to backfire. Chapter 10 explores how and why to provide enrichment. Part 2 concludes with a discussion in Chapter 11 on the importance of learning dog body language to better understand how your dog is trying to communicate with you and others.

Part 3. Good Manners and Basic Training focuses on manners and training mechanics in an easy-to-learn and follow step-by-step roadmap of the nuts and bolts of teaching the basic skills everyone wants their dogs to learn. Chapter 12 explains the top ten tips for successful housetraining. Chapter 13 teaches how to replace puppy and adult dog biting, mouthing and chewing with alternate behaviors. In Chapters 14 and 15, training techniques and trainer "secrets" provide instructions for teaching dogs with the methods that successful force-free trainers use. All of the basic training needs including calm greetings, no jump, sit, down, wait, lightning recall (come) and leash-walking skills are found in Chapter 16. Part 3 includes numerous examples making sometimes complex learning principles and techniques easy for anyone to teach and understand.

Part 4. When Things Go Wrong addresses behavior problems rooted in emotions that professional trainers and pet parents often find difficult to understand and treat. Largely written for the advanced-level behavior consultant, Chapter 17 focuses on aggression of all kinds providing trainers with the tools they need to address the most challenging cases. This chapter provides easy-to-understand and use protocols for problem-solving on aggression topics including red flags, an assessment intake form for private behavioral consultations, a liability contract, and a veterinary behavioral report. Chapter 17 also explores desensitization and counterconditioning exercises and techniques for frustration reactivity, human and dog-dog aggression, sibling rivalry in multi-dog households, resource guarding and a *Do Not* list for family, friends, and visitors. Chapter 18 provides assessment, management and adjunct treatment of allergies to the veterinary plan. The nuanced triggers for barking and how to decrease barking and stress are explored in Chapter 19. Chapter 20, helps the pet parent and the consultant develop a dogs and babies plan that begins, ideally, far before the new baby comes home. In Chapter 21, the causes and treatment of fear are explored. In closing, Part 4, Chapter 22, provides a comprehensive assessment and treatment plan for separation anxiety disorder and related behaviors.

I hope this book may help dogs and the people who love dogs, whether they work with dogs professionally, or touch dogs' lives in any way. Let's help them to thrive.

PART 1

THE HIERARCHY OF DOG NEEDS®

Hierarchy of Dog Needs®

Standards of Care and Best Force-free Practices

Force-free Training: Choose any or all methods

- **Management**
  To Increase, Redirect or Decrease Behavior: Rearrange environment. Remove or distance triggers. e.g., baby gates, dog-friendly fencing, puppy-proofing

- **Antecedent Modification**
  To Increase, Decrease or Redirect Behavior: Change events (triggers) that happen before the behavior

- **Positive Reinforcement**
  To Increase Behavior: Reward desired behavior. e.g., capture, lure, shape, model

- **Differential Reinforcement**
  To Redirect, Decrease or Increase Behavior: Reward for preferred incompatible, alternate, other, or change in the rate of behavior

- **Classical and Counter-Conditioning**
  To Change Emotions: Create new associations

- **Desensitization**
  To Decrease Emotional Response: Develop a systematic graduated exposure therapy plan

- **Premack Principle**
  To Increase, Decrease or Redirect Behavior: Use a high probability (preferred) behavior to reinforce a low probability behavior

- **Social Learning/Observational**
  To Increase, Decrease or Redirect Behavior: Use a dog or human model as sample behavior. e.g., imitation, emulation, contagion

There is never a justification to use pain, fear, dominance devices or training methods with our dogs.

~ Linda Michaels, M.A. Psychology

Dogs, like us, need to feel safe, at peace and loved. They depend on us to fill these needs and we are obligated to do so.

~ Dr. Marc Bekoff, PhD - Animal Behavior

Dogs must be happy in order to learn, pay attention and problem solve.

~ Dr. Simon Gadbois, PhD - Animal Behavior

COGNITIVE NEEDS
Choice
Novelty
Problem-Solving

FORCE-FREE TRAINING NEEDS
"Do No Harm"
Management and Learning

SOCIAL NEEDS
Bonding with People and Dogs
Play

EMOTIONAL NEEDS
Security
Love
Trust
Consistency
Benevolent Leadership

BIOLOGICAL NEEDS
Proper Nutrition   Fresh Water
Sufficient Exercise, Air, Sleep
Indoor Shelter   Safety   Temperature Control
Gentle Grooming   Gentle Veterinary Care

STANDARDS OF CARE AND BEST FORCE-FREE PRACTICES

Welcome to a new era in dog training. Marking the emergence of the force-free age in the field of dog training, The Hierarchy of Dog Needs® is a logical and progressive paradigm whose time has come. The Hierarchy of Dog Needs (HDN) is a wholistic system of care that takes a clear and ethical stand on dog welfare needs and dog-training methods and devices. The HDN is a novel adaptation of renowned psychologist Abraham Maslow's *Hierarchy of* (human) *Needs* that emphasizes strengths, positivity, free will/choice, and a belief in the wholeness of animal nature (Maslow, 1943). Research shows that when biological needs, safety needs, and belongingness needs are met for social animals, they are far less likely to display abnormal behavior. The Hierarchy of Dog Needs is supported by scientific evidence as demonstrated in this handbook and makes no apologies for embracing protective ethics concerning our beloved dogs.

The Hierarchy of Dog Needs infographic and this handbook provide teaching tools for all types of industry professionals and pet parents to use as a force-free alternative to the more conventional but dated teaching paradigms currently available. Anyone who interacts with or studies dogs, or any animal for that matter, can use it successfully. The HDN lists dog needs hierarchically but the levels are fluid rather than static. Once basic needs have been assessed and met, the training methods may be used in *any order* of choice, dependent upon the situation, context, and expertise of the handler.

The Hierarchy of Dog Needs is a guide to animal wellness and *Do No Harm Dog Training*. The Hierarchy of Dog Needs was created as a guide to standards of basic care in dog welfare needs and best force-free training practices. The HDN is in use internationally by veterinarians, veterinary behaviorists, dog trainers (including working-dog and police-dog trainers), groomers, shelters, rescues, animal welfare advocates, and pet parents. The HDN has been translated into French, Spanish,

Portuguese, Danish, Chinese, German, Estonian, Korean, Greek and Arabic to date, with many more requests awaiting translation.

The Hierarchy of Dog Needs is a tool for animal wellness and serves as an essential companion to the *Do No Harm Dog Training Handbook*. HDN *Force-free Training Needs* methods and this handbook may be used for both common behavioral problems and the most challenging issues, such as housetraining, loose leash-walking, excessive barking, separation anxiety, fear, dog-dog aggression, human aggression, resource guarding, and more. It can help to identify the primary, secondary, and other problems affecting the dog and help guide the path of training.

There is an increasingly strong dog-human bond in society and it makes sense that a more dog-friendly, dog-needs paradigm was needed and thus developed. Too often basic needs are not met or are under met. Dog needs are not considered in punitive or "balanced" training approaches where the focus is on punishing unwanted pet dog behavior and not on dog welfare. *Do No Harm* training makes dogs' lives better because it is more effective, safer, and has longer lasting effects. *Do No Harm* is truly dog friendly.

The Hierarchy of Dog Needs infographic is not intended to be a treatise on learning theory. Science has examined many different types of learning that include: Habituation, sensitization, desensitization, positive reinforcement, positive punishment, negative reinforcement, negative punishment, extinction, imitation, mimicry, and social learning. In other teaching paradigms, understanding behavior uses Skinnerian-related quadrants as a means to categorize response frequency. Placing every behavior response into a quadrant is not always helpful or the best approach to understanding emotional and behavioral modification and training needs. Only those methods that are physically and emotionally safe for dogs are included on the HDN and taught in the handbook.

The HDN pyramid infographic was designed to be a stand-alone guide covering as much critical territory for dog welfare and training in a one-page format as feasible. The HDN addresses as many primary needs and force-free training methods as possible, however, no infographic can convey all things to all pet professionals. Scientific advisor Dr. Luis Suoto Soubrier aptly points out, "The main message and the paramount goal of The Hierarchy of Dog Needs are clear. By introducing further nuances and provisos, even after writing an exhaustive (and exhausting to read) set of rules, we would still, unavoidably, be simplifying reality anyway" (L. Suoto Soubrier, personal communication, 2015).

The joys, challenges, and responsibilities of pet parenting involve loving care and fit well with The Hierarchy of Dog Needs model. Of primary importance is the enhanced relationship the pet parent nurtures with their dog by using the HDN. Nurturing and developing social skills and confidence in your dog sets the stage for optimal well-being, using force-free training, instead of instilling fear and potentiating aggression.

Do No Harm is fast becoming the gold standard of care throughout the dog-training field. Pet parents and professionals are now applying emotional and behavioral modification methods using the *Do No Harm* model. The time has come to chart a new course making responsible dog training method the best practice.

I. THE *DO NO HARM* ETHICAL CODES

Ethics are at the very heart of *Do No Harm Dog Training and Behavior Handbook* and the HDN. The embedded *Do No Harm* ethical code follows force-free, aversive-free, punitive-free training methods alone as best practices. To stem the tide of animal abuse in the dog training industry, canine behavior consultants are raising their voices in regulating practices in the field of dog training.

The Pet Professional Guild (PPG) (2020c) is the first international, independent certifying dog training organization to take a clear, uncompromising, antithetical position on the use of shock, prong, choke, dominance, pain and fear-based methods in dog training. Members are fully vetted and must conform to a non-negotiable ethical code of conduct and standards. Members forfeit their membership status for violations of the ethical standards. We need more of these organizations to help protect and defend our dogs' well-being.

Professional organizations caring for and treating sentient beings all have ethical codes guiding their members and detailing acceptable standards of care. Let's take a look at what the most highly esteemed and prestigious organizations in related fields have to say about ethics.

The American Veterinary Medical Association (AVMA)

"Principles of Veterinary Medical Ethics of the AVMA" from the AVMA webpage (AVMA, 2019).

The Principles

4. A veterinarian shall respect the law and also recognize a responsibility to seek changes to laws and regulations which are contrary to the best interests of the patient and public health.

The Principles with Supporting Annotations

1. A veterinarian shall be dedicated to providing competent veterinary medical care with compassion and respect for animal welfare and public health.
2.1 Veterinarians should first consider the needs of the patient: to prevent and relieve disease, suffering, or disability while minimizing pain or fear.
3.3 Veterinary Medical educators should stress the teaching of ethical issues as part of the professional veterinary curriculum for all veterinary students. (AVMA, 2019)

American Animal Hospital Association (AAHA)

"Changing Behavior, Behavior Modification, Aversive Techniques" (AAHA, 2015).

This Task Force opposes training methods that use aversive techniques. Aversive training has been associated with detrimental effects on the human–animal bond, problem-solving ability, and the physical and behavioral health of the patient. It causes problem behaviors in normal animals and hastens progression of behavioral disorders in distressed animals. Aversive techniques are especially injurious to fearful and aggressive patients and often suppress signals of impending aggression, rendering any aggressive dog more dangerous. Aversive techniques include prong (pinch) or choke collars, cattle prods, alpha rolls, dominance downs, electronic shock collars, lunge whips, starving or withholding food, entrapment, and beating. None of those tools and methods should be used to either teach or alter behavior. (AAHA, 2015, p. 212)

The American Medical Association (AMA)

"AMA Code of Medical Ethics"

In 1847 the American Medical Association (AMA) was founded establishing educational and ethical standards for the profession. The AMA's Code of Medical Ethics, the world's first national ethical code of professional conduct, embodies medicine's commitment to the professionalism and self-regulation on which public trust rests. Nearly 100% percent of medical schools administer the Hippocratic Oath as a guide to moral conduct in treating those under the care of their members, urging medical school graduates to "Do No Harm" to the best of their ability (Tyson, 2001).

The *AMA Journal of Ethics* has a dedicated website page entitled, *First Do No Harm* (2019). AMA Principles of Medical Ethics (1995–2021) standard of conduct include

Principles of Medical Ethics

3. A physician shall respect the law and also recognize a responsibility to seek changes in those requirements which are contrary to the best interests of the patient.
8. A physician shall, while caring for a patient, regard responsibility to the patient as paramount. (AMA, 2021)

American Psychological Association (APA)

The American Psychological Association (APA) published the first edition of the *Ethical Standards of Psychologists* in 1953, more than 60 years ago. The APA ethical standards of care undergo continuous review and are now known as the APA's "Ethical Principles of Psychologists and Code of Conduct". These mandates not only require adherence to the law but raise the bar on ethics. From the "Ethical Principles of Psychologists and Code of Conduct" official webpage: Including 2010 and 2016 Amendments (APA, 2017).

Introduction and Applicability

In the process of making decisions regarding their professional behavior, psychologists must consider this Ethics Code in addition to applicable laws and psychology board regulations… If this Ethics Code establishes a higher standard of conduct than is required by law, psychologists must meet the higher ethical standard. This Ethics Code is intended to provide specific standards to cover most situations encountered by psychologists. It has as its goals the welfare and protection of the individuals and groups with whom psychologists work and the education of members, students and the public regarding ethical standards of the discipline.

General Principles. Principle A: Beneficence and Nonmaleficence

*Psychologists strive to benefit those with whom they work and take care to **do no harm** [emphasis added]. In their professional actions, psychologists seek to safeguard the welfare and rights of those with whom they interact professionally and other affected persons and the welfare of animal subjects of research.*

Section 2: Competence

2.03 Maintaining Competence
Psychologists undertake ongoing efforts to develop and maintain their competence.
2.04 Bases for Scientific and Professional Judgments
Psychologists' work is based upon established scientific and professional knowledge of the discipline. (APA, 2017)

Harsh methods are not a viable treatment for emotional and behavioral modification in sentient creatures or a treatment for aggression. Harsh methods are commonly a *cause not a cure* of aggression (Overall, et al., 2006; FDA, 2014).

II. BEHAVIORAL MODELS

Behavior is complex. No single model of behavior can comprehensively understand, explain and predict behavior. The Hierarchy of Dog Needs however is multi-modal, multi-dimensional, and based upon a number of behavioral models providing a more complete and eclectic representation of learning and behavior than any one of the classic models of behavior do alone. Below are some popular *schools of thought* and theories about the nature of behavior.

The Behavioral Model

The Behavioral Model attributes behavior to the environment. The environment drives behavior through antecedents and postcedent consequences. Behavioral Analysis is based upon the *if, then contingency*. Behavior is learned, that is conditioned through

1. *Classical Conditioning:* Associations learned by pairing one stimulus—the antecedent, to another stimulus
2. *Operant Conditioning:* Reinforcement or punishment also known as consequences or postcedents

More often than not both classical conditioning and operant conditioning occur simultaneously and are inextricably linked with each other. However, these two types of learning are typically spoken of independently so students and trainers may more easily understand the concepts of behaviorism. With this clarity, practitioners can identify the underlying principles leading to the formulation of a plan for treating a specific problem, behavior, or emotion. The researchers most notably responsible for developing these representational systems of behavior are research scientists Ivan Pavlov and B. F. Skinner.

This model theorizes that a dog bites a person because the dog has been reinforced or punished for biting, or the dog associates the person with something that previously caused an involuntary physiological response and/or a learned aversive response.

The Affective Neuroscience Model

The Affective Neuroscience Model of behavior attributes behavior to functions of the brain modulated by hormones. The emotional systems model theorizes that environment, behavior, and emotion cannot be isolated from each other, resulting in the activation of multiple emotional and behavioral systems in any given schema. Some of the most notable researchers in this area include Charles Darwin, Jaak Panksepp, and Joseph E. Ledoux.

This model theorizes that a dog bites a person because the dog is experiencing fear, panic, or rage on the neurological and hormonal levels.

The Ethological Model

The Ethological Model of behavior attributes behavior to evolutionary adaptive traits with a focus on field studies in natural environments. The identification of *Modal Action Patterns (MAP)*, inherited tendencies to make specific and complex responses to specific environmental stimuli, helping scientists to understand behavior. Some of the most notable researchers in this area include Charles Darwin, Konrad Lorenz, Niko Tinbergen, and Simon Gadbois.

This model theorizes that a dog bites a person because it is adaptive to survival to bite when threatened or to compete for resources.

The Medical Model

The Medical Model of behavior attributes behavior to wellness or the lack thereof. Veterinarians and veterinary behaviorists build their treatment plans based upon this model.

This practice theorizes that a dog bites a person because the dog has a pathological condition or is in pain.

The Biological Model

The Biological Model of behavior attributes behavior to genetics or DNA, determined by heredity and breeding.

This model theorizes that a dog bites a person because of the propensity for aggression acquired through the dog's lineage.

III. MASLOW'S HIERARCHY OF NEEDS—THE *THIRD FORCE* IN BEHAVIOR

Students of psychology are familiar with *The Hierarchy of* [human] *Needs.* The Hierarchy of Dog Needs is a novel variation of renowned psychologist, Abraham Maslow's Hierarchy of Needs, adapting a human model of behavior to fit dogs. Similar needs occur in all species.

Animal models of human needs are traditionally used in research where the results and conclusions are extrapolated to humans to help us understand disease and develop treatments in medicine and behavior. Pavlov developed his theories of classical conditioning using dogs as his subjects in research. Skinner developed his theories of operant conditioning using pigeons as his research subjects. The field of comparative psychology explores cross-species comparisons, including those between humans and animals (Tinbergen, 1963).

Maslow, disenchanted with the popularized behaviorist paradigm of his time, cofounded the school of thought in psychology called *humanism*, the *Third Force* that emerged subsequent to psychoanalysis and behaviorism (Leahey, 2001). During the summer of 1938, Maslow conducted anthropologic research on a Blackfoot Native American reservation that is believed to have inspired him to theorize a new understanding of the fundamental features of human nature (Taylor, 2019).

Humanistic psychology emphasizes strengths, positivism, choice, and a belief in the wholeness of animal nature. In Maslow's own words: "Self-actualized people have the wonderful capacity to appreciate again and again, freshly and naively, the basic goods of life, with awe, pleasure, wonder and even ecstasy, however stale these experiences may have become to others" (Maslow, 1943, pp. 370–396). Does this not definitively describe what we often observe in our dogs? We witness our dogs taking great joy in simple things, over and over again. Taking a (w)holistic view of the sentient dog, The Hierarchy of Dog Needs combines both wholeness and behaviorist templates for wellness and emotional and behavioral modification understanding that both mental events and previously reinforced learned behaviors are causal. Humanism asserts that the present and the future and the past influence us.

Following on the heels of Maslow's work and others, the former President of the American Psychological Association, and renowned research scientists, Martin Seligman, became the face of *Positive Psychology* (Seligman, 2020). He called for an alternative to psychology's "relentless focus on the negative" and for research into growth, mastery and drive. Today, much research and many academic textbooks explore topics including well-being, the science of happiness, and peak performance. Seligman's most famous work on *learned helplessness* (Seligman, 1972) demonstrated that dogs that had previously learned that escape from shock was impossible, would not even attempt to escape once escape was on option. His breakthrough research shows that *mental events are causal, even in our dogs* (Seligman cited in Schultz & Schultz, 2008).

Maslow further developed his theory in *Motivation and Personality*, highlighting the significance of relationships (Maslow, 1954). *The Hierarchy of* [human] *Needs* remains a very popular framework in secondary and higher education psychology instruction and research. The nature of our relationships with our dogs deserves more attention, thus introducing this adaptation to dog care and training is a unique pleasure.

Dogs have the opportunity to reach an optimal state of well-being when all their needs are met. This is the singular objective of The Hierarchy of Dog Needs principles and procedures, standards of care and best practices. All needs highlighted in the Hierarchy of Dog Needs are interconnected. Needs are similarly dynamic in humans. Researchers find those whose needs for safety and belongingness are met are far less likely to display distraught and disordered behavior than those who have not had these needs satisfied (Schultz & Schultz, 2008).

Note: While a pyramid has become a popular way to represent *The Hierarchy of* [human] *Needs*, Maslow himself never used a pyramid to illustrate his levels in any of his writings on the subject.

FOR THE PET PROFESSIONAL

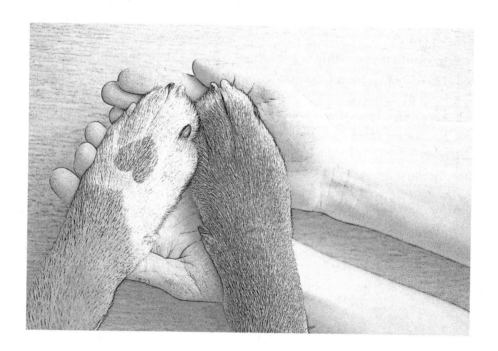

HOW TO USE THE *DO NO HARM DOG TRAINING AND BEHAVIOR HANDBOOK* IN PRACTICE AND BUSINESS

There is a cry for help from shelter facilities to veterinary offices for a new framework to successfully modify behaviors without causing physical or psychological harm to our dogs. *The Do No Harm Training and Behavior Handbook* answers that call. This handbook illustrates how specific needs and force-free training methods are inherently connected, opening the door for conversations with other pet professionals and with clients. In addition, it elucidates how to inspire professionals to invest in a total program of care and training. By design, this handbook encourages collaboration between force-free pet professionals to refer to and support other force-free professionals to achieve optimal well-being for the whole dog. The Hierarchy of Dog Needs (HDN) graphic is used in speaker presentations at veterinary conferences and lectures at local humane societies and pet expositions.

Developing Training Plans

The *Do No Harm* handbook identifies primary, secondary, and other problems affecting dogs and guides the reader on the assessment, treatment, and training path. It accounts for both dog and client needs, helping the pet professionals or pet parents to create a comprehensive training plan. This training handbook also provides an outline for class and private consulting.

Increasing Workflow

Review The Hierarchy of Dog Needs infographic with your client and take notes about problem areas; this will assist in uncovering additional training needs. Creating a *to-do list* helps the professional to set the training focus on the specific needs of their client and dog, providing a comprehensive plan for both.

When working up the pyramid, identify unmet and under-met needs and areas of particular interest or concern. Working down the list of training methods on the left side of the pyramid outlines how to address behavioral issues. Details explaining each method are also discussed in Part 1. The remainder of the handbook contains information regarding the application of these methods, which may be used in any order or combination. In this manner, pet professionals may establish the required number of sessions needed for a comprehensive approach to address the underlying motivations of problem behaviors and identify the various contexts where such behaviors occur.

Using The Hierarchy of Dog Needs

The *Do No Harm* handbook is designed for use in media and the development of professional treatment plans. Consider the following uses:

Media

- Speaking engagements
- Social media groups
- Virtual training
- Blogs
- Websites
- Television spots
- Webinars
- Podcasts

Pet Professionals

- Veterinary behaviorists
- Allopathic, progressive, integrative, and holistic veterinarians
- Veterinary technicians and assistants
- Pet chiropractic and acupressure specialists
- Manners trainers
- Agility trainers
- Working dog trainers
- Service dog trainers
- Therapy dog trainers
- T-touch practitioners
- Pet therapists
- Dog walkers
- Pet sitters
- Gentle groomers
- Rescue group directors, staff, and volunteers
- Animal shelter management and employees
- Foster pet parents
- Responsible breeders
- Dog daycare operators
- Pet store owners
- Pet food manufacturers and distributors
- Pet photographers

EXAMPLES FOR THE PET PROFESSIONAL

What follows are examples of the many ways various professionals can use the *Do No Harm Dog Training* handbook.

Examples for Speakers

Use this handbook as a guide for explaining either very specific issues identified in the hierarchy's pyramid, force-free training methods, or both, during speaker, lecture, or other formats of presentation. Each section can also serve as a standalone topic for a presentation tailored to the interest of a sub-population of dog lovers. For example, one topic of interest is the need for proper temperature control and how to avoid hyperthermia in the summer, and hypothermia in winter. Or a speaker for a breed rescue group might create a presentation on brachycephalic airway obstruction from the section of the handbook devoted to the need for air.

Examples for Pet Bloggers and Television Interviews

The topics in this handbook and The Hierarchy of Dog Needs make excellent blog material. Force-free advocates can easily use the HDN to explain dog needs and force-free training during television spot presentations.

Examples for Classes

Do No Harm Management and Best Force-free Practices methods illustrated by The Hierarchy of Dog Needs are a great segue laying a foundation for force-free training.

Consider developing a lesson guide of basic skills using the *Do No Harm Dog Training Handbook* as a foundation, using The Hierarchy of Dog Needs infographic as a handout for discussion during class. Use the training techniques and trainer "secrets," such as capturing, luring, shaping, linking, and real-life reinforcement to teach force-free best practices in the context of teaching name response, sit, down, wait/stay, come, and leash-walking. Trainers who teach classes may rearrange the topic material and teach a basic skill in each class. Referencing the HDN throughout lessons with clients helps to emphasize the importance of meeting needs and learning force-free methods. The goal for any class is empowering clients to use force-free methods for problem-solving when training issues arise when you are not there in class to guide them. Include a copy of the HDN in take-home training packets.

Examples for Private Consultations

Review the HDN infographic with your client during the first consulting session. Assess training needs and identify the methods you will use from the force-free training methods chart on the left side of the handout. Help address unwanted behavior with explanations of differential reinforcement, counterconditioning, and desensitization methods. Take notes on a master copy. Private consultants can identify behavioral problems needing attention and lead to the development of a treatment plan to determine which basic skills are missing from a family's repertoire to help the troubled dog and client. Address the needs and topics you feel most competent and comfortable teaching. For example, the client may want recommendations on nutrition and exercise. A conversation on *Emotional Needs* and trust often reveals fearful or aggressive behavior only a qualified behavior consultant can safely and adequately address. A discussion on *Social Needs* and attachment may uncover a separation/attachment issue or disorder associated with pet parents, or with other dogs in the family.

Another idea is to create a poster of the HDN for your facility or classroom wall. Have a print company create an unaltered, uncropped (as is) poster from a print-ready file available to force-free advocates from the author.

Examples for Veterinarians

The Hierarchy of Dog Needs (HDN) includes gentle veterinary care as an essential biological health need. As the primary contact professionals, veterinarians are in a position to make the greatest impact on the physical and psychological well-being of the dogs under their loving care. Veterinarians can take a leadership role with pet parents and other pet-related professionals in the animal welfare and force-free movement by using The Hierarchy of Dog Needs and the accompanying *Do No Harm Dog Training and Behavior Handbook.* They are encouraged to share The Hierarchy of Dog Needs with colleagues, patients, trainers, and at speaking engagements, such as in seminar presentations for veterinary conferences. Veterinarians are encouraged to refer only to force-free/*Do No Harm* dog trainers and consultants. (See Chapters 1 and 8, Gentle Veterinary Care.)

Examples for Rescues and Shelters

Make your rescue or shelter truly force-free by adding a copy of the HDN infographic to the take-home packet with each newly adopted dog. Post a laminated copy on the gate to each dog's kennel as a reminder to everyone who enters of how to use force-free handling and training techniques with the focus on meeting emotional needs and decreasing stress. Ensure that all management, staff, volunteers, and foster parents have access to a copy of the infographic as a means to educate everyone connected to your adoption agency. Post a copy on your website and social media sites.

Examples for Groomers

Groomers may blog or offer presentations on the benefits of gentle grooming, the importance of proper hygiene, removal of fur nests that may serve as havens for bacteria, and proper nail clipping to prevent long nails from impeding a dog's natural walking gait or the structural functions of the spine. Use the handbook to develop a training packet that includes information about pet grooming provided in the gentle grooming sections to help the client's dog learn to tolerate and even enjoy grooming.

Examples for Responsible Breeders

Provide a copy of The Hierarchy of Dog Needs infographic in the educational and guidance packets of each new pet parent and discuss the needs and do no harm training practices you want to guarantee to your adoptees.

Note: *The reproduction, use, or modification of the Hierarchy of Dog Needs* ® *is strictly prohibited in any product sold for profit where the primary value of the product is the reproduction itself, such as on t-shirts or coffee mugs.*

FUTURE DIRECTIONS IN RESEARCH, LAW, AND THE ROLE OF CELEBRITIES

The time has come to chart a new course. *Do No Harm* principles and ethics are fast becoming the gold standard of care throughout the dog training profession. Scientists, legislators, and celebrities are urged to take a clear and unwavering position against the physical and psychological harm our dogs suffer, pioneering the cultural change essential in creating truly dog-friendly societies. Worldwide, progressive zoos and sanctuaries have moved away entirely from using punitive and other aversive methods, even when working with large and potentially dangerous animals.

Dog bites are a serious and growing public safety issue and it is well-documented in scientific literature that inflicting pain is frequently a cause of aggressive behavior. Bite incidents may result from the direct administration of shock (Polsky, 2000). Aggression is not the only emotional disturbance stemming from punitive and aversive training methods. According to an article in the *Journal of Veterinary Behavior*, "Good Trainers: How to Identify One" (Overall et al., 2006), investigators placed shock collars, prong collars, and choke collars at the top of the list of equipment that causes anxiety, fear, and arousal, which often contributes to an increase in aggression. A growing number of governments in progressive animal-welfare sensitive nations ban the use of these devices on pet dogs.

Canine research scientists are encouraged to take a leadership role in the ethical treatment of companion animals. Evidence illustrates there is no place for shock, prong, choke, or other aversive variables in companion animal research. The rationale against the use of shock and positive punishment is well established in scientific literature. Dr. Karen Weigle (2019), clinical psychologist, affiliated with the University of New Hampshire spoke out on shock saying, "This has gone on for this long because this is a population who cannot adequately speak for themselves." Who will speak for the dogs? If not us, who? If not now, when? Professional positions opposing the use of aversives in dog training are based on both a sophisticated academic grasp of the neurochemical and behavioral mechanisms at play, and a desire to promote animal welfare in a civilized world (Michaels, 2015d). The hallmarks of leadership in science highlight the detrimental effects that painful devices and practices have on our companion animals. The advent of the Pet Professional Guild (PPG) gives medical professionals, research scientists, and other pet professionals a clear option for affiliation with an international, science-oriented organization. PPG members subscribe to No Shock, No Pain, No Choke, No Fear, No Pain and No Physical Force in dog training. It is understood that science cannot take a stand—but scientists can.

Scientists can easily design research studies that *do no harm,* thus supporting the instrumental and necessary steps leading to a ban on shock devices used with pet dogs. A survey using the extensive Canine Behavioral Assessment and Research Questionnaire (C-BARQ) database (Serpell, 2020), or a separately designed survey, exploring the co-relational relationship between shock training and bites would be of practical value to scientists, animal welfare advocates, trainers, and the public. A survey study based upon a collection of statistics from veterinarians on the injuries and deaths from choke and prong collars would inform and illustrate the true extent of the problem using these devices.

Scientific presentations have real world impact on audiences, and moreover, on our companion animals. Pet professionals from an array of dog-related fields often incorporate these scientific interpretations into their practices and hold them up as a gold standard. New evidence-based practices are the driving force in social commitment to animal welfare policy legislation and the subsequent enforcement of sanctions prohibiting intentional harm to dogs. Scientists who adopt a clear and ethical stand on dog handling and training can help drive social change and shape laws governing animal welfare legislation. Governmental representatives will look closely at what scientists have to say about shock, prong, choke, and dominance training practices. The adaptation of ethics driven science into law puts to rest the unwarranted justification of the use of painful devices and training methods.

Celebrity impact on cultural change is also a powerful and a much-needed force for good. The dog-loving celebrity community can be leading spokespersons for *Do No Harm* training methods. Celebrities can affect the well-being of dogs across the globe with just a few, clear, and well-spoken words about dog training methods. Employing force-free dog trainers and encouraging the production of truly dog-friendly television shows and films will further endear fans to stars and their pets.

Together a commitment to strengthening animal welfare laws and regulations based upon dog-friendly ethics will bring about a transformation—a sea change in dog training that is long overdue. Increasing penalties for dog abuse and neglect, and developing regulation in the field of dog training ensures trainer competency and a *do no harm* ethic for dog-related activities. This will accomplish our collective goal. It is incumbent upon each of us to take a clear and unwavering stand on these issues by adopting a force-free ideology concerning the care and welfare of our dogs.

1

M eeting your dogs' *Biological Needs* is the foundational base for a happy and healthy life. Here are the biological needs that should be met, per The Hierarchy of Dog Needs®

- Proper nutrition
- Fresh water
- Sufficient exercise
- Sufficient air
- Sufficient sleep

- Indoor shelter
- Safety
- Temperature control
- Gentle grooming
- Gentle veterinary care

Proper Nutrition

A dog's focus on food springs from the need for proper nutrition, which is a basic essential need along with air and water. Dogs are completely dependent upon us to provide a sufficient amount of high-quality, biologically appropriate food. They cannot go to the grocery store or open the refrigerator to retrieve what their body is craving! Taking a look at the world from a dog's perspective, allows us to better appreciate our responsibility to provide biologically appropriate nutritious food. Improper diet and poor-quality food may cause behavioral problems and medical issues in dogs. Poor quality food invites allergies and illness. Many medical and behavioral problems are directly affected by diet, so keeping a beloved dog physically and temperamentally fit by meeting their nutritional needs is essential. You want your dog to thrive, so provide high-quality dog food.

While experts disagree about nutrition, most will agree that any diet you choose must be nutritionally balanced. Sadly, ". . . much of the research supporting clinical pet diets does not undergo peer review and is never published in full journal form. Whereas obtaining patent rights to protect intellectual property is understandable, the field as a whole will benefit only if data are published" (Deng & Swanson, 2015, p. 825). Veterinary nutritionists do agree that a poor diet is the biggest obstacle to achieving overall canine health. It is a daunting task to stay up to date on the latest nutritional theories, brands, and recalls. It is important to take nutritional recommendations from reliable sources whose opinions are not influenced by commercial interest as much as possible. If your dog is healthy there are many choices in biologically appropriate diets. However, if there is illness or disease you will want to follow the recommendations of your trusted veterinarian. You will want to

- Select healthy ingredients.
- Avoid questionable additives.
- Understand the effects of dog food processing when choosing meal type such as kibble, freeze-dried, dehydrated, air-dried, raw, or home-cooked.
- Proactively research manufacturer reliability.

Feeding a Biologically Appropriate, Nutritionally Balanced Diet

Feeding a truly nutritionally balanced diet requires selecting quality sources so that all essential vitamin, mineral, amino acid, macro and micronutrient requirements are met. A balanced diet requires a variety of healthy meats and veggies. Most vegetables and some fruits can and should be a part of your dog's diet. For many pet parents, that means finding a few reliable brands and rotating between whole protein sources such as chicken, beef, and salmon, within and between brands. Transition between brands or protein sources over the course of a week or two, gradually adding the new food to the old. Continuously feeding the same food may create allergies and nutritional deficiencies.

Dr. Karen Becker, a leading integrative veterinarian specializing in nutrition recommends a carefully planned biologically appropriate diet for you dogs. She tells us,

And while nutritionally balanced, fresh whole food isn't the cure for every disease that afflicts cats and dogs, it is the very best foundation upon which to build a protocol that can return a sick animal to good health. Simply put, when your pet's organs must work overtime to digest and absorb species-inappropriate nutrients from a processed diet, it inhibits the body's capacity to achieve and maintain a state of homeostasis. (Becker, 1997–2020)

Both canned foods and kibble undergo extreme processing to make them shelf stable. Commercial pet food processing can impact digestibility, the availability of nutrients, and safety (Buff et al., 2014).

Read the Ingredients List

Many properties of commercially prepared dog food are not sufficiently regulated. We suggest that you

- Read the ingredients on labels and choose a food with a specifically named protein source as the first ingredient.
- Avoid the vague term "meat," by-products, corn syrup, and sugar.
- Meat meal is generally rendered meat made of by-products and that is why you will not see meat meals in human foods. Avoid meat meals when there are higher quality alternatives.
- Avoid artificial flavors, colors, and preservatives, especially BHA, BHT, and ethoxyquin that may be linked to carcinogens. Artificial preservatives may be toxic to your dogs: Some artificial preservatives are also used as pesticides.

Consider the following questions when choosing a brand of dog food (Case, 2014).

- **Sources.** Where do the ingredients come from?
- **Recalls.** What is the manufacturer's safety record?
- **Marketing and customer service.** Is the company transparent about its products and responsive to inquiries?

Choose human-grade ingredients that are subject to inspections to meet the strict criterion to be labeled human-grade if within your means. Otherwise, you may be feeding your dog meat ingredients that can contain pathogen-laden diseased or medication-laden euthanized animals. Home-cooked meals can also be great for your dog! If you choose to home-cook, start with trustworthy recipes or prepare a healthy meal for yourself and cook a little extra for your dog: Take care to avoid human foods on the dog toxicity list. Find nutritionally balanced recipes using human-grade ingredients. Reliable sources such as BalanceIT® (2004–20), founded by board certified veterinary nutritionist Sean Delaney, DVM, DACVN, who co-authored a leading textbook on veterinary clinical nutrition, formulates every recipe online for the specific needs of each pet.

Protein should come mainly from animal versus plant sources. Choose a protein-rich, not carbohydrate-rich diet. Canines have few dietary requirements for carbohydrates; however, some commercial dog foods may contain up to 90% grains because grains are inexpensive and increase calories. Grain-free processed kibble is also too often overloaded with calories and carbohydrates. Dr. Doug Knueven, DVM, holistic nutritional expert and sought-after veterinary conference speaker, suggests that you choose a food with a small percentage of healthy whole grains that provide complex carbohydrates. High-protein diets are generally linked to high performance, whereas high simple carbohydrate diets are linked to obesity in dogs (Knueven, 2008).

There are some excellent dehydrated, air-dried, and freeze-dried foods as well. However, if you choose to feed kibble, try to feed a kibble that contains as many organic ingredients as possible. Purchase a 2-week supply of kibble and keep it refrigerated. Oxidation may degrade the essential nutrients that have been supplemented. Do not pour the food out of the bag into another container. Add water or a scoop of wet food to the kibble: Kibble does not provide enough water during a meal. Chewing kibble does *not* clean the teeth.

Feeding Raw

There is a controversial and sometimes contentious debate about feeding a raw diet, however, the evidence against it is inconclusive. Some veterinary organizations, such as the American Veterinary Medical Association (AVMA) and the American Animal Hospital Association (AAHA) have taken positions against feeding raw food for what they believe to be public safety issues. They say,

> *The AVMA discourages the feeding to cats and dogs of any animal source protein that has not first been subjected to a process to eliminate pathogens because of the risk of illness to cats and dogs as well as humans. Cooking or pasteurization through the application of heat until the protein reaches an internal temperature adequate to destroy pathogenic organisms has been the traditional method used to eliminate pathogens in animal source protein, although the AVMA recognizes source protein, although the AVMA recognizes that newer technologies and other methods such as irradiation are constantly being developed and implemented.* (AVMA, 2019, September 5, para. 1).

If you choose to feed raw, ensure that your dog is eating a nutritionally balanced diet. If you are creating meal plans, include raw meat, organ meat, shredded fruits, vegetables, ground and raw meaty bones, and the appropriate supplements. Raw meaty bones are typically half meat with bone that is consumed, such as chicken necks, backs and legs; turkey necks; pork and lamb necks and breasts, and canned boney fish such as sardines, salmon, and mackerel. Canned fish is pre-cooked. Conveniently frozen raw meals of meat, bone, and vegetables are now widely available. Take precautions with food handling hygiene as you do with any raw meat to prevent possible bacterial or parasitic contamination of hands, surfaces, and utensils. Special precautions must be taken for immune-suppressed individuals who are particularly susceptible to pathogens.

A popular public service resource for comparing both wet and dry brands is DogFoodAdvisor.com. The website's research team of professionals dedicated to canine wellness includes a veterinarian. Dog Food Advisor reviews hundreds of dog food brand products from A–Z, interprets nutritional content, evaluates additives, and publishes recall notices. Their reputation for fairness has made them a leader in helping pet parents and business owners. Another source in the form of an annual review for pet parents is *The Whole Dog Journal*, which rates dry and wet food brands.

The *Whole Dog Journal* in "Diets, Dogs, and DCM", Straus and Kerns (2019) analyzed data released by the FDA, in an attempt to determine if there is a link between reported cases of dilated cardiomyopathy (DCM) and the affected dogs' diets. They report, "No one knows for sure what might explain a link between certain types of diets and DCM in some dogs" (2019, October 22, para. 6). The article provides safety precautions, recommendations, and references to the updates, and reports of medical interest. Legumes, namely peas are currently suspected.

Obesity is the most common nutritional disorder in dogs. An excess of 15% over the ideal bodyweight is considered obese and is most often caused by either excessive caloric intake or inadequate exercise, or a combination of the two. Studies indicate that 18 to 44% of dogs are either overweight or obese. Risk factors for obesity include: Dietary practices, female gender, neutering, age, and breed, namely, Labrador Retrievers, Cairn Terriers, Cocker Spaniels, Dachshunds, Shetland Sheep Dogs, Basset Hounds, Cavalier King Charles Spaniels, and Beagles. The socio-economic and dietary habits of the pet parent are factors in dog obesity as well (Collard et al., 2006). A scientific meta-analysis review of causes of obesity in dogs says that we should not use body weight alone to evaluate a dog's nutritional needs when planning meals. Your dog's lifestyle, neuter status, activity level, age, medical condition, and health history must be considered as well (Birmingham et al., 2014).

FRESH WATER

Although truly fresh water is often overlooked for pets, water unfit for you to drink is also most very likely harmful for your dog. Pet parents often mistakenly take the quality of the tap water they give their pets for granted. If you drink spring, distilled, filtered, or bottled water, consider providing quality water as a must for your pet, hand-in-glove with a nutritious diet.

Fresh water is vital for all known forms of life. Unless you are feeding a wet or raw diet, drinking water is most likely your dog's *only* source of hydration for metabolic processes. Water regulates temperature, carries nutrients and oxygen to all cells, lessens the burden on the kidneys and liver by flushing out urine and feces and other toxins, aids in digestion, and dissolves minerals and other nutrients so they are accessible to the body. Water also lubricates joints, moistens tissues such as those in the mouth, eyes, and nose, helps prevent constipation, and protects the body's organs and tissues (Mayo Clinic, 2020a).

A National Resource Defense Council (2003) study cites an article, "What's on Tap," revealing that the tap water of scores of United States cities is compromised.

Pollution, old pre-World War I pipes, and outdated treatment facilities and processing put dogs at risk from contaminants that breed bacteria and fail to remove toxins such as pesticides, industrial chemicals, and arsenic which can be found in tap water. Diarrhea is often linked to food choice, yet the role that contaminated water may play in diarrhea and cancer is often overlooked. In a recent meta-analysis (Ercumen et al., 2014), aging water distribution systems in the United States and other developed countries were found to allow pathogens that cause diarrhea. Most cities are not in violation of the national standards, yet the Environmental Protection Agency (EPA) standards are weak. For example, the EPA allows 10pps of arsenic although scientists concur there is no safe level of arsenic in drinking water.

Note: Water should *not* be rationed for housetraining. Your dog can perish within a few days without water.

SUFFICIENT EXERCISE

The well documented benefits of exercise for people also apply to your dog. There is irrefutable evidence that regular physical activity is vital to help prevent several chronic diseases such as: cardiovascular disease, diabetes, cancer hypertension, obesity, depression, osteoporosis, and premature death (Brendin et al., 2006). In *Decoding Your Dog:* "All Dogs Need a Job," Dr. Mary Klinck, DVM, tells us that a dog's need for exercise is dependent on life stage, breed, and personality; however, individuals within each breed can vary significantly (Klinck, 2014).

Exercise needs are unique to each dog. Have an integrative force-free veterinarian complete a wellness check for your dog before beginning an exercise regimen. Too much, too little, or the wrong type of exercise and mental stimulation can lead to medical and behavior problems (Marcellin-Little et al., 2005). Sadly, there has been very little research about the optimal frequency, intensity, and duration of exercise for dogs. However, if your dog is overweight, monitor your dog carefully, slowly increasing frequency, intensity, and duration of exercise because the heart rate in overweight dogs during exercise is higher (Kuruvillaa, 2003).

Provide frequent and regular physical and mental exercise appropriate for your dog's medical condition, age, and breed. Proper exercise not only keeps your dog fit, but it also decreases stress. It is up to us humans to provide sufficient exercise that is fun, while at the same time keeps our dogs safe. Remember our dogs play by their own rules and they simply cannot be trusted to make good decisions, by our standards, on any regular basis!

Exercise, Mood and Behavior

Scientists have studied the euphoria known as *runners high* that is experienced during and after long-distance running and strenuous exercise. Is it any wonder our dogs love to run? The *opioid theory* is believed to be involved in mood enhancement during and after exercise. The increase in the body's naturally produced opioid endorphins released during exercise has a positive effect on depression and anxiety as well (Boecker et al., 2008). In a recent study, a lack of sufficient daily exercise was associated with canine anxiety. Dogs who exercised less suffered more noise sensitivity and more separation anxiety distress. More exercise may provide a solution for anxious dogs (Tiira & Lohi, 2015).

Types of Exercise for Life Stages

Exercise for Puppies—They Have Special Needs

Puppies have special exercise needs. Frequent self-regulated free-play sessions are encouraged for puppies. Arranging casual play dates with dogs who "play nice" are great for exercise and wonderful socialization for your puppy. Protect your puppy by preventing jumping and falling down. More than 50% of fractures occur in animals less than one year of age (Animal Medical Center of Southern California, 2016). Jumping off of beds, couches, and people's laps, are major causes of spinal and other bone fractures in puppies. Avoid running, long hikes, and long walks until your dog is between 10 and 18 months old, dependent upon size and breed. Here's why:

The bone growth plates are soft cartilage areas that sit at the end of long bones (limbs and pelvis) in puppies and adolescent dogs who are still growing. Bone plates are a weak link, soft and vulnerable to injury. Sex hormone changes in puberty cause the growth plates to close and the plates then calcify and become a stable inflexible part of the bone. Puberty is a landmark for both growth plate closure and for slowly increasing exercise. In puppies the closure is, on average, completed by approximately 10 months of age in large dog breeds, a few months earlier in small dog breeds, and a few months later in giant dog breeds—up to 18 months of age (Provet Healthcare Information, 2013; Marcellin-Little et al., 2005). Specific cautionary measures and additional breed-specific orthopedic concerns should be discussed with your trusted force-free veterinarian.

Exercise for Adult Dogs

Providing daily runs or alternate opportunities to run and play is vital to your dog's physical health and emotional well-being. Most healthy dogs love to run! Make sure your dog is properly conditioned before participating in strenuous or athletic activities. Always prepare the muscles to reduce the risk of injury with a warm-up by starting with slow walking and then increasing intensity to jogging gradually over 5–10 minutes. Be certain your dog is comfortable with the level of intensity before increasing duration, distance, or intensity. Consider enrolling your healthy adult dog in an aerobic dog sport class or joining a local group for swimming, agility training, fly-ball, dog dancing, hoops, lure-coursing, or terrain-intensive scent work.

Your dog, more than likely, will not be cautious about excessive exercise so it is up to you to monitor activities carefully. Excessive frequency, intensity, or duration of exercise can have a negative impact causing injury or making an existing condition even worse. Be sure to provide rest breaks, and build endurance slowly, to avoid cardiovascular fatigue. Fatigue can result in injuries. Be on the lookout for limping, excessive panting, or a reluctance to exercise. Exercise should be joyful. Involving other dogs makes physical activity even more stimulating.

Generally speaking, exercise gear may be a topic of heated discussion but not in the force-free training community. Force-free dog trainers recommend a back or front-clip harness for walking and running in order to distribute the pressure across the dog's chest and body, rather than around the neck and throat structures. If safe for you, your dog, and others, let your dog run naked just with a collar and identification tags.

The benefits gained from safely practiced aerobic and non-aerobic exercise are enriching for both you and your dog. Look for unique trails, parks, beach areas, and neighborhoods to explore. If you prefer to watch rather than run, arrange for a play date with another friendly dog, or visit a safe leash-free dog park *if* your dog is a well-mannered social butterfly. (See Chapter 9, Dog Parks and Dog Play.)

Exercise for Aging or Senior Dogs

For the most part, just like humans, senior dogs continue their desire for activity and exercise, but at a slower pace. Arthritis may negatively impact your dog's ability, comfort, and desire to exercise. Understanding both the physical and the behavioral factors involved in our aging dogs provides the best exercise guidance.

Find ways to include your aging dog in your daily activities—being left home alone often quickens the decline of your senior dog's mental and physical condition. Pay attention to your dog's comfort limit with distance and other endurance factors on walks. A dog stroller or wagon will allow your dog to continue to be part of family activities. Walk for a short distance and then let your aging dog enjoy a ride in the stroller or wagon even if you have a multi-dog household, keeping everyone together if possible. "Sniffari" walks, mainly to sniff, are highly enjoyable for most aging dogs. Sniffing is the window to the world where they can experience novelty.

For dogs who have always loved riding in the car, keep riding! If your dog is too large for you to lift into the car, make a small investment in stairs or a ramp. These aides may be the most practical way of including your dog on these visually enriching and olfactory stimulating adventures.

Scent tracking and interactive toys can be a wonderful source of mental enrichment when physical activity is limited. Therapeutic supervised swimming using a life jacket, socializing with appropriate playmates on the same activity level, or even playing with a respectful puppy whose playstyle is monitored, may help keep your aging dog stimulated.

For more guidance about senior dog exercise, Dr. Karen Overall (2013, pp. 690–697) has a brilliant section, i.e., "Protocol for Understanding and Helping Geriatric Animals", in her *Manual of Clinical Behavioral Medicine.*

If You Cannot Exercise Your Dog

If you cannot exercise your dog, a training-savvy and trustworthy friend or vetted force-free dog walker can help. Do not let anyone else use a choke, slip, prong, or shock collar on your dog. These collars have been shown to cause injuries to dogs. Make it clear to your dog walker that your dog is to be walked on their harness. (See Chapter 16, Leash-walking.)

If your dog needs more exercise than you can provide or if you have limited space, when safe for your dog's age, medical condition, and morphological structure, consider exercising with a lure/chase toy. Some physically challenged pet parents who are unable to exercise their dog outside of the home find a lure-chase toy a convenient way to make sure their dog runs each day. This toy is also recommended for pet parents who do not have enough time to exercise their dog on any given day. The chase-lure toy is especially beneficial for prey-driven, high-activity level dogs or powerful breeds that love and need to run. It works great for small breeds as well and is a lot of fun for the handler.

Lure-chase Toy Rules

There are some important caveats regarding lure-chase toys.

- The lure should be kept near the ground, not lifted into the air. Jumping and twisting of the spinal column may cause injury.
- Once your dog catches the lure, always trade-up, by offering a high value treat tossed away from the lure, giving you a chance to retrieve it safely. Better yet, teach "Drop It." Otherwise, dogs may resource guard the lure, as if it were a prey item they've just caught.
- Allow your dog to catch the lure on occasion or the lure-chase toy game causes undesirable frustration. Exercise should be fun!

Another at home exercise technique for adult dogs without medical conditions, arthritis, or a predisposition to back injuries, and who are natural retrievers is *upstairs fetch*. If you have a carpeted staircase in your home and a healthy dog, upstairs fetch is like having a stair-stepper exercise machine for your dog. Toss treats, one at a time up the stairs. Do not toss anything down the stairs as this could result in injuries to dogs tripping and falling down the stairs.

Digging is another great natural exercise for your dog that does not require daily time or physical effort from pet parents. Get a sand box or designate a special spot in the yard reserved for a *dog zone digging pit* where you regularly bury goodies.

SUFFICIENT AIR

A puppy's first breath is a critical sign of life outside of the womb. Air is a metabolic requirement for survival, and it is the need that must be met first. Abraham Maslow's original work, *A Theory of Human Motivation* (1943, The Basic Needs section, para. 16.) delineates the basic physiological needs to maintain the body's homeostasis. One of the most basic of these needs is the need for oxygen. Oxygen travels through the lungs and is then transferred to red blood cells that carry the oxygen to all of the organs in the body that require oxygen to function.

If your dog is having breathing problems, see your veterinarian as soon as possible. Breathing difficulties can quickly become life threatening. Air is a *deficiency need* (Maslow, 1943) and if dogs are unable to satisfy their need for air, at a minimum they are uncomfortable and at the extreme, they are suffering and often medically endangered. The body cannot function properly with inadequate oxygen and will ultimately fail.

Airway Injuries from Choke and Prong Collars

Dogs are not morphologically built for collars around the neck. Choke and prong collars *when used correctly*, choke. The use of choke and prong collars exacerbate breathing problems, particularly in our brachycephalic breeds, and may cause medical injury to the trachea, which is essential to breathing.

Choking collars are typically made of metal, chain, or rope euphemistically called a *slip lead*. Rope is the device of choice used for hanging, therein, the purpose of the slip lead and a noose are much the same i.e., to choke. The metal spikes on prong collars are, additionally, often sharpened to inflict more pain and pressure, resulting in injury. The use of choke and prong collars which exert enormous pressure in pounds per square inch on the spikes, impair breathing and may cause medical injury. According to Eileen Anderson, in "Why Prong Collars Hurt", the pressure on the prong collar is concentrated into multiple small areas (like spike heels) instead of being dispersed. The pressure exerted to the throat by the average prong collar is approximately 155 times that caused by a flat collar (Anderson, 2017, para. 32).

Dr. Sophia Yin, DVM, on Choke Chains

So why do I avoid the choke chain . . . there are many medical and safety reasons. Not surprisingly, strong yanking on the neck with a chain can cause health issues. If the force from a dog pulling on a flat collar raises intraocular pressure [pressure inside the eyes], imagine how high that pressure must rise when you actually yank the dog with a thin chain! Even if your dog has no eye issues, the choke chain is notorious at exacerbating airway issues. For instance, it can worsen coughing in dogs prone to collapsing trachea (weak trachea that flatten more than they should) and affect the ability of dogs with small tracheas, such as pugs and bulldogs, to breathe. (Yin, 2012a, Choke Chain section, para. 5).

This report from a senior veterinary clinician appears in the *New York Post*, "Pet owners might use choke or prong collars to help train a dog that pulls on the leash, but accidents with these devices can cause serious injury, including permanent neurological problems—or even death," said Dr. David Bessler, senior emergency clinician at Blue Pearl Veterinary Partners in Manhattan. "The whole point of a choke collar is that it applies force 360 degrees," he explains. If a dog surprises an owner and takes off running, the collar snaps the pet back, causing whiplash, or choking. Bessler recalls a fatal case where an owner stepped on a leash as the dog started to run: "It caused an upper-airway obstruction and that dog drowned in its own fluid" (Bessler (n.d.) cited in Sala, (2014). Punitive training with a choke collar, such as strangulation by holding a dog off the ground by a choke collar (a not uncommon practice), can cause severe brain damage (Dickomeit et al., 2013).

Brachycephalic Obstructive Airway Syndrome (BOAS)

Short noses and wide set eyes might make dogs look cute and childlike, but these features are often associated with breathing difficulty and may come at a very high price to our dogs: Make no mistake, BOAS is a painful condition in dogs. The risk increases as the morphology becomes more and more exaggerated.

Breeder and Veterinarian Responsibility and BOAS

Brachycephalic airway syndrome (BOAS) may affect puppies as young as three months of age (Meola, 2013). Veterinarians and kennel clubs must discuss the problem openly with colleagues and pet parents. Due to the serious medical and welfare implications and the increasing popularity of the brachycephalic breeds, efforts to separate fashion from health are needed. Risk factors should be used to guide breeding decisions. In a study on the impact of facial conformity on canine heath, Packer et al., (2015) warns, "As such, breeders and buyers should be aware of these risks when selecting a dog and breeding organizations should actively discourage exaggerations of this high-risk conformation in breed standards and the show ring." A fundamental rethink in brachycephalic breeding is necessary to save the breeds.

Breathing disorders increase as muzzle length shortens. Breed-related air obstruction disorders are commonly associated with some of the extreme conformation standards established by breed and kennel clubs. Breeds such as the Pug, English Bulldog, Boston Terrier, Cavalier King Charles Spaniel, French Bulldog, Boxer, Pekingese, Shih Tzu, Japanese Chin, Shar-Pei, Lhasa Apso, and short-nosed crossbreeds are at great risk of developing BOAS because the soft tissue is crammed within the skull (Burn et al., 2012) often resulting in chronic and debilitating respiratory dysfunction. Thicker necks and obesity are additional exacerbating factors in brachycephalic dogs (Burn et al., 2015).

Pet parents too often dismiss labored chronic breathing difficulties and respiratory noise as normal despite their dogs' obvious difficulty breathing, overheating, gagging, and choking while on short walks. Dogs may physically collapse and die due to lack of oxygen. Although these pet dogs often show severe clinical signs of BOAS, many pet parents do not recognize that their dog has a breathing problem. Pet parents may believe that these breathing abnormalities are normal signs of aging. Too often these dogs have acute attacks or lose consciousness before a pet parent recognizes breathing is a problem and seek medical help. In a recent study (Liu et al., 2015), 60% of French Bulldog pet parents failed to recognize BOAS in their dogs. Indeed, research finds that 58% of surveyed pet parents of brachycephalic breeds may be suffering because pet parents believe that breathing difficulties, noisy and labored breathing, gagging and choking are "normal" for that breed (Burn et al., 2012b). Some pet parents describe the medical symptoms of respiratory dysfunction as "cute."

According to Dr. Gerhard Oechtering (2010), faculty of veterinary medicine at the University of Leipzig, Germany, "Malformations and collapsibility of the upper airways are much more complex than previously thought." A dog's nose is thought to be essential for effective thermoregulation. Stenotic nares are pinched or narrow nostrils that make it difficult to breathe and cause snorting and snoring. Laryngeal collapse may occur as a result of stenotic nares and tracheal narrowing and lead to death.

Jemima Harrison, producer of the 2008 BBC Documentary, *Pedigree Dogs Exposed*, highlights the serious nature of some of the health and welfare problems in purebred dogs. Harrison sheds light on the reality of the suffering of many brachycephalic breeds. She reports, "Many flat-faced dogs try to sleep sitting or even standing up because their airways block when they drop their heads. It means that some brachycephalic dogs are chronically sleep-deprived" (Harrison, 2016, para. 1). The Royal Veterinary College at the University of London (O'Neil et al., 2015), reports, "These dogs may not be able to enjoy the simple pleasures in a dog's life such as exercise, play, food and sleep."

Polluted Air

Do your best to protect your dog from both indoor and outdoor air pollution when reasonably plausible, just as you would for yourself. Exposure to air pollution has been shown to produce cognitive deficits and brain lesions in dogs as shown by a magnetic resonance imaging (MRI) study published in the *Journal of Brain and Cognition*. The study examined the effect of pollution on brain abnormalities in dogs and children (Barragan-Mejia et al., 2008). Use air purifiers in your home. Avoid smoke-filled rooms and walking your dog when the *Air Quality Index* (n.d.) is high for humans.

SUFFICIENT SLEEP

Sufficient sleep is a fundamental biological need for our dogs. Sleep, along with food, water, and oxygen is essential to survival. Sleep is a critical requirement for optimal health and emotional well-being. Puppies and dogs need to get the quality sleep and the rest their bodies crave. Your dog's species-specific need for sleep is both similar and different from what humans need. Although sufficient sleep is not discussed frequently, veterinarians, breeders, pet parents, trainers, shelter workers and foster parents are responsible for seeing that the dogs in their care have adequate sleep opportunities. Sleep needs vary with age, health, lifestyle, and among individuals. Sleep strengthens the immune, skeletal, and muscular systems. Dogs suffer physically and psychologically and cannot thrive without sufficient sleep.

Newborn humans require on average twice as much sleep as adults. Similarly, puppies need *lots* of extra sleep to grow, heal wounds and store energy to develop and function properly. Many rescue dogs come from very stressful environments, sometimes unavoidably so, with little opportunity for true relaxation. They may be at critical risk for exhaustion and thus, have special sleep needs. To read more about sufficient sleep, see Diane Garrod's book, *Stress Release For Dogs: The Canine Emotional Detox* (Garrod, 2021).

Sleep Deprivation

Sleep deprivation has been found to increase aggressiveness and decrease effective social interactions (Kahn et al., 2006). Sleep deprivation is associated with a compromised immune system, diabetes, weight gain, obesity, depression, hormonal imbalances, and can more than double the risk of cardiovascular disease (Brown et al., 2012). According to Bentivogliio & Grassi-Zucconi (1997, pp. 570–576), "Pioneering canine experimental studies going as far back as 1894 show that sleep is a vital function, and that the lack of sleep causes brain damage and eventually death. The complete absence of sleep was found to be fatal for puppies in a few days. Adult dogs died after 9–17 days without sleep."

Sleep deprivation shortens attention span, increases anxiety, impairs memory, and has a negative effect on mood. The relationship between sleep deprivation and anxiety is well documented in clinical research (Pires & Anderson, 2012). Anxiety is one of the most insidious emotional consequences of both dream sleep (REM) deprivation and deep-sleep deprivation. Generalized anxiety disorder and phobias are associated with sleep deprivation, so anxiety may also cause sleep deprivation.

Dog vs. Human Sleep Patterns

There may be a genetically hard-wired reason for your dog's rumbling about during the night. Periodically scanning the environment may be an innate, residually adaptive behavior, which served to detect predators and protect survival in the wild.

The 24-hour internal clock drives all animals. Circadian rhythms are biologically built-in, even in nocturnal animals (Edgar et al., 2012). One study on dog sleeping habits shows that your dog's rest occurs mostly at night, but their activity increases approximately 2 hours before dawn, and they become most active at dawn, on average. Dogs often nap around the noon hour and have slower activity during the afternoon hours (Tobler & Sigg, 1985). Approximately 44% of your dog's time is spent in alert wakefulness and 21% in the drowsy state. Adult dogs sleep approximately one-third to one-half of a 24-hour-cycle, with an average internal bedtime of 9 pm and rising time of 4 am, according to a classic dog sleep study (Lucas, et al., 1977). Dr. Alexandra Horowitz (2009) also suggests dogs may have a burst of energy in the evening because of their species-specific sleep-wake patterns.

As stated above, sleep-wake *patterns* are species-specific. Humans most commonly sleep for several hours in a single session whereas dogs do not. A 1993 study of sleep-wake activity in dogs showed that the typical pattern of sleeping and waking in dogs is very different than that in people, contrary to popular belief (Adams & Johnson, 1993). Within an 8-hour period, the 24 dogs in the study had 23 sleep-wake cycles on average, of 21 minutes each: they would sleep for 16 minutes and then spontaneously awaken for 5 minutes! Unlike humans, these dogs appeared to become fully conscious during those 5 minutes of wakefulness. When two or more dogs slept together, they each had their own sleep-wake cycling, unaffected by the other dogs cycling. Think of your dog needing power naps throughout the day. Power naps promote performance and learning, help to restore balance to immune and neuroendocrine systems, and are ideal for the genetically hard-wired canine sleep-wake cycle.

Carefully choose the placement of your dog's bed. Wolves have dens, humans have bedrooms, and so your dog ought to have some sanctuary as well. For daytime power naps, your dog may prefer an open-door crate in a corner of a bedroom or other room, a cloth covered open crate, or an orthopedic bed set apart from the line of traffic in your home. Puppies require more sleep than adult dogs. Keeping puppies in the center of the living room, with human activity continually disturbing their sleep, fosters stress.

When setting up containment areas for newborn puppies, responsible breeders should keep each puppy's sleep needs in mind, balancing *Biological Needs* with *Social Needs*. Senior dogs often require more sanctuary space as a safety net apart from other animals in the home to protect their aging bodies and allow for additional sleep needs.

People pay close attention to the type of spinal and back support our own mattresses provide and understand how important proper sleep support is for our own well-being, however, pet parents often make the mistake of choosing the cutest or cushiest beds for their dogs. All dogs, particularly dogs with long spinal columns such as Dachshunds and giant breeds, need a bed with sufficient spinal support. Why not give your dog the best of both worlds—orthopedic support and cute blankets and pillows if you wish. If the only soft bed for your dog does not allow your dog to stretch fully, a remodel of the *dog zone* is in order to provide a truly optimal sleep environment for your best friend.

Separate, but close sleeping quarters may help both canines and humans sleep better at night. As a social and domesticated species, emotionally healthy dogs generally want and need to be in close proximity to us. However, just as humans need a quiet environment for restful rejuvenation, so do our dogs. Consider a change in sleeping locations or quarters if your need for sleep is out of sync with your dog's sleep-wake cycles. When choosing restful sleeping quarters, the National Sleep Foundation (2016) reminds us to factor in proper temperature control, sound, and light.

Dog Dreaming and Deep Sleep

Approximately 23% of your dog's time is spent in deep-sleep, and 12% in the dream state associated with rapid eye movement (REM) (Lucas et al., 1977). During REM sleep, your dog's eyes may roll, they may whimper, shake, whine, growl, and even bark on occasion. They often appear to be chasing something with all four legs pumping the air! Fascinatingly, because a large portion of your dog's brain is devoted to processing scent, your dog may be dreaming in the scent sensory mode as well! "Those who see smells must remember in smells, too: When we imagine dog's dreaming and daydreaming, we should envisage dream images made of scents," Dr. Horowitz reports in *Inside of a Dog* (2009, p. 88).

Puppies spend a greater percentage of time in the dream state than adult dogs, very likely processing all of the new information they are absorbing each day. Dreaming may be a bridge between the brain and behavior, having useful functions similar to dream function for humans.

Dogs adopt many different sleeping positions, some by choice, some as a security measure—and some because the only bed provided is in the shape of a donut. Feral dogs and wolves curl up into a ball with their paws tucked under their body and tails wrapped over the face to conserve body heat and protect their limbs, face, throat, and vital organs. This is the least vulnerable and least restful position for sleeping, however this position allows for a quick leap to the feet for fight or flight. Some dogs sleep on their stomach, also allowing them to jump to their feet easily in the event of a threat or an interesting activity they would like to follow. We also see the "splotz" tummy position (rear legs outstretched) that is often more restful, but still ready to leap into action. Dogs that sleep outstretched on their side are genuinely able to relax and are most often feeling secure in their surroundings. Some dogs sleep belly-up with their legs in the air. Generally, this indicates a secure and confident dog because it is a vulnerable position that exposes vital organs and the throat.

INDOOR SHELTER

Dogs deserve and need to have indoor shelter. Because the natural sleep-wake cycles of dogs differ sharply from sleep-wake cycles in humans, your dog needs a quiet, safe *dog zone,* and a truly comfortable bed to take refuge from a busy daytime household to truly thrive.

It is Dangerous for Dogs to be Left Outdoors Unsupervised

All pet professionals and pet parents should be aware of the considerable and potentially severe ramifications of keeping a dog in an outdoor pen or running loose, unmonitored in a yard. Leaving a dog outdoors unattended may result in medical, emotional, behavioral, and sometimes even legal problems. Of course, there are great benefits to being outdoors, such as fresh air, sunshine, plenty of sniffing opportunities, and the freedom to eliminate as needed. Consider the safety and feasibility of a doggy door to have the best of both worlds with indoor and supervised outdoor access.

Inclement weather, or normal weather for your city, can pose some serious medical risks such as hypothermia or hyperthermia resulting in your dog being unable to control their body's temperature leading to life-threatening survival issues, suffering, and death. Heatstroke may result from something as unexpected as fence-fighting with a visiting dog in the next yard, or from playing chase through the fence with your neighbor mowing the lawn. Sunburn is painful and can lead to skin cancer. Protect pink noses, bellies, inside of the ears and top of the head, with a non-toxic sunscreen on short-haired/thin-skinned dogs when your dog is outdoors. Neighbors frustrated with your dog's incessant barking, or children, may accidentally or deliberately release, steal or poison your dog.

Although laws vary between state, chaining or tethering a dog with a rope or a line to a stationary object for any longer than it takes a person to complete a temporary task—approximately 10 minutes—is now illegal in the state of California (Animal Legal and Historical Center, 2014). The Humane Society of the United States tells us, "Dogs (especially small dogs) should not be left outside unattended, should never be chained and should always be kept on a leash in public areas" (2016, para. 11).

Outdoor Emotional and Behavioral Risks

The failure to provide sufficient outdoor supervision and indoor shelter may result in the following emotional and behavioral problems:

- **Isolation and loneliness.** Dogs are now rarely considered farm animals (even if they live on a farm) but more often they are thought of as members of our families. Responsible caretakers and pet parents must recognize that dogs have real social needs that only we have the power to help fill—or to thwart.
- **Stereotypies.** Many dogs develop difficult to treat idiopathic obsessive behaviors such as tail-chasing, fly-snapping, and self-mutilation due to isolation, boredom, and frustration from being left alone outdoors.
- **Anxiety.** Frustration arising from the genetically-driven need or a desire to engage with passing dogs and humans can lead to fence-barrier stress and may devolve into aggression towards people in general and other dogs.
- **Guarding.** Natural guarding behaviors may intensify and create or exacerbate existing human and/or dog-dog aggression.
- **Aggression.** Teasing from neighborhood children and fence-fighting with other dogs may lead to aggression towards children, adults, and other dogs.
- **Lack of rest.** Dogs kept outdoors and working dogs rarely relax sufficiently to achieve healthy, deep, restful sleep.

Parasites, Insects and Wildlife

In "The Great Awful Outdoors" Pat Miller (2001) concurs that keeping your dog outdoors for long periods may lead to a variety of problems. Pet food and water should be kept indoors to avoid attracting wildlife and parasites to your yard. Extended time outdoors results in hazards that can cause psychological and physical damage, even death, and may include:

- **Fly strike.** When left outdoors dogs risk bites by flies attracted to defecation. Flies lay eggs on the dog host leading to maggot infestation in the open wounds which are painful and sometimes fatal (RSPCA, 2021).

- **Heartworm.** The parasitic worm, *Dirofilarial immitis,* are spread through the bite of a mosquito putting dogs in danger of heart failure, lung and other organ damage and death.
- **Tapeworm infection.** If a dog eats a flea carrying the tapeworm larva, the larva grows into a tapeworm attaching to the dog's intestine. Tapeworms may grow to 11 inches in length.
- **Other insects**. Bee stings, ticks, poisonous spiders, venomous fire ants, mites, wasps, and hornets, are dangerous and pose immediate injury or long-term parasite problems for your dog. When left outdoor dogs cannot escape these flying and crawling insects looking for a host. In "Venom Reactions and Treatment Options" The American Society for the Prevention of Cruelty to Animals (ASPCA) tells us that with multiple bee stings, systemic poisoning is not uncommon and a dog may need to be hospitalized for multiple days (ASPCA, 2016).
- **Rabies.** In the United States, rabies is most commonly found in raccoons, foxes, skunks, and bats. The San Diego Humane Society (2020, para. 1) warns us about raccoons in our yards, "They can carry rabies and baylisascaris worms, both of which are contagious to you, and distemper which can be transmitted to your pets."
- **Wildlife.** Fence your yard securely and protect your dog through supervision. Danger from wildlife such as: snakes, rabid raccoons, skunks, foxes, coyotes, eagles, owls, hawks, bats, and stray cats may lie in wait in your backyard ready to defend themselves if disturbed or to prey upon your dog.
- **Coyotes.** Coyotes who disturb dogs are either protecting their pups and their territory or are lured into neighborhoods by well-meaning residents who have been offering food to wildlife. Do not let your dog interact or play with a coyote.
- **Snakes.** A potentially serious threat to your dog's safety outdoors is snakes. How do you keep your dog from being bitten by a venomous snake? Unfortunately, there is no easy answer and there are no guarantees. Neither your family nor your dog is safe from venomous snakes. Some dogs have an inborn aversion to snakes while others find them fascinating. Many snake bites occur on the pet parent's own property. No spray or scatter products have been proven to be effective.

Secure Your Yard

Remove food sources, such as rodents, mice, birdseed, crickets, and outdoor pet food. Secure all garbage cans. Remove habitats where snakes may hide, such as: Woodpiles, vegetation, underbrush, and rocks. Seal holes and block entrances under your house or deck. Install rattlesnake safety fencing.

Leash Your Dog

Do not allow your dog to walk or roam in known snake infested areas. The San Diego Natural History Museum herpetology research center (2020) advises, "Common sense is the best defense. Cultivate an attitude of alertness. Never let a dog run loose; always keep a dog leashed no matter how good it normally is." Keep your dog safe and happy by providing exercise in secured environments such as at a dog park, an agility class, swimming, kayaking, paddle boarding, surfing, dock diving, fly-ball, shopping with you, chasing a lure toy or asking your dog to fetch your tennis serves into the swimming pool!

Snake Venom Vaccine

Snake bites must *always* be treated as a veterinary emergency immediately. The vaccine is not a substitute for an emergency visit to your trusted integrative veterinarian. Make sure your vet carries antivenin. If you live in or visit areas where rattlesnakes roam, ensure your dog receives the snake venom vaccine which is generally effective for venomous rattlesnakes. Side effects are rare. The vaccine cost is minimal and may dramatically reduce the effects of venom, the cost of treatment, and recovery time in the hospital. It may save your dog's life.

Snake Aversion Training Using Shock

Promotional claims, anecdotal reports, and unverifiable statistics abound about the benefits of shock training for your dog for snake-aversion. There is no empirical data to support the efficacy of this training or that demonstrates that snake-aversion training by shock does all, or any part of, what it promises to do. Additionally, shock training may give pet parents a dangerously false sense of security. Many snakebites occur by inadvertently disturbing a snake and no amount of shock training will prevent that.

Behavior experts tell us that shock is easily misapplied and can traumatize animals, and result in severe and permanent side effects, such as the fear of the great outdoors, or men, for example. The reaction that snake aversion training promises to teach is flight. However, science tells us that the various responses to fear, pain, and shock include fight, flight, freeze, fawn, and others. The *Fight-flight Syndrome* is scientifically unpredictable according to Nijenhuis et al., in the *Journal of Traumatic Stress* (1998). Other unexpected and undesirable responses are equally as likely, such as:

- The dog could successfully go to *flight* but because of the fear associated with shock, in the dog's panic, get bitten by the snake.
- The dog could go to *fight* and get bitten by the snake.

- The dog could go to *freeze* and become paralyzed in fear and get bitten by the snake.
- The dog could go to *fawn* in submission and get bitten by the snake.
- Dogs can lose their flight response reaction over time and get bitten by the snake.

Pet parents who work with a trainer must be sure that the trainer's methods are safe: Trainers must never use shock collars. No competent dog trainer uses shock for any purpose. Learning should never hurt. Alternative, non-aversive, snake avoidance training methods are springing up because of the need to find an alternate, more effective, and safer method than shock. Popular and effective new courses in real life scenarios of an outdoor hike, teach your dog to alert you immediately upon encountering a snake, similar to basic service dog training. That is—the sound of a rattlesnake is your dog's cue to come to you.

SAFETY

To protect your dog, puppy-proof your home, yard, and pool area just as you would for a toddler. Many everyday household items can pose a threat to your dog—even some items specifically meant for pets can be dangerous. However, pet parents should never use any product or substance on their dog that was not specifically created for them.

Poisons, Toxins, and Household Hazards

Read the labels and toxicity warnings on all household cleaning products. Diluted vinegar and water are a typically safe alternative to commercial cleaning agents. Beware of holiday hazards and toxins that may be sniffed or absorbed through the pads of your dog's feet. Potentially toxic agents should be avoided if at all possible. Never use any potentially toxic product or application, such as essential oils, without first consulting a veterinarian (ASPCA, 2015). If you suspect your pet has been exposed to any poisonous substances, contact your veterinarian, or call the ASPCA Animal Poison Control Center hotline at (888) 426–4435 immediately (2019).

Here's a partial list of things to avoid:

- **Insecticides, mosquito repellants, and rodenticides** are used in many over-the-counter flea and tick remedies. Prescription flea and tick control products may also be toxic.
- **Human and veterinary medications** such as pain killers including aspirin, acetaminophen, ibuprofen, and naproxen (pets metabolize and eliminate these drugs differently than humans), cold medicines, anti-cancer drugs, anti-depressants, vitamins, diet pills, and many prescription drugs can all be toxic to animals. Keep medicine containers and tubes of ointments and creams away from dogs because they can easily chew through them.
- **Creams and ointments** applied to your own skin can cause serious, even life-threatening dangers if your dog licks your skin after a recent application. Read the label, keep your skin covered, and wash your hand thoroughly after use.
- **Poisonous household plants**, including azalea, dieffenbachia (dumb cane), lilies, philodendron, poinsettias, and mistletoe.
- **Chocolate** is toxic to dog because it contains theobromine and caffeine and the sensitivity to these substances is far greater in dogs than in humans. The darker and more bitter the chocolate the greater the danger.
- **Human foods** to avoid include xylitol, grapes, raisins, onions and onion powder, alcoholic beverages, yeast dough, coffee grounds, salt, macadamia nuts, avocados pits, tomato, potato and rhubarb leaves and stems, and anything with mold growing on it.
- **Essential oils** whether inhaled or ingested may lead to central nervous system depression and liver damage. Inhaled oils may lead to aspiration pneumonia (Pet Poison Helpline, 2020).
- **Cigarettes, nicotine patches, e-cigarettes, and marijuana**, whether inhaled or ingested are toxic.
- **Bar soaps**, especially those made with essential oils or glycerin are toxic.
- **Bleach** must be properly diluted followed by a thorough rinsing and airing out.

- **Fabric softener sheets** contain harmful chemicals if chewed or ingested, even if already used, and may also result in gastrointestinal obstruction.
- **Grout sealer** of the alkaline type is poisonous to dogs leading to drooling, vomiting, and sores in a dog's mouth.
- **Rawhide dog chews** may be contaminated with salmonella, which can infect pets and humans who come in contact with the chews. These types of chews may also pose a choking hazard.
- **Xylitol** is a sugar substitute commonly found in peanut butter. Many breath mints and gum contain xylitol or menthol which can lead to seizures and liver damage.
- **String, yarn, rubber bands, and dental floss** are easy to swallow and can cause intestinal blockages or strangulation. Rope chew toys are notorious for threads that can be pulled out and swallowed and then wrap around internal organs such as the stomach and intestines requiring surgery.
- **Electric cord burns and electrocution.** "Electrocution from chewing on an electrical cord is the single most common type of electrical injury for household pets. These types of injuries can result in burns to the surrounding areas, e.g., mouth, whiskers, or facial hair. The current alters the electrical conduction in the heart, muscles, and other tissues" (PetMD, 2016, para. 1). Turn off the electricity before moving your shocked dog and seek immediate veterinary treatment.
- **Toys with movable parts** especially squeaky toys or stuffed animals with plastic eyes can pose a choking hazard to animals. Take the same precautions with your dog as you would with a small child.
- **Slick wood floors and uncarpeted stairs** are slipping hazards and often instill fear in dogs because of an experience with the unstable slippery surface. Many dogs have long fur between the digits, making slipping a real danger.
- **Holiday decorations and lights**. Ornaments appear like a toy ball to your dog but contain glass. Lights contain glass components and chewed cords may lead to electric shock. Topped holiday trees are common. Keep these items out of reach and if possible, confine your dog to an undecorated area of the home particularly while you are away from home.

Swimming Practice and Drowning

Never throw your dog into the water to "see how it goes"—because your dog can easily drown, struggle or thrash and any trust you may have established will be broken. The safest, least stressful, and most effective way to teach a dog to swim is to use a properly-fitted life jacket. A life jacket often helps new swimmers relax enough to paddle with all four legs. Desensitize your dog to wearing a dog life jacket to keep him afloat and to provide peace of mind for you. Your dog's innate ability to swim or ease in learning to swim is, in part, determined by breed and body morphology. Even some retrievers need a helping hand to learn and find the confidence to swim for fun and exercise. Breeds with short legs and wide chests such as Bulldogs, Boston Terriers, Corgis, and Pugs, simply were not bred for swimming. Large, muscled breeds such as the *bully* breeds, require a great deal of energy expenditure in the water due to their significant body mass. Sight hounds, such as Salukis, Whippets, Italian Greyhounds and Greyhounds, have the disadvantage of both large muscles and little body fat to keep them afloat.

According to an article in the *Whole Dog Journal* (Colman, 2019), a common but dangerous dog myth is that our dogs already know how to *dogpaddle* and keep themselves afloat in the water. However, new, and panicked swimmers tend to concentrate their efforts on the front legs alone forgetting to use the back legs. One of the most important things you must teach your dog is how and where to exit the pool, should your dog accidentally fall in or literally get lost while swimming. Do not allow your dog to drink excessive amounts of chlorinated water from the pool and always make fresh water readily available. Rinse your dog off thoroughly after swims in the pool and out in nature. Dry your dog's ears and dry under the collar. Learn CPR for pets. Avoid contaminated still pools of water and green algae-ridden ponds. Home pools should be fully fenced to protect your dog from swimming unsupervised.

TEMPERATURE CONTROL

Homeostasis. Temperature control is one central process that is necessary for life in response to environmental changes. According to Modell et al., (2015), "Homeostatic regulation refers to mechanisms related to maintaining consistency of the internal environment." Serious and life-threatening hyperthermia (too hot) or hypothermia (too cold) are often seen in dogs who are exercising, left outdoors in the elements, or locked in cars where homeostasis may be critically compromised.

Normal and Abnormal Dog Temperature Guidelines

Dr. Janet Merrill, DVM, of the Urban Search and Rescue Veterinary Group (2020, para. 3), provides these normal and abnormal canine temperature parameters:

- **Normal**—rectal temperature between 101.0—102.5°F
- **Hypothermia**—rectal temperature less than 98.0°F
- **Hyperthermia**—rectal temperature between 102.0—108.0°F
- **Heatstroke**—rectal temperature greater than 105.8°F accompanied by central nervous system dysfunction (Merrill, 2020).

Hyperthermia, Also Known as Heatstroke

An extreme rise in body temperature is a medical emergency requiring immediate treatment to prevent disability or death (Flournoy et al., 2003). Hyperthermia, more commonly known as heatstroke, is an environmental or exertion caused life-threatening medical emergency in dogs. Dogs regulate their temperature and cool themselves by evaporation (panting) and conduction (transfer of heat to a cool surface). Panting creates a cooling effect through evaporation of saliva in the mouth, on the tongue and from the lining of the lungs. The primary cooling mechanism for dogs is panting with the mouth open (Coren, 2010).

Unlike humans, sweating is not a significant mechanism of cooling for a dog. Dogs have no other efficient way of getting rid of body heat other than panting. Dogs do not have sweat glands, except in their feet. Your dog's fur coat can easily make your dog susceptible to overheating. Fur is an insulator that keeps the heat (and cold) out, as long as your dog is not in a continuously hot environment. Once the body temperature rises, however, fur slows the cooling process because heat from the body cannot escape. Dogs not properly conditioned to exercise in the heat and humidity, and older dogs may suffer heatstroke very quickly.

Dogs left outdoors or locked in cars may suffer hyperthermia where the dog's body temperature becomes elevated because it is producing or absorbing more heat than it can release. Other major risk factors associated with heatstroke in dogs according to Dr. Janet Merrill (2020) include:

- Weight greater than 66 pounds but not associated with obesity
- Obesity
- Brachycephalic breeds
- Environmental conditions—either external temperature and/or high humidity
- Dark coat color
- Fatigue
- Previous episodes of heat exhaustion
- Muzzling

Nylon muzzles that restrict breathing and impede panting are particularly dangerous, disabling your dog's ability to cool itself. To prevent hyperthermia, *never* use a nylon muzzle in hot weather or when exercising your dog. If necessary, use a basket muzzle properly sized to allow room for a full-mouthed pant.

Temperatures at or above 105°F can cause brain damage. If the body becomes overwhelmed by a rise in temperature because of excessive heat and humidity, heatstroke occurs. According to the National Institute of Health (2016), heat waves pose risks for susceptible individuals such as the very young, old, overweight, and the health challenged. The sweltering heat waves of summer and the long-term effects of sudden temperature changes shown in climate change models are predicted to become more frequent.

Heatstroke Prevention

Avoid exercising your dog in hot and humid conditions. Proper hydration is critical to dogs, particularly when exercising in warm conditions. Hydrate, hydrate, and hydrate. In hot weather, before, during and after exercise, use a garden hose or spray bottle frequently to dampen your dog's fur with water to create an evaporative effect to help your dog stay cool. A child's plastic swimming pool placed in the shade can also help your dog regulate internal temperature.

Heatstroke may be easily prevented in healthy dogs by following these recommendations:

- Plan exercise for cool periods of the day
- Provide adequate ventilation
- Provide free access to plenty of shade

- Provide free access to fresh cool drinking water and ice cubes
- Do not lock your dog in the car. Heatstroke often occurs when dogs are confined in cars where temperatures rise suddenly and dramatically
- Do not leave your dog outdoors alone unmonitored
- Consider a cooling device such as a sleeping pad or doghouse
- Condition your dog with progressive acclimation to exercise, heat, and humidity.

Symptoms

Hyperthermia begins when signs of heat stress go unheeded. Dogs who are panting heavily and if the environment permits, seeking shade, cool surfaces, and drinking water to bring body temperature down are experiencing heat stress. A staggering gait and the appearance of "drunkenness" means your dog may be falling victim to heatstroke. According to Flournoy et al., (2003), "Signs of heatstroke are: increased panting, drooling, vomiting, bloody diarrhea, rapid heart rate, and dry, sticky, and discolored (bright pink, reddish or purple) gums and tongue. Cortical blindness, cardiovascular collapse, unconsciousness, seizures, coma, central nervous system dysfunction, shallow breathing, and death may follow if veterinary care is not sought immediately."

Know your dog's normal gum and tongue color so you will recognize changes in gum color should you suspect hyperthermia. If your dog is panting heavily and the gums are a dark pink—stop, rest, come indoors and offer cool water immediately.

Treatment

Treatment should be rapid and aggressive. Measures should be taken immediately and during transport to the veterinarian to lower the body temperature by spraying your dog with cool (*not cold*) water and allowing evaporation, opening windows, and using air-conditioning to dissipate the heat. Cool, wet towels along the back of the neck, groin, and armpits (sites of major blood vessels) with airflow can begin the cooling process while on the road to your veterinarian.

Cool the body gradually—do NOT immerse your dog in cold water, administer cold-water enemas, or cover your dog's body with a wet towel: this can inhibit your dog's cooling mechanisms (Flournoy et al., 2003). Cold water immersion makes the core temperature rise, rather than decrease. Cold water also causes shivering generating heat and making it counterproductive to cooling.

Hypothermia

Hypothermia is a medical emergency that occurs when the body is losing heat faster than it can produce heat, causing a critically low body temperature. Hypothermia, in healthy dogs, is caused by either exposure to cold weather, wet fur and skin, or immersion in cold water (Mayo Clinic, 2020b, PetMD, 2010). Dogs at risk for hypothermia include puppies, seniors, those with low body fat, heart disease, kidney disease, and hypothyroidism.

Prevention

Short-haired, thin-skinned, and toy breed dogs may lose heat particularly fast. If your dog is sensitive to cold, do not hesitate to add a sweater, or hoodie for sensitive ears, to provide extra warmth indoors and out. Add boots to protect tender pads when pads may suffer chemical burns from deicing salt or literally stick to icy pavement. Generally, avoid harsh weather, ice, and snow.

Symptoms

Shivering is probably the first thing you would notice as your dog's body temperature drops. Shivering is the body's attempt to warm itself. If you notice your dog shivering on any occasion, barring a medical condition or fear, take action. However, be aware that *shivering stops* as hypothermia worsens. Lethargy often follows shivering and paleness (Miller, 2019). When your dog's body temperature drops, the heart, nervous system, and other organs are unable to function properly. Hypothermia can lead to coma, heart, and respiratory failure and ultimately to death.

Treatment

The standard of care for hypothermia is to use warmed blankets from the clothes dryer, or a warm (*not hot*) hair dryer plus a hot water bottle wrapped in a towel against your dog's abdomen: an unwrapped water bottle may burn your dog's skin. Check your dog's temperature every 10 minutes. If the rectal temperature is below 98°F, seek immediate veterinary care. The successful outcome of treating hypothermia warms the body back to a normal temperature.

GENTLE GROOMING

Force-free training and force-free husbandry care go hand in glove. Although grooming is often considered a cosmetic practice, The Hierarchy of Dog Needs highlights proper and gentle grooming as an essential *Biological Need* and health issue. Positive experience in grooming is critical to our dogs' physical and emotional fitness. A gentle groomer is worth her weight in gold. (See Chapter 8, How to Find a Good Veterinarian and Groomer.)

Health Benefits of Grooming

A shiny coat is an indicator and mirror of your dog's overall health. A dull coat indicates that something is amiss in your dog's health. Proper hygiene of your dog's coat is important for your dog's health, including the removal of excess hair fur nests or mats that may serve as havens for bacteria, parasites, and fleas. Seasoned, knowledgeable groomers can identify possible medical issues during grooming procedures that might otherwise go unnoticed such as: Abscesses, skin conditions, ear infections, tumors, cysts, insect bites, wounds, foxtails, pebbles, splinters, small bits of broken glass, worm infestations such as maggots, and areas of sensitivities where your dog has been biting or scratching. Head shaking may mean an ear infection. If a dog rubs his head against objects, your dog may be trying to scratch itchy, infected ears.

Nail Trims Are a Must

Nail trims are not simply a cosmetic concern. Overgrown nails that reach and touch the floor can cause serious functional problems and deformities in your dog. Many dogs are either kept indoors or only run outdoors on soft grassy surfaces, so nails are not gradually worn down by running on concrete or blacktop. Regular nail clipping is necessary so that overgrown nails do not impede your dog's walking gait or cause skeletal deformities of the limbs and spine, which are often accompanied by pain (College of Veterinary Medicine, Washington State University, n.d.). Dewclaws on the inner side of the paw do not reach the ground so they are not worn down naturally as the dog walks, runs, and plays.

Health Problems and Pain Created by Overgrown Nails

Overgrown nails lead to a vicious repetitive cycle of pain and avoidance. Dogs avoid having the nails and paws touched because of pain and fear, which leads to painful and unpleasant nail-trimming sessions, which leads to both the dog and pet parent avoiding nail trims, which leads to longer and longer intervals between nail trims, which in the end just leads to more pain. And the cycle repeats (Flaim, 2016). Below find a list of injuries and trauma a dog suffers from overgrown nails.

- Long nails can curl into a semi-circle and grow into the toe pad
- Pain in the nail bed caused by the pressure of overgrown nails pressing back into the nail bed
- Deformity of forelimb joints can result from nail bed pressure against the bones
- Unnatural weight distribution results in a predisposition to injuries
- Postural abnormalities, particularly in older dogs
- Painful and difficult walking and running
- Painful split and torn nails
- Elongated blood vessels in overgrown nails make mail trims more difficult

Outdated and Dangerous Grooming Standards

Potentially Dangerous Grooming Equipment

Just as equipment and restraint devices in the dog training and veterinary professionals are moving quickly toward force-free, pain free, and fright free options, this is the wave of the future in grooming also. However, trainers, other professionals, and pet parents may be surprised to learn of the potential danger and discomfort, physically and emotionally, in what is currently considered standard equipment in grooming.

Standard equipment used by many groomers include:

- **Nooses.** A noose attached to a grooming arm that prevents dogs from jumping off the grooming table. Dogs left unattended for a very short period of time may be hanged from attempts to jump off the table or from accidental falls.
- **Straps.** A strap under the stomach that prevents dogs from sitting.
- **Slings.** A cloth sling, often used to immobilize dogs for nail trims, is raised, hanging the dogs off the ground.
- **Nylon muzzles.** A nylon muzzle that prevents dogs from using the mouth to pant and bite.

- **Drying cages and boxes.** Dogs may suffer hyperthermia, heat exhaustion, severe burns, and death from malfunctioning equipment, or from not being properly supervised while in a drying cage with the equipment inadvertently left running. Even when properly supervised your dog's body temperature can rise quickly. Additionally, stress makes body temperature rise faster.
- **Clippers.** Buzzing clippers may cut or nick mats that are close to the skin.
- **Scissors.** Sharp scissors may injure eyes or other body parts.

Potentially Dangerous Grooming Practices

Grooming is an unregulated field. There is a pressing need for the grooming industry to embrace more dog-friendly ethics and practices, making animal welfare the priority—and for pet parents to accept less than perfect grooms. Dangerous grooming practices and negligence can cause injury and even death. Some of the most egregious examples include:

- **Raising the grooming arm.** If your dog struggles while being groomed, it is not uncommon for some groomers to raise the grooming arm again and again until the dog stops struggling. The dog may be literally hung from the grooming arm and must devote all energy to breathing.
- **Calling for "reinforcements."** An alternate practice to raising the grooming arm is to call on another groomer to physically restrain the dog while being groomed. The more the dog struggles, the more the groomer and assistant restrain the dog until the dog stops struggling because of total physical exhaustion or fear, reported as good behavior.
- **Aggressive dogs.** A seldom-considered danger in many grooming facilities is that dogs may be attacked, severely injured, or killed by other dogs in the grooming salon. At a minimum, a dog's socialization with people and other dogs is often negatively impacted by the grooming environment and experience if separation is not consistently used for fearful dogs and those who may aggress.

Improving Standards and Best Practices of Grooming

In an exposé in the *BARKS from the Guild* trade magazine (2016, July), gentle groomer, Michelle Martiya, makes some cautionary recommendations. According to Martiya, "The introduction of restraints can determine whether the next grooming visit will be even more frightening for the dog, or just a mildly unpleasant experience." Groomers should develop a training plan with the pet parent to be practiced between sessions moving toward more gentle grooming practices and restraints.

Here are some suggestions for equipment and practice improvements leading to a more pleasant experience for the dog.

- Equipment and practices should keep the dog and groomer safe from injury.
- Equipment should be the least intrusive temporary solution to an immediate problem, that is, the minimal amount of equipment restraint needed for the task.
- Equipment should be properly conditioned, that is, desensitized, so as not to stress the dog.
- Equipment should be comfortable for the dog; if the dog struggles more, the groomer should try a different restraint (Martiya, 2016).
- The noose should be loose enough to allow the dog to sit or stand comfortably but still prevent the dog from jumping off the table.
- The dog should be allowed to choose the most comfortable body position.
- The grooming arm should not be raised so high as to make the dog uncomfortable.
- The grooming arm should *never* be raised so high where breathing is difficult for the dog.
- Use of an Elizabethan collar for larger dogs are less restrictive and easier to accept than a standard muzzle.
- Use of an air muzzle for small dogs is much less restrictive and easier to accept than a standard muzzle. If a muzzle is necessary, the pet parent should purchase a basket muzzle and classically condition the muzzle *before* going to the groomer and between visits. Use the muzzle like a food bowl or deliver treats through the basket so your dog happily offers to put the head inside the muzzle (Patel, 2010).
- Dogs who cannot stand for long periods of time may be properly and kindly conditioned to slings, maintaining four feet on the ground.
- Wraps used around the head and ears to reduce dryer noise must be used with great care as they may induce *tonic immobility* where fear is mistaken for good behavior. (See Chapter 11, Flooding and Tonic Immobility.)

GENTLE VETERINARY CARE

Gentle veterinary care is a principal component of the foundational *Biological Needs* level of the Hierarchy of Dog Needs. Force-free training and force-free veterinary care go hand in glove. Veterinarians are generally the first professionals who interact with a puppy or rescued dog and some of the only people outside of family who may have a lifelong relationship with each dog. Positive interactions starting with the first veterinary visit and throughout the life of your dog are critical to a dog's physical and emotional fitness. A stressful first visit may be a cause of behavior problems that continue throughout a lifetime of veterinary visits and may negatively affect your dog's social development. We encourage pet parents to be pro-active in being not only their dog's biggest fan, but their dog's most ardent advocate as well. (See Chapter 8, How to Find a Good Veterinarian and Groomer.)

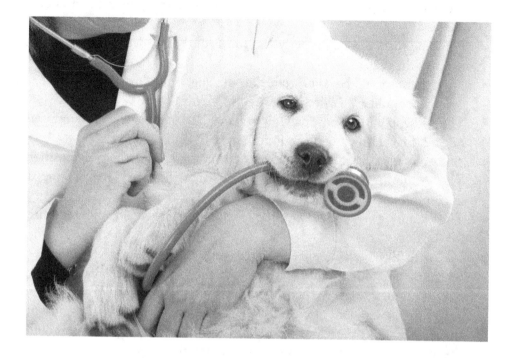

Animal hospital designers have suggested ways to make veterinary offices more environmentally enriched, such as

- Painting walls in pastel colors. Have staff wear pastel-colored scrubs and lab coats. When seen through a dog's eyes, a white lab coat is too bright and may be frightening.
- Removing fluorescent lights. The buzz from those old fixtures can be heard by dogs and may frighten them.
- Providing alternatives to lifting animals up on to high exam tables with cold slippery metal surfaces. Some clinics use yoga mats for animal exams.
- Playing classical music (Lewis, 2016).

Benefits of Regular Veterinary Care

Early Detection of Disease

Annual wellness health exams for the family dog should be scheduled, just as you schedule exams for your family members and yourself. To prevent pain, suffering, and the progression of disease, early veterinary diagnosis and treatment is critical to improve quality of life.

A Belgian awareness campaign highlighting the benefits of veterinary visits provided free pet health care appointments on a voluntary basis (Diez et al., 2015). Seven hundred and ninety-one veterinarians participated in a campaign examining 17,938 pets. According to answers on the questionnaire, 7% of the dogs had never previously received a veterinary visit, 27% had not been seen in the past year, but 66% had been seen in the past year. A large percentage of dogs receiving veterinary care received little preventative care. The most common finding was overweight and obese dogs. The prevalence of disorders reported included obesity (33.5%), dental calculus (31.1%), inflammation of the external ear caused by bacteria (14%), mammary tumors (11.2%), cataract (9.5%), heart disease (6.4%), osteoarthritis (5.4%), and lameness (5.4%).

Basic and specialty veterinary services. Some of the basic and specialty advance care services veterinary professionals offer include: Wellness exams throughout the developmental stages, geriatric health care, vaccinations, urinalysis, microchipping, neutering and spaying, blood panels, treatments for infections and parasites including fleas and worms, dietary prescriptions for dogs who are ill, diagnostic x-rays, digital x-rays, cardiology, EKG/EEG, echocardiography, non-invasive ultrasound (sonogram) to evaluate the condition of internal organs, laser surgery, stem cell therapy, chemotherapy, orthopedic surgery for broken bones, patella abnormalities, joints, muscles, ligament injury, arthritis, tendons, and OFA-X-Ray to detect hip dysplasia, dermatology and rehabilitation for disease and injury. Many clinics and specialty hospitals are increasingly providing essential dental care, including services such as root canals, root planing, crown placement, gum (gingival) surgery, and orthodontics.

Veterinarians and Behavior

Pet parent and dog stress are key reasons why pets are not brought to the veterinarian more often for maintenance care. Many pet parents do not take their dog for veterinary care unless their dog is obviously ill, or they follow up with fewer appointments because both the pet parent and their dog are unwilling to experience the fear too often associated with veterinary visits (Volk et al., 2011). Visits to the veterinarian are essential but are too often unnecessarily stressful and even traumatic for many pet dogs. (See Chapter 11, Flooding and Tonic Immobility, and Chapter 21, Fear.)

The American Veterinary Association and the American College of Veterinary Behaviorists provide some insight and statistics. When veterinary students finish school, they realize they need help with learning animal behavior. Of more than 113,000 veterinarians in in the United States in private clinical, public, and corporate practice, there are fewer than 80 veterinary behavior specialists (ACVB, n.d.).

In a video interview, Dr. Karen Overall, DVM, PhD, and editor of the *Journal of Veterinary Behavior*, discusses the missing gap of behavior education in the veterinary education system and in veterinary medical schools (2011), "People need to realize that vets do not know that much about problem behavior, or even normal dog behavior. Worldwide it is exceptional that veterinary specialists in behavior are faculty in veterinary medical schools and yet the biggest single killer of pet dogs (and cats) are behavior problems." More dogs are relinquished by pet parents and euthanized by animal shelters for behavior problems than as a result of medical problems. Sadly, the average pet parent does not know that most veterinarians, being medical doctors, are not necessarily knowledgeable about dog behavior. This may become a serious problem if a pet parent seeks behavior advice from a veterinarian not academically schooled in behavior as they often provide opinions on behavior or recommend aversive trainers. Behavior management guidelines set forth by the *American Animal Hospital Association* (2020) are reviewed below.

The leading edge "Position Statement on Humane Dog Training" from the American Veterinary Society of Animal Behavior (AVSAB) (2021a) gives clear guidance as to the trainers and behavioral consultants veterinarians should and should not refer their clients to for training. They write,

> *If a trainer is observed using aversive training methods or if a trainer discusses out-dated ideas such as "dominance", "leader of the pack", or "alpha" theories, then clients should be advised against hiring them . . . After the health evaluation the veterinarian can determine if they have the skills and desire to create a behavior treatment plan or if they prefer to partner with a behavior consultant or trainer* (p. 2.)

Veterinarian specialists in Europe are often involved in conducting research, however, veterinary behavior research is rare in the United States as the overwhelming majority of veterinarians are solely clinical practitioners. They may not have a thorough understanding or knowledge of current animal behavior research, familiarity with aggressive incidents or evidence-based understanding of how to address such issues. According to the interview with Overall (2011), "A lot of our veterinarians are not thinking as scientifically as they could be."

Animals who experience stress during a veterinary visit may mask their symptoms. Promisingly, there are a growing number of veterinarians who have sought education and now specialize in the field of behavior. More than ever before, veterinary doctors, behavior consultants, trainers, and pet parents are working together to make visits to the veterinarian more joyful and less stressful for dogs.

AAHA Guidelines for Canine Behavior Management

The American Animal Hospital Association (AAHA) originally developed and published the *Canine and Feline Behavior Management Guidelines* in 2015 (Hammerle et al., p. 219) to help veterinarians and their staff with "concise, evidence-based information to ensure that the basic behavioral needs of feline and canine patients are understood and met in every practice." The guidelines mandate the following: "All team members should be committed to a program of 'behavior prophylaxis,' whereby puppies and kittens are treated in a nonthreatening manner from their first visit." The guidelines for veterinary practices were based on a consensus of expert opinions and clinical experience. The recommendations were researched and written by three veterinarians who specialize in behavior: Karen Overall, VMD, PhD, DACVB, CAAB; Lisa Radosta, DVM, DACVB; Emily Levine, DVM, DACVB, MRCVS; and other esteemed veterinary professionals and technicians, including Sophia Yin, DVM, MS; Marcy Hammerle, DVM, DABVP (C/F); Christine Horst, DVM; and Marcia Rafter-Ritchie, LVT, CPDT, VTS-Behavior.

The *American Animal Hospital Association Canine and Feline Behavior Management Guidelines* stand out as a progressive voice in the veterinary field. In their report, they champion low-fear and low stress clinic environments. The value and scope of regular veterinary visits outlined in the AAHA guidelines (2020) are publicly available and provide recommendations for comprehensive veterinary healthcare programs. These recommendations are designed to help the veterinarian deliver optimal patient care and are of great interest to pet parents and other pet-related professionals who want to see their pets thrive and avoid pain and suffering insofar as that may be possible.

To develop a lifelong healthcare strategy, the guidelines divide a dog's life into five stages: Puppy, young adult, mature adult, senior and end of life (AAHA, 2020). According to Creevy et al., (2019, para. 1) in "The Canine Life Stages Guidelines", "The guidelines provide the following recommendations for managing 10 health-related factors at each of the first four canine life stages: lifestyle effect on the patient's safety, zoonotic and human safety risk, behavior, nutrition, parasite control, vaccination, dental health, reproduction, breed-specific conditions, and a baseline diagnostic profile." The guidelines also offer prevention, diagnostic, and therapeutic plans.

Veterinary Guidance on Aversive Training Tools and Techniques

In regard to training and behavior modification recommendations for veterinarians, the AAHA clearly states, "It is essential that clients ask trainers about specific tools and techniques used. If the tools or techniques include prong collars, shock collars, leash/collar jerks/yanks or if the trainer explains behavior in terms of "dominance" or throws anything at a dog, advise clients to switch trainers" (AAHA, 2011, p. 211–212). Here are some of the AAHA warnings to veterinarians against using aversive techniques:

This task force opposes training methods that use aversive techniques. Aversive training has been associated with detrimental effects on the human-animal bond, problem-solving ability, and the physical and behavioral health of the patient.

- *[Aversive techniques] cause problem behaviors in normal animals and hastens progression of behavioral disorders in distressed animals.*

- *Aversive techniques are especially injurious to fearful and aggressive patients and often suppress signals of impending aggression, rendering any aggressive dog more dangerous.*
- *Aversive techniques include prong (pinch) or choke collars, cattle prods, alpha rolls, dominance downs, electronic shock collars, lunge whips, starving or withholding food, entrapment, and beating. None of those tools and methods should be used to either teach or alter behavior* (AAHA, 2011, p. 213).

The AAHA (2015) guidelines provide detailed information for veterinarians to help develop behavior management as a core competency for their veterinary staff and employees and include:

- Benefits of low-stress handling
- Reducing fear in the veterinary clinic
- Recognizing signs of anxiety and distress in dogs
- Handling anxious and reactive patients
- Behavioral developmental stages in dogs by age
- Potential problems that are likely to arise if exposure during developmental stages is not done properly, including profound panic, fear of humans, heightened reactivity to dogs, sensitivity to touch, fear of new things, inappropriate play, or the absence of play
- Behavior patterns associated with normal development
- Behavior patterns associated with problematic development

While many progressive veterinarians and clinics are aware of the need to change the old approach to behavior, some veterinarians are still seemingly unaware of the trend toward pet-friendly veterinary practice, or resistant to learning new ways. If a veterinarian refers patients to a dominance method dog trainer, or one who employs shock, prong, or choke collars, consider it a red flag pointing to the veterinarian's lack of sufficient and accurate knowledge about appropriate emotional and behavioral modification methods for pet dogs. If your veterinary clinic has not graduated to a dog-friendly approach, it is time to open the dialogue or find a pet centered veterinarian for your dog.

Renowned veterinarian, Dr. Marty Becker, developed the groundbreaking *Fear Free®* initiative and professional certification program (2020b) program. Becker is the chief veterinary correspondent for the American Humane Association and has written 22 books. Dr. Becker tells us, "Once pets know fear, anxiety and stress, you cannot undo it. You can see it. You can smell it because dogs are stained with their own saliva from licking themselves. You can hear it and feel it" (Becker, (n.d.), cited in Manning 2016).

The *Fear Free* program uses a careful approach, gentle control techniques, and a calming veterinary clinic environment for your dog. The removal of anxiety triggers makes veterinary visits more enjoyable, safer, and less stressful for your dog, providing a setting conducive to the delivery of better veterinary care. The *Fear Free Level 1 Certification* (2020a) requires approximately 12 hours of online instruction. The program is designed for all individuals employed at a veterinary practice, including veterinarians, nurse technicians, groomers, customer service representatives and practice managers.

Integrative Veterinary Care

Integrative veterinary medicine is a comprehensive approach to veterinary care that combines the best of *conventional allopathic medicine* (CAM) with alternative, natural, and holistic preventative, diagnostic, and therapeutic practices. Integrative veterinary practice promotes the benefits of natural medicine in support of conventional, allopathic, medicine. The integrative veterinary field is interested in researching new techniques, new products, and new treatments to help veterinarians provide the best possible care to animals.

The internationally renowned author, veterinarian, and force-free training advocate, Dr. Karen Becker, is a proactive and integrative wellness veterinarian. She describes her practice in this way, "My goal is to help you create wellness in order to prevent illness in the lives of your pets. This proactive approach seeks to save you and your pet from unnecessary stress and suffering by identifying and removing health obstacles even before disease occurs" (Becker, 2019).

The Veterinary Institute of Integrative Medicine (VIIM) was formed to help educate veterinarians and pet parents of the benefits of alternative approaches to healing animals and to bring integrative medicine to the forefront of animal healing. Integrative medicine seeks to treat the whole dog with an interest not limited to the medical history, but also genetics, nutrition, environment, family relationships, and stress levels. Integrative medicine asks the question, "Why"? The goal is to treat the underlying disease patterns, seeking to nurture all aspects of an animal's well-being, resulting in lasting physical, mental, and emotional health.

> *There is a dramatic paradigm shift occurring in the animal health care world. This new paradigm, which is called Integrative Medicine, takes a more holistic approach to the treatment of animal disorders than the present traditional medical model, which focuses mainly on pharmacological solutions. The mission of the Institute is to create resources to help educate veterinarians and dog, cat and horse owners about holistic veterinary medicine.* (Veterinary Institute of Integrative Medicine, 2019, para. 1–2)

These therapies include but are not limited to therapies based on techniques practiced in osteopathy, chiropractic medicine, or physical medicine and therapy; veterinary acupuncture, acutherapy, and acupressure; veterinary nutraceutical therapy; and veterinary phytotherapy (AHVMA, 2016).

Veterinarian, Dr. Judy Morgan, *Naturally Healthy Pets*, lists three hallmarks of integrative medicine (2020):

- **Minimize harmful byproducts and chemicals.** Proper diet is the foundation upon which integrative care programs are based. (See Proper Nutrition, Chapter 1.)
- **Minimize vaccines.** Recent research shows that the immunity from vaccines may last for years. Many veterinarians now recommend vaccinating less often than was formerly suggested. Consider a titer test as a possible alternative to many automatically scheduled vaccinations to check on your dog's immunity status.
- **Minimize medications.** While medications may help treat one symptom, they may cause other symptoms, commonly known as side-effects (Morgan, 2020).

The American Holistic Veterinary Medical Association (AHVMA, 2016) promotes techniques that are "humane, gentle, minimally invasive and incorporate patient well-being and stress reduction, centered on love, empathy and respect." Holistic veterinarians use standard therapies, such as drugs and surgery along with holistic therapies.

Psychiatric Medications and Brain Plasticity

Human psychiatric medications to treat animal behavior problems have become an increasingly popular and lucrative practice. Yet studies in brain anatomy and function that demonstrate that *changing behavior changes brain chemistry* both during early development and in the adult brain (Kolb et al., 2003). Many integrative veterinarians suggest that more natural remedies and a solid management and emotional and behavioral modification program must be carefully explored and implemented before turning to medications. Psychiatric medications may be helpful in severe cases as well as cases that have not responded to emotional and behavioral modification, however, unlike humans, dogs cannot self-report on the effects they are experiencing from psychoactive drugs. All drugs have side effects and sometimes unexpected and opposite *paradoxical* effects as well. If medication is being considered, consulting with a veterinary behaviorist is highly recommended.

Dental Care

The importance of regular professional dental care is often overlooked by pet parents and others involved with the care and training of your dog. It was not until the 1980s that there was a surge of interest in veterinary dentistry. According to the American Veterinary Dental Society, more than 80% of dogs develop gum disease by three years of age (Verstraete, 2016). Oral health is as necessary for your dog as it is for you and your other family members. Oral health has a profound effect on your dog's general health, so do not forget to clean and care for those beautiful pearly whites. If left untreated, dental disease is often very painful and can contribute to other oral cavity or systemic diseases (Bellows et al., 2019, 2005). Periodontal disease allows bacteria and toxins to enter the bloodstream with potentially harmful effects to internal organs. Diseases associated with periodontal disease in dogs include bronchitis, hepatitis, endocarditis, kidney disease, and pulmonary fibrosis due to chronic, recurrent low-grade infections (DeBowes et al., 1996).

Signs of Oral and Dental Disease

The American Veterinary Dental College (AVDC) provides a list of signs of oral and dental disease in dogs. If any one of us suffered from any of these conditions, we would be complaining of pain and visiting the dentist immediately. Our dogs cannot complain and are genetically hardwired to hide their pain.

- Bad breath—foul breath very likely means decayed and painful teeth
- Loose teeth or teeth that are discolored or covered in tartar
- Drooling or dropping food from the mouth
- Bleeding from the mouth
- Loss of appetite or loss of weight
- Inflammation of the gums
- Receding gums
- Swelling of the jaws
- Behaviorally, rubbing of the face against furniture or rugs
- Moving away from you when you touch the mouth may indicate serious dental problems (AVDC, 2016).

Begin dental care at an early age. Annual dental check-ups and x-rays with a dental veterinarian are strongly recommended. Removal of dental plaque and tartar is critical to prevent dental disease both in dogs and humans. Disease-causing plaque mineralizes on teeth in two to three days and then cannot be removed by simple brushing. Regular professional dental cleaning is the most effective way to clean beneath the gum line to prevent periodontal disease and identify problems: anesthesia-free dental cleanings do not clean beneath the gum line.

Introduce daily or twice daily brushing slowly by rubbing your dog's teeth and gums with soft gauze wrapped around a finger. Gradually switch to a toothbrush designed for pets or to a very soft human toothbrush. Be patient, especially with older animals. Make brushing a bonding experience and avoid forceful restraint. Meat-flavored toothpaste can help! Fortunately, cavities occur much less frequently in dogs than in people (Hale, 1998).

IN MEMORY OF DR. SOPHIA YIN, DVM, MS

Dr. Sophia Yin, an internationally acclaimed veterinarian and applied animal behaviorist was at the forefront of the humane approach to handling pets in veterinary clinics, zoos, shelters, and in grooming with the goal of reducing fear and anxiety. Dr. Karen Overall, a close colleague of Yin's, tells us, "There was no training program for what Sophia did. She chose to focus on the weakest link—animals who are fearful in veterinary settings" (Overall in Zimlich, 2014, section, A Behavior Pioneer, para. 5).

Dr. Yin was a pioneer in her focus and concern about the emotional well-being of pets. Yin combined science with practical and functional applications while developing low-stress handling techniques for treating and working with animals. She shared her research and methods with professionals and with the public in academic journals, magazines, teaching seminars, workshops, books, and instructional materials, including *Low Stress Handling, Restraint and Behavior Modification for Dogs & Cats: The Small Animal Veterinary Nerdbook*, her best-selling textbook, for veterinary hospitals and individual veterinarian certification (Yin, 2009). Her DVDs include *Low Stress Handling of Dogs and Cats: Creating a Pet-Friendly Hospital, Animal Shelter or Petcare Business* (Yin, 2012b).

Dr. Yin recognized early in her private practice that more dogs are euthanized due to behavior problems than medical issues. Her contributions improved the quality of life for our pets and increased the safety and efficiency of veterinary staff and other pet professionals, while paving the way for future developments in force-free training and animal care. Those involved in force-free emotional and behavioral modification feel deeply that her passing is a great loss to our field.

2

EMOTIONAL NEEDS

Taking care to attend *Emotional Needs* nurtures the relationship between pet parent and dog and helps prevent behavioral problems. Psychological and emotional health is every bit as important as physical health. Physical and emotional wellness go hand-in-glove. The insight that dogs lead rich emotional lives can be traced back to Charles Darwin (1809–1882) who hypothesized in *The Descent of Man* (1871, p. 448) that all animals experience pleasure and pain, happiness, and sadness, and fear.

Emotions evolved to help us communicate with each other and they influence cognition and behavior. Today scientists and researchers, such as Dr. Marc Bekoff and the late Dr. Jaak Panksepp (1943–2017) who coined the term Affective Neuroscience, and Dr. Karen Overall, editor of the *Journal of Veterinary Behavior*, provide evidence on dog emotions. In *The Emotional Lives of Animals*, Bekoff tells us, "It's bad biology to argue against the existence of animal emotions" (2007, p. xviii). Some of the leading researchers in emotional systems models include, Panksepp and Watt, Berns, Bekoff, Ekman and Cordaro, Izard, and Levenson (Tracy & Randles, 2011).

Neuroscientist Dr. Jaak Panksepp theorized that *environment, behavior,* and *emotion* could not be isolated from each other. He developed an Emotional Systems Model in which neurotransmitters called neuromodulators modulate hormones that drive emotion (Panksepp, 2010). Neuromodulators can either potentiate or inhibit nerve impulses.

Panksepp's model posits that there are seven primary emotional systems. Four are *Appetitive/Positive* (+) and three are *Aversive/Negative* (-) (Montag & Panksepp, 2017). However, multiple emotional and behavioral systems may be activated in any given scenario. That is, both positive and negative emotions may be triggered in response to the same event. Panksepp's Emotional Systems Model is explored below.

Appetitive Emotional System: Seek, Care, Play, and Lust

1. Seek (+)

The *Seek* emotion is the most prevalent. It motivates, stimulates, and often drives dog behavior. Dogs seek what they need and want, and also seek to find relief. Some of the more familiar neuromodulators that drive seeking behavior are dopamine, glutamate, and endogenous opioids.

2. Care (+)

The *Care* emotion drives nurturing and social bonding with humans and other animals. Two of the hormones involved in social bonding, including maternal bonding, are oxytocin, which acts as a neurotransmitter, and prolactin. Other neuromodulators that drive care include dopamine and the endogenous opioids.

3. Play (+)

Play drives the dog's learning of social rules and defines social interactions through social bonding and having fun. It is expressed by affection, joy, and the satiation of needs. When needs are met, dogs seek to play. As a puppy, play helps dogs interact better when they reach adolescence and adulthood. Neuromodulators involved in play are glutamate, acetylcholine, endogenous cannabinoids and opioids.

4. Lust (+)

Lust is driven by the need to mate and reproduce—to transfer one's own genome. Hormones involved in driving lust include vasopressin, (which functions as a neurotransmitter), testosterone, and estrogen.

Aversive Emotional Systems: Grief (formerly Panic), Fear, and Rage/Anger

5. Grief (formerly Panic) (-)

Grief is the emotion that drives separation anxiety in dogs, feeling lost in the environment, depression, agoraphobia, sadness, and mourning over death. Grief is inhibited by secure attachment involving the endogenous opioids, and oxytocin and prolactin, the main social bonding modulations. Grief is driven by deficits in these neuro modulations and where achieving secure attachment may have been thwarted.

6. Fear/Anxiety (-)

Fear is the emotion that drives the *Fight/Flight Syndrome*, along with other "F's," notably: Freeze, fawn, fidget, and fornication under stressful situations. A real or perceived threat or a sudden loud noise, for example, drives fear. Fear itself is aversive but it sharpens the ability to escape and avoid potentially dangerous situations. Fear is driven by the neuromodulators, glutamate and epinephrine and norepinephrine which are both hormones and neurotransmitters.

7. Rage (-)

When seeking is interrupted, *Rage* may be aroused, which interacts with the fear systems. The rage core system invigorates aggression when a dog is frustrated or restrained, has its needs thwarted, or seeks to defend itself or its territory. Neuromodulators that arouse this system are Substance P and glutamate, while opioids and GABA inhibit the system.

SECURITY

The need for a sense of security and protection from danger is basic to all mammals and necessary to thrive. It is the pet parent's job to teach their dogs that the world is a safe place, both physically and psychologically. Failure to meet security needs in environments and relationships leads to anxiety and psychological disorders that sometimes mirror those found in humans. The importance of creating a physically safe and secure environment and an emotionally safe and secure environment for our dogs should not be underestimated. Feeling physically and emotionally safe and free of fear at home, and when visiting the veterinarian and groomer are primary needs for your dog. (See Chapter 8, How to Find a Good Veterinarian and Groomer.)

Attachment and Abandonment

Establish and maintain *secure attachments*, particularly with people within the home and with other dogs in and about the home and yard, thus fulfilling your dog's need for connection. These attachments are critical to emotional well-being. It is theorized (Palmer & Custance, 2008) that the human-dog bond may be similar to an infant's attachment to a parent; thus we use the term *pet parent*. The brain chemistry expressed in the human-dog bond is rooted in mutual attraction governed by the *reward system* in bonding. Ethologists in the 1990's showed that dogs have patterns of attachment to humans similar to the mother-infant relationship (Topal et al., 1998). Another notable study demonstrates that the quality of a dog's relationships to people is critical to the dog's social behaviors and also affects problem-solving abilities (Topal et al., 1997). A research study demonstrates that both children and dogs are affected in their performance on cognitive tests by having a secure base (Horn et al., 2013). Dogs use the pet parent as the *secure base* for interactions with the environment, similarly, as do children.

There are four *attachment styles* that are formed primarily by early experience. Although the effects of negative early experiences may be mitigated later in life, they are often difficult if not impossible to eliminate. Thus, the single most important factor of the human-puppy relationship is bonding and becoming a secure base for your dog. The four attachment styles are: Secure, anxious-preoccupied, dismissive-avoidant, and fearful-avoidant. Renowned anthrozoologist, Dr. John Bradshaw, points out that biologists have been reluctant to use the term *love* to describe the bond between a dog and pet parent, so they typically call it "attachment" (Bradshaw, 2011).

LOVE

The Hierarchy of Dog Needs includes love as an essential *Emotional Need* of dogs. This break-through concept has significant implications and offers scientifically and empirically supported rationales. It is not just that we love our dogs, but that our dogs *need* our love. Love is an action word. To love a dog is to treat a dog with compassion, that is, seeking to understand what makes dogs "tick" and to remain steadfastly loyal to them. Ensuring that their social-emotional well-being is met day in, and day out is the number one priority—rather than treating dogs as virtual captives, born to do our bidding making us happy for as long as is convenient for us.

Oxytocin, fMRI's, and Genetics

Scientists in various fields, from neuroscience to anthropology, have suggested that much of what we call love is explained by hormonal and brain chemistry, according to Harvard University paper titled, "Love, Actually" (Wu, 2017). Multiple studies demonstrate that the same systems are activated when dogs interact with us as between people who are in love. Oxytocin is called the love hormone in humans. The scholarly study by Kis et al., (2014) concluded that the oxytocin system also mediates the social behavior of dogs towards people. Oxytocin is essential not only in maternal bonding, but in stress-reduction and social cooperation.

The famed neuroscientist, Dr. Gregory Berns, describes the purpose of his work, "to understand the dog-human relationship from the dog's perspective" in his breakthrough book, *How Dogs Love Us: A Neuroscientist and His Adopted Dog Decode the Canine Brain* (2013). Berns' research was motivated by the death of his dog Newton. Berns wanted to learn if Newton had loved him the way he had loved Newton. He wanted to find out what dogs are thinking and feeling. Berns' discovered that the dog brain looks and functions much like the human brain in some enlightening and analogous ways. His work provides us with a physical description of what happens in a dog's brain when the dog has a pleasant association with "their" person.

"Move Over B. F. Skinner"

Dr. Berns' work in fMRI's (functional Magnetic Resonance Imaging) with unrestrained awake dogs measured cognitive changes in the dog's brain activity, mapping the neurological basis for individual preferences. Dr. Berns' book, *How Dogs Love Us* (2013) is based upon research from his Dog Project (2012–2016).

The Dog Project maps the perception and decision-making function of the dog brain and compares the maps to human brain maps. The same anatomical structure includes a brain region, known as the caudate nucleus which "lights up" in both dog and human bonds, when associated with positive emotions. The data strongly suggests dogs love us and miss us when we are gone. In a *Psychology Today* interview with Dr. Marc Bekoff, Berns tells us, "These data can be further used to move us away from simplistic, reductionist behaviorist explanations of animal behavior and animal emotions and also be used to protect dogs and other animals from being abused" (Berns in Bekoff 2013, para. 9). Bekoff states in no uncertain terms, "Move over, B. F. Skinner and those who defy and deny what we know by continuing to claim that people who say that other animals have rich and deep emotional lives are being overly sentimental and soft, anthropomorphic and non-scientific: They are wrong" (Bekoff, 2013, para. 10). Professor Berns concurs with other leading researchers in animal emotions, "Now using the MRI to push away the limitations of behaviorism, we can no longer hide from the evidence. Dogs and probably many other animals (especially our closest primate relatives) seem to have emotions just like us" (Berns in Bekoff, 2013, para. 10).

Domestication has provided dogs a pathway to form close affectionate bonds with people (Topal, 2006). The genetic basis for domestication and the development of affection toward people is well-established in the work on silver foxes by famed researchers Belyaev et al., (1981) and Trut et al., (2002). According to a study published in *Animal Cognition*, dogs may express empathic concern and comfort-offering behaviors (Custance & Mayer, 2012). Rather than approaching the typical source of comfort, the pet parent, dogs approached strangers who were pretending to cry, and started sniffing, nuzzling, and licking them.

In the chapter entitled "For the Love of a Dog" in his book *The Genius of Dogs: How Dogs are Smarter Than You Think* (2013), Dr. Brian Hare asserts, "Despite the abuse dogs suffer at our hands, no other species is as loyal to the human race as a dog. Dogs behave like children in various ways: following their owners around, vocalizing to get their attention, and clinging to them when they are unsure." Hare's research shows that gentle petting decreases cortisol and releases chemicals in the dog's brain, producing feelings of calmness and affection.

As the scientific scholarly literature about dogs and love progresses, not only is hormonal and brain chemistry evidence for personality characteristics and a need for love in our dogs supportable, but there is also a genetic basis that points to it as well. Canine behaviorist researcher, Dr. Clive Wynne's book *Dog Is Love* (2019) explores dogs' attachment to humans through studies from his Canine Science Collaboratory at Arizona State University and cutting-edge studies worldwide. Wynne collaborated with geneticist Dr. Bridgett vonHoldt et al., (2017) who found evidence in dogs that three genes may be a key to explaining their unique and exaggerated interest in people. These genes are involved in human Williams-Bueren syndrome. In this genetic disorder one of the outstanding personality traits is the hyper social trait of behaving in an overly friendly manner.

In *Psychology Today*, dog researcher and author, Dr. Marc Bekoff, tells us, "We do indeed know what and who dogs want and need, and it isn't rocket science. Dogs (and other animals) want and need to feel loved, safe and secure, want and need to interact and have fun and play with their friends and engage in frenetic "zoomies" when they can" (Bekoff, 2018, para. 3).

Dogs need love. It behooves us to give it freely, consistently and without reservation and to *do no harm* psychologically or physically. Be the soft place for your dog to land, the soft place that can be counted upon to show your dog love.

TRUST

All relationships thrive on trust and good communication. Trust is the cornerstone belief that someone is reliably trustworthy. The hormone and neurotransmitter oxytocin is often referred to as the "trust hormone" because it facilitates bonding. Trust takes time to establish and is easily broken. Sadly, when trust is broken it may seriously damage the relationship and is often irreparable. Establishing and evenly maintaining trust with your dog could not be more important to their emotional health. Assessing your dog's emotional trust level leads to a better understanding of your dog's propensity to experience joy as well as fear, or the likelihood of displaying aggressive behavior.

Stress and Distress

Trust is inversely related to anxiety and distress. Anything that threatens homeostasis causes stress. In a study in the *Journal of Comparative Medicine* entitled, "Animal Well-being II: Stress and Distress", Calpin tells us, "Numerous factors associated with needs, life in captivity, threatening events, or aversive stimuli may threaten homeostasis. An animal's well-being and quality of life is a reflection of your dog's internal somatic and mental state that is affected by what your dog perceives" (Calpin et al., 1997, para. 1).

Can Your Dog Trust You to Recognize a Threat?

Understanding how your dog perceives a threatening situation is key to establishing trust. *You* may know a situation is not a threat, but your dog is not functioning with the same complex cognitive abilities that humans have acquired. In addition, remember, you do not meet other dogs eye-to-eye as your dog does. Another dog may be loudly broadcasting threat signals to your dog that go unnoticed or may be misinterpreted by you. The threat may be quite real for your dog: it may be the human perception that is not in line with reality! As trusted caretakers and pet parents, you need to become experts in recognizing potential stressors for your dog. This is commonly referred to as avoiding *trigger stacking* in dog training. Real and perceived threats to your dog's well-being often lead to abnormal and maladaptive disorders.

Emotional and biological well-being are enhanced by your dog's familiarity with the environment, including dog and human social groups, and also by predictable changes in the environment. When you increase predictability that can be trusted, stress decreases. The result is an increased sense of joy and well-being and often a decrease in fearful behaviors in your dog. Both learning ability and memory impairment are associated with stress, as is long-term depression. Immune dysfunction and shortened lifespan related to disease processes have been shown in research to have a negative effect on health and longevity (Dreschel, 2010).

Building a bond of secure attachment through trust is a responsibility every person with a dog in the family needs to embrace. The high rate at which dogs are surrendered to shelters, breaking the bond of trust, raises serious ethical questions. Since all healthy relationships are based on trust, the obligation to build a secure and lasting attachment with your dog is a must (Hens, 2009).

Both acute and chronic stressors should be regularly and competently assessed with an open heart. As your dog's caregiver, you are your dog's safe haven both physically and emotionally. You want to show your dog that your home is safe, and that the world is a wonderful place to live.

CONSISTENCY

Predictability and Routines

Dogs love routines. It is important to us, as sentient creatures, to be able to predict outcomes. It is equally important that your dog is able to predict outcomes because your dog is dependent upon you. Dogs thrive when daily events are predictable, and when your mood is consistent when you communicate with them. Just as routines are helpful for people to maintain emotional stability, it is even more so with your dog. Continuity and stability go hand-in-glove. Continuity is the flip side of novelty. So much of your dog's life is controlled. Providing activities that your dog loves and can expect to occur, such as scavenging breakfast, walk time, and chew hour; gives your dog a sense of control over an otherwise seemingly chaotic, or boring environment. Predictability lends itself to emotional security. Dependable secure attachment lays the groundwork in forming healthy relationships. Consistency in emotional attachments formed in early puppyhood is essential for your adolescent and adult dog to thrive. Consistency accelerates the learning process for your dog.

Apply dog rules and boundaries consistently. Have all members of your household, visitors, and employees agree upon and reinforce the desired behaviors you want rather than reinforcing the behaviors you do not want. If anyone who interacts with your dog sends your dog mixed messages, your dog cannot learn what is expected or wanted. Do not ignore an unwanted behavior one day and carelessly and inadvertently reward it on another day. That is just not fair to your dog!

BENEVOLENT LEADERSHIP

Dogs Have the Brain of a Toddler

Benevolent leadership is needed if you so much as housetrain your dog. Domesticated dogs are our companions, and it is the responsibility of the trainer and the pet parent to guide them with a patient, kind and gentle hand. Dogs deserve no less.

Dogs Are Cognitively Similar to a Toddler—For Life

Research illustrates, dogs have the cognitive development of a child at approximately two to three years of age and need to be treated with the same understanding and patience afforded to a toddler. Dr. Gregory Berns, professor of neuroeconomics at Emory University led a team of researchers in identifying the small region in dogs' left frontal cortex that regulates self-control. The famed dog researcher, using MRI images, tells us, "Whatever amount of self-control they have must be eked out of a small piece of brain real estate" (Berns in MacLellan, 2016, para. 9).

As opposed to dominance tactics, the need for benevolent leadership is imperative in order for a sense of security, trust, and love to grow. Authentic leadership does not dominate, force, intimidate, or employ other aversive techniques that cause fear or stress and damage the relationship with your dog and other people as well. Yet, positive does not mean permissive. Effective leadership confidently and calmly teaches your dog how to live happily with people.

Modern training never requires you to psychologically intimidate or physically hurt your dog, regardless of what a pet-professional, family member, friend, or neighbor may say. Indeed, harsh methods have deleterious effects on your dog which are far-reaching and may be irreversible. *Do No Harm Dog Training* is not only safer and more humane, but it is more effective than aversive training and it is relatively easy for anyone to learn. No competent trainer uses force or collars that cause pain. Nothing shouts "I have no skill" like a trainer who uses shock, prong, or choke collars—and pain or dominance with dogs.

We already have all of the resources our dogs want and need. It's simple, really. Learn how to manipulate the rewards to get the behavior that you want by communicating in a language your dog can understand. There is never a need for aversive methods.

3

SOCIAL NEEDS

Dogs are social creatures, just as we are, and have characteristics that often mirror our own. Social bonding with humans and other dogs should be guided and encouraged through gentle, two-way, and non-threatening interactions, ideally from a very early age. Importantly, play in all its various expressions has a vital essential role in behavioral development and should be encouraged.

The risk of developing emotional and behavioral problems from the lack of proper, early, and continuing frequent socialization opportunities is significant. However, the expectation that dogs should be social butterflies is unrealistic because it is not abnormal for animals to compete for resources. Without laws and cultural social taboos to govern humans, our competitiveness would take other forms as well. In addition, dogs appear to fall on a spectrum of sociability from introvert to extrovert similar to humans. Some dogs prefer the company of people, while others prefer the company of their own kind.

BONDING WITH PEOPLE

Animals are a source of social support as more and more people identify their dogs as a family member. Not surprisingly, dogs look to humans for social support as well. Research has shown that dogs are capable of some empathic abilities toward humans, by demonstrating contagious yawning (Arnold, 2017). Pet parents often cite situations where their anxious dogs clearly look to them for comfort, support, and direction. Dogs can read our facial expressions often better than humans can read each other's facial expressions.

The health benefits to people who interact with dogs is well documented in the scientific literature. *The Human Animal Bond Research Institute* (HABRI) at Purdue University is an online research resource that classifies and archives research on the science of the human-animal bond. Under the direction of the human-animal bond scholar, Dr. Alan Beck. HABRI reports that, "Positive human-animal interaction appears to be related to changes in physiological variables both in humans and animals, particularly dogs" (HABRI, (n.d.). This is evident by a decrease in blood pressure and heart rate when animals and humans interact. The hormones associated with well-being in both humans and dogs, e.g., cortisol, oxytocin, b-endorphin, and dopamine, are triggered and expressed when animals and humans interact.

We can easily see areas where dogs help people, such as: Child health and development, search and rescue, disability and guide dog companions, autism spectrum disorder, dementia, Post Traumatic Stress Disorder (PTSD), trauma, relief from social isolation and loneliness, workplace wellness, cardiovascular health, cancer detection and recovery, healthy aging, and general quality of life, among many others. The list is long.

Best of Friends?

Conversely, however, pet parents may dismiss their dog's genuine need for companionship. The primary relationship is the most critical factor influencing a dog's welfare and well-being. Emotional arousal and physiological measures are taken to understand better how dogs experience their daily interactions with pet parents. The quality of a relationship with dogs is indicated by a high frequency of positive interactions with them (Beck, 2003). The Hierarchy of Dog Needs leads us to ask: "What do we do in return for our dogs to meet their social *need for us* as their dependable and gentle caretakers, steadfast companions, and protectors?"

An insightful doctoral thesis by Dr. Therese Rehn, "Best of Friends? Investigating the Dog-Human Relationship" looks at how dogs experience the relationship with their pet parents (Rehn, 2013). She asks, "What is the impact that we have on our dogs?" Rehn's research is based upon attachment and social support theories in human psychology and anthrozoology in *I Like My Dog, Does My Dog Like Me?* (Rehn, 2014). Recent studies have shown that oxytocin levels increase in dogs interacting with their primary attachment figure versus interacting with a stranger. Humans have bred dogs through artificial selection to be companion animals and working partners: science indicates that we may have bred a hyper-social behavioral system into our dogs. If our dogs are denied or thwarted in their natural inclination to connect with us, serious emotional and social deficits and behavioral problems are likely to develop.

A dedicated lifelong commitment to your relationship with your dog is essential for your dog to thrive and not suffer unnecessarily. Dogs need to bond with humans to form reliable secure attachments. When bringing a dog into our home, it is our responsibility to see this *Social Need* is met. Provide your dog with enriching experiences, such as going for rides in the car to new, secure environments. Be the trusted, benevolent leader your dog turns to when feeling unsure or frightened.

If your puppy misses out on appropriate puppy-friendly play opportunities, the communication deficits may be difficult for your adolescent or adult dog to overcome. Social deficits with people and low dopamine levels increase the risk for addiction to one-way style games. One-way games using prey drive, such as tossing a tennis ball or chasing a lure-toy, may be high intensity, but your dog is not truly interacting with you (Kaufer, 2013).

Biddability

Princeton University evolutionary biologist, Dr. Bridgett vonHoldt, studies the underlying genetic basis for social behavior in dogs. Dr. Gary M. Landsberg, DVM, DACVB and author of "Social Behavior of Dogs" in the *Merck Veterinary Manual*, reports that relationships with people are not established by dominant/submissive signaling but are a result of genetics and shaped by learning (Landsberg, 2020). As a result of human intervention and selective breeding, humans have bred *biddability* in our dogs, so it is our responsibility to follow through and care for their emotional well-being with a lifetime of commitment and gentle care, even when the going gets tough, or when we are having a bad day. Bradshaw (2011, p. 171) reminds us, "Since we humans have programmed this vulnerability, it's our responsibility to ensure that our dogs do not suffer as a result."

Recognizing when dogs want to engage and when they do not and training them with the methods detailed in The Hierarchy of Dog Needs truly enhances your relationship with your dog.

BONDING WITH DOGS—DOG-DOG BONDING

How do we know that dogs need other dogs? What are the genetically determined social bonds that exist between dogs? The propensity for bonding in dogs runs deep because "All dogs are domesticated wolves" (Safina, 2015, p. 222). Wolves have complex social structures. Many wolf races have the most complex form of social organization among wild canids, that is, the pack. The pack is typically comprised of related individuals with just one male and one female breeding at a time while the other members assist in raising the young. Co-operation is essential in the rearing of young and is also involved in co-operative group hunting (Serpell, 2007). High social attentiveness and tolerance in wolves are believed to be an important factor in the evolution of cooperative dog-human relationships (Range & Viranyi, 2015). Similarly, with dogs, these social behaviors may be genetically driven (Safina, 2015).

However, domesticated dogs are genetically altered from their naturally evolved wild ancestors. Dogs often live lives of isolation from one another. The range of diversity across breeds suggests there may be other social system differences between breeds. Similarities in wolf-like traits vary, as do social behaviors from one situation to another. These factors make designing within and between group interactions difficult to research.

Critical Periods of Learning from Others During Development

During puppyhood, the importance of early and frequent positive developmental experiences with a wide variety of dogs enhances a predisposition to pro-social behavior later in life especially during the critical, *sensitive period* of development. Puppies learn *bite inhibition* from other puppies and older puppy-friendly dogs during fair play. Learning bite inhibition helps to prevent miscommunication and overstepping boundaries with other dogs. Dogs may form secure attachment bonds with other dogs similar to the secure attachment bonds they ideally form with humans. Rightly matched individuals and groups of dogs generally bond. A fearful dog can learn to overcome fear from a more confident dog. One dog may help another dog grieve loss.

To develop and maintain social relationships, clear and effective communication between two dogs or the members of a cohort group is essential. Communication and relationships between dogs (*intraspecific* aka within the species) are established through visual signals, vocalization, scent, and pheromones. Visual signals include body posture, tail and ear carriage, facial expressions, and piloerection. It may be very challenging for a dog to accurately interpret the signals of other dogs because of selective breeding and the wide variation in body morphology across breeds, breed behavioral traits, cropped ears, and docked tails.

A failure to understand your dog's social developmental needs may lead to a lifetime of heartache for you both. Our dogs need not be social butterflies and we should not have that expectation of them. However, the ability to tolerate the proximity and hopefully to have friendly interactions with others of the same kind, can go a long way toward a happy partnership between you and your dog, and your dog and the larger world. Nevertheless, dog-dog aggression need not be a deal-breaker. (See Chapter 17, Dog-Dog Aggression.) The Pet Professional Guild has an excellent resource page that includes my contribution, "Puppy Socialization and Vaccinations Belong Together" (Michaels, 2012; Pet Professional Guild, 2012, 2020d).

PLAY

Play is an important type of enrichment and positive reinforcement because it elicits positive emotions. Most healthy dogs love playing by themselves, with people, with other dogs, and with toys and objects when given a chance and if it feels safe. Play should be, by definition, voluntary and self-rewarding. Play is an integral part of your dog's life, particularly in puppyhood, as it is in our own lives. Puppies learn a great deal from fair play, just as we do.

Benefits of Play

Play has a vital role in healthy adult dog development and social interactions. Dogs need to play. Play is biologically, emotionally, socially, and cognitively beneficial to your dog. Dr. Stuart Brown, founder of the United States National Institute of Play is clear about the mental health imperative of play. He tells us, "The opposite of play is not work—the opposite of play is depression" (Brown, 2008, TED). Dr. Mechtild Kaufer in the highly rated book, *Canine Play Behavior* (2013) tells us that frequent players have lower cortisol levels and typically live life in a more relaxed manner, whereas, dogs raised in isolation suffer from a permanent reduction in their dopamine, noradrenaline, and serotonin levels, in the long term. Carefree social contact involving tactile stimuli such as physical contact that includes petting, stimulates the release of oxytocin and helps bond dogs to each other and to us. Thus, for your dog to truly thrive, you must begin recognizing play as a need.

Your dog can work off excess energy during play and get those endorphins flowing whether your dog is playing with you or another dog. Play is great physical exercise, increases coordination and keeps your dog in tip-top shape while practicing dodging, running away, and chasing. These valuable skills are *adaptive to survival*.

Fair Play

One indispensable benefit of play is learning how to cooperate, trust, and be fair to others by learning social rules. Play requires self-control and teaches empathy. Fair play facilitates resiliency. Play trains dogs for the unexpected challenges in life within a typically low-risk setting, creating greater emotional flexibility in your dog, enhancing the ability to cope, and navigate fear-inducing conditions.

Fair Play Rules for Dogs

All dogs should be given the opportunity to practice and improve upon their social skills during play. Dr. Marc Bekoff, PhD in *Animals at Play* identifies the four features of fair play rules for dogs:

1. Ask first
2. Be honest
3. Follow the rules and
4. Admit when you are wrong with a play bow! (Bekoff, 2008)

There are discrete, concrete things to look for and recognize in appropriate play between dogs whether on a playdate or at a dog park. Do not listen to people who tell you to "Let them work it out." It is your responsibility to protect your dog's physical and emotional well-being when it comes to play. Normal, healthy play can be rowdy, noisy, and include body slamming, gestures, and vocalizations that may frighten pet parents. There are very specific things to put on your "acceptable" or "caution/ danger" list. (See Chapter 9, Dog Play Rules, Dog Parks and Dog Beach Safety Tips.)

4

COGNITIVE NEEDS

MENTAL EVENTS ARE CAUSAL

The father of positive psychology, Dr. Martin E. Seligman (born 1942), is known best for his break-through research on learned helplessness, happiness, and resilience. Seligman further conducted experiments demonstrating that *mental events are causal.* His research opened the door to the study of cognition, contrary to the theory and practice of the radical behaviorists of his time (Schultz & Schultz, 2008). Cognitive scientists illustrated that the rich internal lives of dogs are more complex than can be understood or explained through Skinnerian consequences and Pavlovian responses. The cognitive exercise of choice, problem-solving, and experiencing novelty at home and in the environment crowns our pyramid.

Cognition involves internal mental processes, such as motivation, attention, memory, perception, decision-making, and problem-solving—the conscious processes interfacing between stimuli and responses. Cognitive science celebrates many types of intelligence, not just learning in the behavioral sense. Hare and Tomasello (2005) suggest that the process of domestication afforded dogs advanced socio-cognitive abilities. Examples of dogs' intelligence include understanding human gestures, learning new words, facility at communicating, making inferences, and recruiting help and cooperation with others. Dr. John P. Pilley helped redefine intelligence in dogs by teaching his dog, Chaser, the names of more than a thousand different objects by means of exclusion. Play was the main reinforcer for Chaser's learning. "Dogs are smarter than we think," Pilley confirms (2013, [Video]. YouTube).

Dr. Brian Hare, PhD in Biological Anthropology, founded the Duke University Canine Cognition Center where he tests both pet and working dogs. Dr. Hare illustrates human-like responses in dogs, suggesting there are many similar cognitive processes guiding both humans and dogs (Barrows, 2011). Hare's *Citizen Science* enterprise, Dognition, has analyzed a large amount of data from pet parents. The array of data collected help researchers understand dogs more quickly and on a much broader scale than single studies typically do. There are 5 cognitive dimensions: Empathy, communication, memory, reasoning, and cunning. Hare discovered that each dog has a unique set of cognitive skills and a style to navigate their environment and the world. Some dogs are great communicators, some have great memories and yet others are best at the connecting with their humans (Hare, 2020).

In a book review published in the *American Scientist*, Dr. Bekoff, a self-described rich cognitivist, points out, "Many observations show that members of some species imitate other animals, empathize with them, are able to take another's perspective in certain situations (there is neurobiological evidence to support the conclusion that some animals have a theory of mind), and have culture and rather sophisticated patterns of communication" (Bekoff, 2004).

Chewing and sniffing activities enrich your dog's life through mental and physical stimulation. Intellectual exercise, such as learning new skills, tricks, and playing with interactive toys, complements aerobic exercise and helps to decrease stress and boredom. Scent work is a popular choice for senior dogs, dogs recovering from injuries, and dogs suffering from debilitating medical conditions. These are engaging alternatives for dogs who are unable to participate in aerobic exercise safely.

CHOICE

Naturally, we want to teach our dogs to make good choices that will become regular habits. Dogs being virtual captives, are given the choices that you alone allow them to make. Insomuch as the pet parent controls all of a dog's resources and freedoms, they can either provide generous opportunities for choice, or restrict their dog's ability to make choices for themselves. The latter generates stress, and moreover, may open the door to mental illness. A happy dog's life is not an unrelenting series of if/then contingencies imposed upon our dogs by us.

Unlike traditional, balanced or even positively oriented formal obedience training, empowerment-based training increases the amount of control our dogs have over the environment thus meeting their own needs and decreasing stress. In *Behavior Adjustment Training* 2.0 Grisha Stewart tells us, "Exerting too much control disempowers the learner, whether it is done through threats or treats" (2016, p. 8).

In psychological terms, *Locus of Control* refers to the degree to which your dog feels control over the outcome of events rather than feeling helpless. The effect of perceived control and the exercise of choice are self-rewarding and help your dog regulate emotions (Cho, 2017). Controlling circumstances and behavior that revolve around safety issues is critical for your dog. Your guidance must enhance experiences and provide enrichment. One of the ways this is accomplished is by providing choices. Asking for *consent* in various known or potentially stressful conditions, particularly those that involve touch, approach, strangers, and other dogs will give your dog situational and environmental control.

Consent

Dr. Hope Ferdowsian, MD, physician and animal protection advocate writes, "Like many vulnerable humans, animals are capable, though often deprived, of making informed decisions about their lives. Animals can express assent and dissent, but we rarely respect their personal sovereignty in ways that acknowledge their aptitude for making choices. Play and cooperation among animals are examples of how animals can express consent with one another, but we do not speak the languages of other animals, and they typically do not speak ours. Even when they express dissent to us, their feelings are often ignored" (2016, para. 8). Cooperative veterinary care and grooming are using Choice in voluntary husbandry more frequently, just as progressive zoos have already been doing for some time. Allowing your dog the option of saying, "yes" or "no" is an invitation - however, the pet parent must be ready to accept, "no" as an answer! Respecting your dog's choices through voluntary cooperation built upon trust, will go a long way toward helping your dog cope in what can too often be a very stressful human-dominated universe.

Yes, No, and Not Now

The founder of Horse Charming, Max Easey, is a pioneer in the area of science-based, force-free education and training for horses. Easey makes "consent training" for horses the basis for initiating, continuing, or stopping interaction with horses (Easey, 2014). She explains,

> Consent training gives the horse a simple way to directly control our behaviour, by teaching the horse to use cues they can give to us that tell us when to proceed AND when to retreat or take a break. What we want is a two-way conversation that gives the animal the right to change their mind, even if they've just given consent. This turns most training on its head because for the most part trainers train animals to be able to control their own behaviour (M. Easey, personal communication, October 11, 2019).

In dog training, Chirag Patel's novel technique he coined *The Bucket Game*, he provides dogs the option of giving consent to the continuation of training . . . or to do something else, should the dog say "no" or "not right now." It is a game of *choice*. According to Patel, "We're teaching dogs that their behavior has function" so that we're empowering our dog's choices rather than suppressing them (Patel, 2015, [Video] YouTube).

NOVELTY

Novelty-seeking is behavior of an exploratory nature. Exploration allows animals to gather information about their environment. A study by Kaulfub & Mills (2008) demonstrates that dogs are naturally predisposed, attracted to, and prefer novel rather than familiar stimuli. Novelty-seeking is thought to be one of the temperament dimensions of personality and risk-taking. The degree of seeking novelty balances the need for consistency. Assessing your dog's needs at each stage of their growth helps you achieve a proper balance between the two.

Novelty is associated with learning and has many benefits for your dog such as participating in self-rewarding, species-specific activities, and enhancing confidence. Puppies raised in a visually barren environment with an early separation from their mothers are often excessively fearful of novel situations (Bronson, 1968). Puppies and dogs of all ages must be provided with an enriched environment in a sometimes otherwise rather dismal world that lacks dog-centered stimulation and activities.

Types of Enrichment

Enriching your dog's environment empowers your dog by giving your dog the satisfaction of controlling some of the outcomes of their behavior while experiencing the excitement of exploration. Customizing enrichment to meet your dog's needs improves health and wellness. Adding complexity to the environment has many benefits and increases normal behavior patterns, often reducing problem behaviors that may result from boredom and frustration. Novelty enhances your dog's ability to cope with challenges. A barren environment causes chronic stress that may result in self-injury such as excessive chewing of the feet, tails or other body parts and stereotypies. Providing scent enrichment activities which activates their novelty-seeking interests is important. Conversely, taking great care in protecting our dogs from scents that may be offensive or toxic to them is critical.

The Center for Animal Welfare at Purdue University published a paper wherein researchers from the College of Veterinary Medicine outline five types of enrichment: Social, occupational, physical, nutritional, and sensory (Garvey et al., 2016).

1. **Social Enrichment** meets the need for novelty and interaction with people and other dogs.
2. **Occupational Enrichment** provides a novel challenge, a "job" that facilitates both mental and physical exercise, such as fly-ball or playing fetch and solving food puzzles "games."
3. **Physical Enrichment** enhances the quality and the complexity of your dog's living environment, providing novel toys, digging activities, doggy doors that

allow choice over social and physical space, a view of the great outdoors, and perhaps a sanctuary to hide within when frightened.

4. **Nutritional Enrichment** includes natural foraging/scavenging, hiding food, and proper species-specific nutrition.
5. **Sensory Enrichment** stimulates the senses of smell, sight, sound, and tactile enrichment suited to your dog's needs. Some examples of novel enrichment are visual images, music, grazing, nose games, and sensory gardens which can decrease stress.

A New Paradigm for Dog Enrichment

In *Canine Enrichment: The Book Your Dog Needs You to Read* (2019, p. 9) author Shay Kelly asks, "What have dogs got? Only what we give them. Our modern lives are full, often too full, but a dog's life is empty, far too empty." Kelly has developed a uniquely progressive roadmap to providing enrichment for our dogs, known as "The Five Elements of Canine Enrichment."

1. **Safe Environment** is essential to the enjoyment of life and decreasing fear.
2. **Food Enrichment** delivers high value calories in a setting that enhances emotional as well as physical well-being through seeking.
3. **Non-Food Enrichment** includes play toys and outdoor activities.
4. **Companionship and Bonding** recognizes the need for secure attachments and sociality.
5. **Natural Behaviour** enrichment provides opportunities for dogs to engage in sniffing, play and running.

(See Chapter 10, Enrichment and Grazing Games.)

PROBLEM-SOLVING

There is a growing research interest in the cognitive abilities of dogs because they show more than expected success in problem-solving skills, which may involve higher cognitive abilities (Viranyi et al., 2006). Here are some examples that have spurred interest among scientists.

- Researcher Kaminski et al., (2004) found that the Border Collie, Rico, was able to acquire the names of novel items through fast-mapping and exclusion learning. Some dogs use cognitive process, which are remarkably similar to human processing of information.

- Search and rescue missions employ dogs in problem-solving activities for the purpose of finding missing people, avalanche victims, and survivors at disaster sites, and in cadaver detection.
- Dogs are also skilled in finding missing pets and other animals including locating endangered mammals and birds for conservation such as scat-detection of bears, kit foxes, wolves, and even tigers and seals.
- In the field of medicine, dogs are the experts in detecting some types of cancer and alerting humans prior to the onset of a seizure or hypoglycemic attack.
- Dogs are also important for detecting illegal drugs, explosives, and accelerants in arson cases. Dogs can detect substances at a far lower concentration than humans and they can locate a target scent while ignoring non-target scents in search activities (Browne et al., 2006).

Dogs' scent-sensitivity is far beyond our human ability to perceive the world through smell. We cannot and do not experience the world as dogs do. Therefore, it is not surprising that we have a hard time understanding what it's like to be a dog. "How Do Dogs "See" with Their Noses?" A video created by Dr. Alexandra Horowitz (2015) explains how dog intelligence in scent-detection is superior to human intelligence in scent-detection. Dogs can "see backward and forward in time." Scent trails proceed and linger after a dog or person passes, providing dogs with information about the past and providing them with information about the future to literally sense who may have passed and who may be approaching. Humans have no intelligence or ability in this type of awareness or learning from the environment. Dogs have several hundred million scent receptor cells compared to approximately just five million scent receptors in the human brain. As a result, a much greater proportion of the dog brain is dedicated to information processing of *odor profiles* when compared to the human brain. The vomeronasal organ in dogs detects hormones that humans and other animals release into the body and air that alerts dogs to both the emotional state and health status of others. Dr. Horowitz reports that "Stress and anger manifest as a cloud of hormones" to our dogs!

Intelligence

Intelligence evolved as an adaptation to solve evolutionarily novel problems. Intelligence comes in many forms. For example, the standard human IQ test predicts the likelihood of success in college through reading comprehension, mathematical, and analytical skills measures. In addition, some people have enhanced athletic intelligence, some have emotional intelligence, and some have powerful memories or navigational skills, while others are mechanically inclined geniuses. However, we should not make the mistake of assessing dog intelligence by human measures because when we do, we miss out on celebrating how intelligence actually manifests in our captivatingly unique dogs.

A wolf's skills needed for survival and thriving cannot be fairly compared to the skills needed by humans. Our dogs are domesticated wolves. Being socialized to humans, dogs are generally more exploratory with less fear of novel objects, known as decreased neophobia. Decreased neophobia has led to a correlation between human socialization and problem-solving abilities (Reid, 2019). Dr. Brian Hare, a leading scientist in animal cognition, tells us in *The Genius of Dogs: How Dogs are Smarter Than You Think*, "Learning is just one type of intelligence" (Hare & Woods, 2013). Hare's Dognition study reveals that compared to other mammals, dogs are at a genius level in comprehending and at signaling others with body language and vocalizations, learning new words, understanding their audiences' perspective, copying other actions, and recruiting help from others.

Enhanced environments increase problem-solving abilities and positive social interactions too. Environmentally enriching interactive games using brain skills such as, finding hidden food and puzzle-feeders can increase a sense of general well-being in our dogs in what is often a sterile environment from their point of view.

5

BEST FORCE-FREE PRACTICES FROM THE HIERARCHY OF DOG NEEDS

Force-free training is safer, *more* effective, and *more* reliable than aversive training, when taught with good technique. The professional attributes of competency, accountability, and transparency in advertising, deliver the optimum dog-friendly care and training that our dogs need and deserve. Learning force-free training is also easier for pet parents. We now know that the fear of pain is traumatizing for our dogs, just as it would be for us. The chronic stress of never knowing when punishment may occur creates distrust of humans in dogs and leads to bites. The so-called "balanced trainer" who practices a mix of punishment and rewards is a contradiction of terms. Alternating rewards with punishment creates distress in our dogs and has been shown to interfere with learning and relationships and may be a cause of aggression.

DEFINING FORCE-FREE DOG TRAINING

All behavioral terms and activities are rooted in scientific definitions for practical usage, so everyone involved in academic discussion is on the same page. Leaders in each field of study define new concepts resulting in a collectively agreed upon definition known as an *operational definition*. Scientifically and operationally defining force-free dog training establishes common ground and sets the stage for educating and teaching the broader community on emerging best practices within the field.

Pet Professional Guild (PPG) and The Hierarchy of Dog Needs formally adopted the term *Force-free/Force-Free*. The Pet Professional Guild Mission Guidelines explains behavior modification techniques appropriate for animal care and training. The *Do No Harm Dog Training and Behavior Handbook*, and the *Do No Harm Dog Training* social media group, among others, also define force-free similarly. Force-free means using methods preventing physical and emotional suffering in dogs in the moment and for the long-term.

Intent in Training

Importantly, force-free dog training is defined by the training practice itself, and by the *intent* motivating the training practice. We ask, "Does the training cause physical or psychological harm to the dog? Is the trainer dominating or intimidating the dog? Is the trainer using forceful or fear-based tactics to gain compliance?"

PPG recognizes, however, "Any definition can never be so expansive and explicit that every possible situation is addressed" (2020b, para. 3). In the context of the PPG Guiding Principles framework, physical force is defined as "any intentional physical act against a pet that causes psychological or physical pain, harm or damage to the pet" (Pet Professional Guild, 2020b, para. 4).

Force-free Training

- Places dog safety and emotional well-being first
- Is the absence of physical and psychological pain and/or the threat of it
- Manages and resolves the difficult problems of our dogs in a systematically positive manner

- Monitors the willingness of our dogs at each step during training before moving forward
- Avoids making our dogs feel worried or uncomfortable

The priorities, best practices and the exclusions define what force-free training is and in addition what it is not. Force-free training is categorically and qualitatively different and unique from traditional or so-called "balance training" by virtue of the operational definition of *what we do and what we do not do* as described below.

Force-free Dog Training Exclusions

What we *do not* do. Specifically:

- No shock
- No prong
- No choke
- No pain
- No fear
- No dominance or intimidation
- No compulsion methods
- No physical force
- No hitting with any object, including rolled up towels
- No throwing items
- No swatting with a newspaper
- No shaking cans of coins or rocks in our dogs' sensitive ears
- No spraying water in the face or body
- No yelling

CHOOSE ANY OR ALL METHODS

Nurturing biological health and psychological well-being enhances emotional stability, social skills, and cognitive abilities by meeting our dogs' real needs. The Hierarchy of Dog Needs describes the emotional and behavioral modification methods that force-free behavior modification consultants and trainers endorse. Effectively using these techniques serves to increase, decrease, and redirect behavior, and also to change emotional responses. We set the stage for optimal well-being by using force-free training, and eliminating the potentiality for fear, stress, and aggression.

According to an article in the *Journal of Veterinary Behavior,* "Good Trainers: How to Identify One" (Overall et al., 2006), shock collars, prong collars, and choke collars are at the top of the list of equipment that causes anxiety, fear, and arousal, and may contribute to an increase in aggression. Polsky (2000) describes severe attacks on humans by dogs who were being trained or maintained on electric shock fences, euphemistically marketed as *invisible* fences. The promise of fast results may appeal to pet parents. Guaranteed quick results are often touted as a benefit of using punitive dog training methods. However, punitive training is akin to putting a small Band–aid® on a deep wound that is likely to cause an infection.

A Lifetime of Fear?

Using a shock collar and later deciding to try positive reinforcement is detrimental to your dog's emotional well-being. The damage done by the shock treatment is sadly, often irreversible. Research shows that one-trial (one shock) learned fear lasts a lifetime. American neuroscientist, Dr. Joseph LeDoux (2011) explains it in simple terms everyone can easily understand:

> *We'll start with the simple behavior that we use when we study all of this, and it is Pavlovian Fear Conditioning. So, a rat is placed in a small chamber, and the rat hears a sound, and if nothing happens the rat begins to ignore the sound, but if the sound is paired with electric shock - and you only have to do this one time - then the rat develops a fear of*

the sound because it predicts the electric shock. And this becomes a lifelong fear. As long as you present the sound to the rat again, as long as the rat lives, the rat will be afraid of this sound unless you've done things during the rat's life to weaken that stimulus. But even if you weaken it through, for example, extinction processes, the fear always comes back. **The fear is almost, more or less, permanent and is a characteristic of the animal for the rest of its life in one way or another** *[emphasis added].* (LeDoux, 2011).

The widely cited Department for Environment, Food & Rural Affairs (DEFRA) study measured the behavioral and physiological impact on dogs when shock collars were used during training compared to the impact on dogs when no shock was used. This study demonstrated that dog welfare was negatively impacted with training conducted by professional shock collar trainers (The Department for Environmental Food and Rural Affairs, 2010). BanShockCollars.ca (2007) provides an updated list of numerous scientific studies supporting the movement to ban shock collars worldwide. There is a fast-growing list of countries where these devices are now illegal. The No Shock, No Prong, No Choke logo is a free download on The Hierarchy of Dog Needs website and is currently available in 15 languages.

Force-free Training Best Practices

Being kind to your dog is good science. Wonderfully, barring neurological damage, all behavior is effectively modified using The Hierarchy of Dog Needs Best Force-free Practices. The force-free training and *Do No Harm* Management and Learning methods are not listed in any particular order. The force-free best practices methods listed below may be used in any order or combination to address training problems:

- Management
- Antecedent Modification
- Positive Reinforcement
- Differential Reinforcements of DRI (Incompatible), DRA (Alternate), DRO (Other—no undesired behavior in a predetermined amount of time), DRL (Lower frequency in a predetermined amount of time)
- Classical and Counterconditioning
- Desensitization
- The Premack Principle
- Social Learning

The first step in any successful behavior modification program is visiting a gentle veterinarian to rule out any possible organic cause, pain, disease, or condition, for a sudden or chronic change in behavior.

Note: Parts 2, 3 and 4 of this handbook provides examples of each training method for many of the most common and the most difficult behavioral problems, such as housetraining, excessive barking, jumping, aggression, fear, and separation anxiety.

Management

"To increase, redirect, decrease or eliminate behavior: rearrange environment. Remove or distance triggers. e.g., baby gates, dog-friendly fencing, puppy-proofing" (Michaels, 2015/2020). From The Hierarchy of Dog Needs [Pyramid Graphic].

Preventing Undesirable Behavior

The benefits of effective management are often under-rated. Management prevents problems and undesirable habits from developing. Typically, it is more difficult to modify behavior once it becomes a habit than preventing it before it is repeatedly rehearsed. Preventing your dog from making undesirable decisions by managing the environment sets your dog up for success in training.

Puppy-proofing your home, yard, and garden makes the environment safe for your puppy, preventing bad habits from developing and preventing property loss. As responsible pet parents, creating a safe environment for your dog is much like baby-proofing a home for a child.

Sometimes the easiest answer for a behavior problem is managing the situation. Containment as a management technique may prevent frustration for both your dog and you. For example, you could spend ten years teaching your dog to stay in the yard and not chase the wildlife your dog sees in the canyon beyond your property. It would take a great deal of effort and time, moreover, it would not be reliable. If the right rabbit crossed your dog's path, your dog may take chase and never look back. Alternately, you could build a fence to solve the problem with management. We very frequently want to choose the method that is easiest for all.

Here are more examples of good management:

- Pantry doors. Use a hairband or plastic tie to secure pantry doors and low-lying kitchen cabinets. Use an adhesive note to remind others to close the doors. Use a weight or spring so the doors close on its own.
- Toilet. Keep the bathroom door and the toilet lid closed: use small adhesive notes to remind guests. (Keep the toilet free of toxic chemicals).
- Cats. Place x-pens around the cat areas to prevent litter munching by your dog. Separate the dog and cat for mealtime to avoid competition and swapping of food.

Antecedent Modification

"To increase, decrease, eliminate or redirect behavior: change events or Associations (triggers) that happen before the behavior" (Michaels, 2015/2020). From The Hierarchy of Dog Needs [Pyramid Graphic].

Changing your dog's environment can prevent or solve problems. An antecedent is the event, activity, stimulus, or trigger immediately preceding a behavior. In the functional analysis model of behavior modification, the Antecedent is the A in ABC, B is the Behavior and C is the Consequence. Antecedents can be manipulated to either encourage desirable behaviors or to decrease undesirable behaviors. Classically conditioned respondent behavior is controlled by *antecedents* as opposed to being controlled by *consequences* as are operantly conditioned behaviors.

Modifying Stimuli That Precede a Trigger

In *How Dogs Learn*, Burch and Bailey (1999, p. 157–160) list six methods of *antecedent control* that modify behavior:

- **Remove the trigger for an undesirable behavior.**
  Example: If your dog barks at other dogs passing by the window, cover the window or use a baby-gate to block the dog's view out of the window.
- **Add a cue for a desirable behavior.**
  Example: If during a walk, your dog fixates on another dog, call your dog's name to distract and redirect your dog back to you *before* a bark and lunge occur.
- **Add an *establishing operation* to increase a desirable behavior.**
  Example: If your dog does not want to leave the dog park after a recall, play with your dog for a short time after "Come," and *then* leash your dog and leave the park. The play session is the added establishing operation.
- **Remove an *establishing operation* to decrease an undesirable behavior.**
  Example: If your dog typically jumps on guests after rushing to answer the door with you, first let your dog calm down outside of the range of guests. The establishing operation of rushing to the door is removed. Later, allow your dog to say "hello" when your guests are seated. Rushing to the door is the removed establishing operation.
- **Decrease the effort needed to engage in a desirable behavior.** Decreasing the effort needed to practice desirable behaviors increases the probability that desired behaviors will occur. This makes desirable behaviors an easy choice for your dog.
  Example: If your dog whines during your dinner, feed your dog before you eat and provide an interactive food toy for your dog to enjoy during dinner.

- **Increase the effort needed to engage in an undesirable behavior.** Increasing the effort needed to practice undesirable behaviors decreases the probability that the undesirable behavior will occur. This makes the undesirable behavior less appealing.

  Example: If your dog acts like every inch of a walk is a "sniffari," walk in the middle of the sidewalk and quicken your pace.

Positive Reinforcement (+R)

"To increase behavior: Rewards for desired behavior using capturing, luring, shaping, and modeling" (Michaels, 2015/2020). From The Hierarchy of Dog Needs [Pyramid Graphic].

Increasing Frequency Using Rewards

Positive Reinforcement is a procedure or experience where the frequency or intensity of a desired behavior increases or continues because the behavior was previously associated with a reward such as food, toys, praise, or love (Overall, 2013). Positive reinforcement increases the likelihood a behavior will be performed *in the future* because a reward was given *after* a behavior was practiced in the past. Therein, the frequency or intensity, that is, the strength of the desired behavior is increased through positive reinforcement.

A positive reinforcer is typically something your dog seeks out. A reinforcer must increase the frequency, intensity, or duration of a behavior, or maintain a behavior as the *consequence* of something being *added*, that is, a reward. Thus, the reinforcer is in the eye of beholder. Keep in mind that what *you* think will be reinforcing as opposed to what your dog actually finds reinforcing may be two different things. For example, if your dog does not find tennis balls attractive, playing a game of fetch will most likely not be reinforcing, and fetching will not increase in frequency. The key is to figure out what your dog likes best and use those things as rewards in teaching your dog so your dog can easily understand what you like. If your dog loves cheese, using low-fat cheese as a food reinforcer can speed learning and training by increasing the frequency of the behaviors you find desirable. Positive reinforcement is associated with the release of dopamine in the brain, known as the *pleasure chemical,* one of the feel-good chemicals: the others being endorphins, oxytocin, and serotonin.

Positive reinforcement is one of the ideological foundations and the preferred operant treatment for learning new behaviors in force-free training.

Learning Based Upon Past Consequences

Positive reinforcement is one of the four *quadrants* and helps explain voluntary behavior. In his classic research tome, *The Behavior of Organisms* (Skinner, 1938), American psychologist, B. F. Skinner (1904–1990), defined operant learning as experiences where behavior is either strengthened or weakened by the consequences of that behavior. Skinner's behaviorism was devoted entirely to the study of responses to stimulus in observable behavior rather than any internal processes that drive behavior (Schultz & Schultz, 2008). Operant learning is also called consequence learning, contingency learning, instrumental learning, response learning, and R-S learning (Chance, 2014).

The founder of the Pet Professional Guild, Niki Tudge, explains operant learning for us here:

> *With operant learning, new behaviors are learned, and existing behaviors are modified based on the past consequences of doing them. Behaviors that are reinforced are repeated and behaviors that produce aversive consequences are suppressed. Operant behaviors help the learner control their environment and with positive consequences empowerment takes place.* (N. Tudge, personal communication, 2015).

Note: The term *reward learning* is seen not only in scholarly journal literature on learning but even more so in neuroscience scholarly literature on reward pathways and biological scholarly literature (Chance, 2014, p. 133).

Differential Reinforcement (DR) of DRI, DRA, DRO, DRL

"To redirect, decrease, or increase behavior: Reward for preferred incompatible, alternate, other, or change in the rate of behavior" (Michaels, 2015/2020). From The Hierarchy of Dog Needs [Pyramid Graphic].

Redirecting Undesirable Behavior

Differential Reinforcement is one of the most useful operant behavior modification tools in the force-free toolbox. This is a type of operant training where some behaviors are systematically reinforced while others are not, combining positive reinforcement for an appropriate response and *extinction* of a previously reinforced behavior simultaneously (Pam, 2013, Chance, 2014). That is, differential reinforcement increases the probability of the frequency a desirable behavior *while at the same* time it decreases the probability of an undesirable behavior (Burch & Bailey, 1999). DR *redirects* the unwanted behavior. When choosing a differential reinforcement protocol decide first whether your goal is decreasing the frequency of the behavior, such as excessive barking, or replacing one behavior with another, such as sitting instead of jumping on you and your guests. Successive approximation, or shaping is a form of differential reinforcement (Skinner, 1953). Differential reinforcement is a type of operant counterconditioning (Overall, 2013).

Incompatible, Alternate, Other and Lower Rate Reinforcement

Each type of differential reinforcement (DR) has varying rates of effectiveness in different contexts and with different dogs. Here are four types of differential reinforcement: DRI, DRA, DRO, and DRL.

- **D**ifferential **R**einforcement for an **I**ncompatible behavior (DRI)
  DRI reduces the frequency of an undesirable behavior by reinforcing a *new replacement behavior* that is incompatible. This is one of the most effective means of differentially reinforcing your dog. Your dog is unable to do two things at the same time. The beauty of DRI is that it captures the desired behavior while preventing the undesired behavior at the same time.
  Example: When greeting people, reward your dog for Sit, Stand, or Targeting your hand as desirable behavior replacements to jumping on people. (See Chapter 16, Greetings, and No Jump.)
- **D**ifferential **R**einforcement for an **A**lternate behavior (DRA)
  DRA reduces the frequency of an undesirable behavior by reinforcing a *different and alternate, but not incompatible behavior*. DRA demonstrates to your dog that desirable behaviors result in rewards, while undesirable behaviors do not.

Example: For barking, reward your dog for an alternate behavior such as lying down instead of barking. This teaches that lying down earns the reinforcement whereas barking does not. Your dog can still bark while lying down but is less likely to do so.

- **Differential Reinforcement for Other behavior (DRO)**
(DRO) change in the rate of behavior or no undesired behavior in a predetermined amount of time (Psychology Dictionary Professional Reference, 2019).
DRO reduces the frequency of an unwanted behavior by providing periodic reinforcements only if the dog does something different than the undesirable behavior for *a given amount of time, intensity, or duration.*
DRO is also known as *omission training* procedure.
Example: When your dog whines at the dinner table, reward your dog every five minutes for lying in bed or playing with a toy. This teaches that lying in bed or playing with a toy is more reinforcing than whining.

- **Differential Reinforcement for Lower frequency behavior (DRL)**
DRL is the *lesser rate, that is, lesser frequency* of an undesired behavior in a predetermined amount of time. This is also called differential reinforcement of long response times dependent upon the interval between responses being greater than the minimum.
DRL reduces the frequency of an undesirable behavior by reinforcing when the undesirable behavior is practiced less often.
Example: Reward your dog every five minutes for barking just a couple of times, instead of incessant barking. If your dog barks more than twice, reset your clock. This teaches your dog that low frequency barking is rewarded.

Dog behaviour expert and driving force behind the *UK Dog Behaviour and Training Charter*, Andrew Hale, cautions, "Operant solutions should be a tool in the toolkit: they shouldn't be the toolkit. We want to reinforce something that is innately useful to the dog. If we just switch one behavior for a different behavior even when using positive reinforcement, we risk ignoring the need for *relief-seeking* that prompted the original behavior" (Hale, 2021).

Note: Ignoring behavior as the singular treatment for the purpose of extinction is typically effective only in laboratory settings where other confounding variables are controlled. In real life, however, intervening variables such as other reinforcements in the environment affect behavior. For example, if your dog jumps up on you and you ignore your dog by turning your back, your dog may be content in jumping at your back to touch you. Perhaps you did not turn quite fast enough, or the movement of turning away further aroused your dog. Importantly, we do not purposely use extinction techniques alone in force-free training. Extinction alone often causes frustration and stress for your dog.

Classical and Counterconditioning

"To change emotion: Create new associations" (Michaels, 2015/2020). From The Hierarchy of Dog Needs [Pyramid Graphic].

Classical conditioning is also known as Pavlovian respondent conditioning and is based upon *associations* or the *bonding of two stimuli*. This type of learning occurs when a neutral stimulus (such as the sound of a bell) is paired with another stimulus (food). The sound of the bell becomes associated and reflexively connected with the delivery of food. Therefore, a dog who previously salivated for food alone (unconditioned response) will salivate at the sound of the bell, without the presentation of food (conditioned response). One event becomes a reliable predictor of another event occurring, teaching the dog that the first event predicts the second event. The dog learns to have an anticipatory reaction to the first event.

Pavlov's work demonstrates that hormonal glands and reflexes govern involuntary behavior. Animals experience many of these events as emotions (Chance, 2014). Increased heart rate, increased respiration rate, and even changes in immune system responses are reflexes. Emotions are involuntary; however, associative learning can modify an emotion called a Conditioned Emotional Response (CER). Conditioned "reflexes" are not inborn but rather learned. Learned reflexes may vary dependent upon conditions and are subject to behavior modification (Chance, 2014). Additionally, Pavlov demonstrated that even higher mental processes can be described in physiological terms (Schultz & Schultz, 2008).

Creating Positive Associations and Modifying Negative Associations

The founder of the Pet Professional Guild, Niki Tudge, explains respondent learning for us here:

> *Learning occurs with both respondent and operant behavior but what is learned during each one is very different. First, let's look at respondent learning, also known as classical conditioning or Pavlovian conditioning. With respondent conditioning new eliciting stimuli, not new behaviors, are learned. This learning occurs through the process of repeated and close pairing of a neutral stimulus with an existing conditioned stimulus. This is the stimulus-stimulus-response (S-S-R) learning, and it is this process that accounts for responses through associations such as the elicitation of salivating at the sound of a tin of food opening. It is also through this S-S-R process that emotional reactions are triggered such as a change in heart rate. In this same way, fear or calmness are elicited by conditioned stimuli* (N. Tudge, personal communication, 2015).

From *A History of Modern Psychology* (Schultz & Schultz, 2008, p. 287), we learn Pavlov also tested buzzers, lights, whistles, tones, bubbling water, and metronomes with the same results. Pavlov, in his own words taught us that, "Footfalls of a passer-by, chance conversations in neighboring rooms, slamming of a door, or vibration of a passing van, street cries, even shadows cast into the windows of the room," are all variables that change the nature of the association learned (Pavlov, 1927).

Example: The leash becomes associated with going for a walk. This is why your dog gets excited when you pull out the leash.

Example: Crinkling the bag of dog treats becomes associated with treats, so crinkling the bag of dog treats can be used as a Recall *cue* all by itself!

Associative Learning

Classical Conditioning, the learning of *new associations*, and *Counterconditioning*, the learning of alternate associations for *previously learned associations*, are a primary method in molding and modifying behavior in the field of force-free dog training. Counterconditioning reverses the effects of unwanted conditioned responses by teaching new associations (Chance, 2014).

Example: Counterconditioning creates a new association to an already established one. If a previously learned association paired the sound of the doorbell with strangers appearing at the door, teach a new association pairing the sound of the doorbell with something your dog loves. For example, if your dog barks at the door when the doorbell rings, countercondition the sound of the doorbell by pairing it with hot dog bits delivered on the back patio. With multiple pairings, your dog learns to respond to the sound of the doorbell by happily running to the back patio for hot dogs!

Multiple pairings are typically required but not in the case of learning fears. Fear can be learned in just one single exposure called *one-trial learning*. For example, in shock training, dogs may associate people, places or things with being shocked. Unrelated or *unintended* associations, such as a child walking by your dog can become an unexpected, an unintended, and unwanted learned association. The dog may now fear children because the dog associates children with being shocked.

The Little Albert Experiment

The classic research study known as The Little Albert Experiment, demonstrated the power of classical conditioning and how fears may generalize by associating a rat *(Neutral Stimulus*, NS) with a loud bang (*Unconditioned Stimulus*, UC). A baby

(Albert) who was previously unafraid of a rat was conditioned to become afraid of rats (*Conditioned Response*, CR) and other furry animals by pairing/associating the rat with a loud noise. This breakthrough research showed that the emotion of fear is learned, and generalized to other similar objects or any stimuli present (Watson & Rayner, 1920).

Example of learned fear by association in dog training. If, your puppy is frightened or attacked by another dog on the first night of training class, your puppy may not want to go back into the building *and* may develop a fear of dogs that may last a lifetime. The puppy (or adult dog) has associated the building with an aggressive dog and generalized that fear to other dogs, just as Little Albert generalized his fear of a rat to other furry animals.

Desensitization

"To decrease emotional response: Develop a systematic graduated exposure therapy plan" (Michaels, 2015/2020). From The Hierarchy of Dog Needs [Pyramid Graphic].

Systematic Graduated Exposure

Building upon Pavlov's research in counterconditioning, psychiatrist, Joseph Wolpe, developed the process of *Systematic Desensitization;* a treatment for fear and anxiety disorders used to treat human patients suffering from debilitating phobias (Chance, 2014). Systematic desensitization is a type of counterconditioning and is the gold standard in treating fear and aggression in dogs when applied carefully, slowly, and systematically. This treatment exposes the dog to a realistic fear stimuli, but at a much lower intensity. Systematic desensitization involves overcoming fears gradually while ensuring the dog is free from anxiety at each step before proceeding to the next step (Burch & Bailey, 1999).

It has three main components:

1. Relaxation
2. A hierarchy ranging from the least or easiest, to the most problematic or intense version of the trigger stimulus
3. Counterconditioning

In practice, we expose a dog to a *sub-threshold* version of the trigger where there is no observable response, then follow immediately by a positive, high value, counterconditioning stimulus (reward/reinforcement). The intensity of the trigger is gradually heightened as long as there is no observable response, such as body language displays. The procedure is repeated with incremental increases in intensity as long as there is no observable response. (See Chapter 17, Desensitization and Counterconditioning Techniques.)

Teaching Your Dog to Relax

Dr. Karen Overall (2013, p. 581–584) created a "Relaxation Protocol" as a foundation for desensitization and counterconditioning where the physical changes associated with relaxation are rewarded. First, the dog learns to perfectly focus on the pet parent or trainer for 15 seconds, preferably lying down. Then, in a slowly, graduating format, duration, distance and distractions are increased. The protocol teaches dogs to accept everything from the handler answering the doorbell, to the absence of the handler for a short time. The dog is rewarded every second or third task. If signs of anxiety or stress are observed, the pet parent or trainer immediately returns to an easier step where the dog was successful, showing no anxiety, or they should both take a break from training.

The combined terms, *Desensitization and Counterconditioning*, referred to as D&CC, are frequently used in concert in force-free dog training. In desensitization training, the dog learns *not to react* to stimuli that slowly and incrementally increases in intensity. In counterconditioning the dog learns a different emotional response, and may learn "response substitution" i.e., a different behavioral response than the current reaction to the stimulus. This combination of techniques may result in both emotional and behavioral modification.

In the dog trainers' classic, resource guarding treatment book *Mine* (2002), author Jean Donaldson constructs step-by-step desensitization hierarchies for food, object, and location guarding, handling and the generalization of counterconditioned responses to other items and people.

Flooding is considered the antithesis (opposite) of desensitization. Flooding pushes the dog *over-threshold* resulting in possibly serious and damaging results, often making the subject worse rather than better.

Premack Principle

"To increase, decrease or redirect behavior: Use a high probability (preferred) behavior to reinforce a low probability behavior" (Michaels, 2015/2020). From The Hierarchy of Dog Needs [Pyramid Graphic].

Preferred Behavior Can Reinforce Less Preferred Behavior

The *Premack Principle* method of learning uses a high probability (preferred) behavior to reinforce a low probability (not preferred) behavior. David Premack (1959, 1965) discovered that a *reinforcing stimulus,* such as food, could also be seen as the behavior of eating food. Understanding the Premack Principle is commonly illustrated by a parent who tells the child to eat their peas *first* (low probability/less preferred) and the child may eat dessert *afterwards* (high probability/preferred behavior), that is, *one behavior can reinforce another behavior*. Engaging in one behavior can be used as a reinforcer for increasing the frequency of another behavior (Chance, 2014). Eating dessert is *contingent* upon eating peas first. Here's an example most people are familiar with that you may already be using—A hungry dog has a high probability for eating treats, but a lower probability of sitting, making the opportunity of eating treats dependent upon sitting and resulting in the reinforcement and increased frequency of sitting. However, the Premack Principle is not dependent upon a physiological function or primary and secondary reinforcers but on behavior reinforcing behavior.

Any behavior your dog enthusiastically seeks, such as: opening the door, playing fetch, sitting on the couch, or walking to the hydrant to read "pee mail," may be used as the reinforcer for performing a less preferred behavior first.

Examples

- A dog that loves to chase a ball only gets another throw when the dog brings the ball back directly to your feet first.
- If your dog prefers herding sheep rather than to "Coming" to you for a cheese treat, teach your dog that herding sheep is contingent upon "Coming" to you. In other words, a non-preferred activity is reinforcing *because* it precedes engagement in a preferred activity.

Social Learning—Also Known as Observational Learning (Bandura, 1965)

"To increase, decrease or redirect behavior: Use a dog or human model as sample behavior. e.g., imitation, emulation, contagion" (Michaels, 2015/2020). From The Hierarchy of Dog Needs [Pyramid Graphic].

Dogs learn new behaviors by observing another dog or a person. Social learning is learning from observing the activity and the consequences of that activity from the behavior of a *model* (Chance, 2014). Social learning helps the learner either acquire similar behaviors, or to try something different if the model's behavior does not result in a resource or in acquiring a new skill.

Imitation, Emulation, Social Facilitation and Emotional Contagion

Imitative learning occurs when the learner uses the same method observed and achieves the same result. For example, a dog learns to open a door by pushing down on the handle with a paw after observing a human opening a door by pushing down on the handle with a hand.

Emulation learning occurs when the learner uses a different method to achieve the same result.

Social facilitation learning occurs when the presence of others enhances behavior (Zentall, 1996). For example, if the lead dog in a dog team pulls to the left, all dogs will pull to the left. The dogs may also run at a greater speed when on a team.

Emotional contagion learning occurs when dogs mirror an emotional state, either intraspecies/conspecific (dog mirroring another dog) or interspecies/heterospecifics (dog mirroring their human). This may have either a positive or a negative effect on the dog. Additionally, there may be long-term stress synchronization between a dog and the dog's human in the home, resulting in the human mental condition affecting the mental condition of their dog.

Social learning may be especially useful when helping a fearful dog. For example, by having the fearful dog observe a confident dog enter into a swimming pool. This approach is known as *conspecific learning*. Using a teacher-dog as a *model rival* also motivates a dog to try a similar behavior such as fetching.

Recent research in social learning includes that of Dr. Adam Miklosi of Eotvos Lorand University in Budapest, Hungary (Miklosi & Kubinyi, 2016). The proposition is a technique called *Do As I Do,* and teaches the instruction, "Do It", as a *rule rather than a cue* (Fuguzza, 2014). The researchers reported that the *Do As I Do* technique is useful for teaching a dog to interact with an object, which may be of some importance to service dog training (London, 2015). Additional research is needed by independent investigators to further demonstrate validity and reliability.

PART 2

SETTING YOUR DOG UP FOR SUCCESS

6

HOW TO FIND A DOG THAT FITS YOUR LIFESTYLE *BEFORE* YOU FALL IN LOVE

A new dog romping about the house provides constant entertainment and unconditional love. However, be prepared to train, exercise, and care for the puppy or rescue dog through adolescence, adulthood, and old age. Adding a dog to your family is a lifetime commitment. The decision to bring a dog into your family is a serious responsibility requiring planning, forethought, and commitment. Once you fall in love, it is often too late to turn back, so plan carefully and choose wisely.

Choose a Dog That Fits Your Lifestyle and Family

To provide a proper forever home, choose a dog or puppy that fits in as closely as possible with your family, home, and lifestyle. Your dog will have a distinctive personality and quirks making their own character part of your dog's unique charm.

- Choose a dog whose personality and genetic traits are a good match with all the members of your family, particularly the primary caretaker.
- Choose a dog that is the right size for you. If you love lap dogs, a large or giant breed may be too big to sit on your lap, although Great Danes have figured out how to do it.
- Choose a dog whose activity level matches your family's activity level. If you are a couch potato, a herding breed will not likely lay around the house with you. If you are looking for an easy-going house pet who is a social butterfly, dogs who have specifically been bred to guard may not suit you and may be the wrong choice.

Whatever dog you do choose, remember you are making a life-long promise to not only care for your dog and meet their needs, but to train them gently using

Do No Harm methods. A 10+ year commitment should be made thoughtfully, not impulsively.

All puppies are adorable so make a list and stick to your list of

- Must have traits
- Flexible traits
- Do not want traits

There are many far-reaching factors to examine when choosing a dog. These considerations will help ensure you find the best fit for you and your family.

- Age
- Size
- Activity level
- Predisposition to medical problems
- Hair length, shedding, and grooming maintenance needs
- Average longevity
- Breed

Learn how to care for a new dog before you bring one home, just as you would prepare for the arrival of a new baby into your home. *Before You Get Your Puppy*, by pioneering puppy expert, Dr. Ian Dunbar, DVM, PhD (2001) is an informative free resource you can download to help you prepare your family and home for a new dog.

All breeds can be wonderful or problematic with children. Successful interactions between dogs and children are dependent upon both the dog and the child receiving proper training for appropriate interactions with each other. Pet parents must remain vigilant and actively supervise any dog-child interactions with any child under the age of 5 years old.

ADOPTING A DOG OR PUPPY

Shelters and rescue groups are wonderful sources to help connect you with your forever companion—and what a great feeling you will have when you provide a loving home to an abandoned dog and very possibly save a life! Adoptable dogs are most likely already neutered or spayed and have up to date vaccinations and microchips. Although puppies are extremely and impossibly cute, a house-trained adult dog may make an easier transition into your home life. A senior dog can be a wonderful addition to the right home. Local and breed-specific adoption agencies, shelters, and rescue groups have thousands of good dogs of every breed, size, age, and description who need forever homes.

Check out Petfinder.com (2020). Research the rescue or shelter and try to find a rescue group or facility that has met not only your dog's biological needs, but is aware of a dog's emotional, social, and cognitive needs. Find a rescue that supports *Do No Harm*/force-free training methods and that already uses The Hierarchy of Dog Needs when possible. Adopting during the holiday season is especially popular and many shelters and rescues now encourage families to do so. However, puppies are a lifetime commitment. Do not give a puppy as a gift to someone who may not be prepared or want to provide a loving forever home.

AVOIDING PUPPY MILLS

The first quantitative evidence demonstrating that puppy mills produce puppies with fears, phobias, learning deficits, and a generalized lack of resilience resulting in a seriously impaired ability to cope with normal stressors, was published in *Applied Animal Behavior* (McMillan et al., 2011).

In the eye-opening report by Jeanine Kunkel-Jones, in "Puppy Mills: The Horrific Truth", prospective pet parents are advised *never* to purchase a puppy from a pet store, unless the puppy can be directly traced to a reputable rescue and *never* purchase a puppy sight unseen off the Internet. According to Kunkel-Jones,

Pet parents who desire a physically sound, healthy, happy, sociable puppy are often severely and sadly disappointed after purchasing a puppy. When you purchase a puppy, you may unknowingly support cruel and inhumane treatment of dogs. While no puppy seller will admit to sourcing a puppy from a mill, the sad fact is that puppy mills are big business and a major supplier of puppies. Breeding is done regardless of genetic heath issues, both visible and invisible, from deformed body parts to elbow, knee, hip, and eye problems. Female dogs are typically bred every heat cycle until they can no longer produce, then they are killed, dumped, or sold. (Kunkel-Jones, 2019, para. 7, 9)

Health care is virtually non-existent, and most dogs spend their entire lives in dirty, cramped wire cages without any kind of enrichment. In many puppy mills, wire cages are stacked upon each other so waste falls onto the dogs below. Cages are often dirty, and food is of the poorest quality. Diseases and parasites are prevalent, including those communicable

to humans. Proper veterinary care is an expense that eats into the bottom line. In addition, cruel practices such as medical procedures without anesthesia are practiced. Puppies are shipped all over the country, taken from mothers at an early age and often subjected to inhumane treatment in transport. When dogs exhaust their usefulness, they are rarely euthanized humanely. Shooting, drowning, and beating are common. The "lucky" ones are dumped at shelters. (Kunkel-Jones, 2019)

SELECTING A GOOD BREEDER AND A HEALTHY PUPPY

Avoid supporting online puppy mills that typically ship a puppy to you. The first step is to verify the breeding protocols so you receive a healthy puppy. Just like people, the best predictors of puppy health are the longevity of parents, grandparents, and great-grandparents. Temperament is genetic and personality is the result of how that temperament is modified by socialization and the dog's environment.

Best Breeder Practices

The best breeders raise puppies indoors around a variety of people, including strangers and children outside of the immediate family. The best breeders also safely introduce puppies to other puppy-friendly dogs outside of the litter and the home, so all puppies are given the necessary opportunities to become both people and dog friendly.

By the time puppies are eight weeks old, they should have

- Been handled every day
- Met dozens of people, including calm children
- Heard all sorts of noises on a low to medium level
- Met numerous vaccinated friendly dogs of all ages and breeds
- Had remedial housetraining, chew toy training, and separation anxiety prevention training

---

Visit the mother dog and inspect the entire kennel grounds to be certain the facility meets your standards of kind treatment and cleanliness. Adult breeding dogs should never be fearful or aggressive. Be prepared to wait for a puppy. Good breeders will not release a puppy under eight weeks old and only breed a limited number of litters per year. If everything is in order, try to visit your puppy regularly from 4–8 weeks of age to nurture the human-animal bond and the bond with you.

Here are some questions to ask prospective breeders:

- May I visit the place where your puppies are bred?
- What can you tell me about the health of your dogs' ancestors?
- Who bred each parent and how do I get in touch with the breeders?
- How did the grandparents die, and at what age?
- What are the temperaments and personalities of the parent dogs?
- What kind of socialization do you give your puppies?
- What do you feed them?
- Do you vaccinate them before they leave for their new homes?

A *reliable breeder* provides medical records of tests performed. You must receive the genetic testing records recommended by a national breed club for eyes, luxating patella, hip dysplasia, and other breed-related predispositions to disease. If the breeder has not posted their dogs' certifications of health on their websites, request to see documentation of tests given. If appropriate paperwork cannot be provided, then immediately remove the breeder from your prospective list. Choosing a breeder who does not meet these basic requirements creates a substantial financial risk for you, but more importantly creates a situation where puppies may suffer greatly. These risks often result in long-term painful emotional experiences for the buyer. This is why a reputable breeder always provides health guarantees, encourage you to contact their veterinarian and other references, and offers documentation of several generations of pedigree lineage.

Note: Having "papers" generally denotes American Kennel Club (AKC) registration and pedigree lineage but often has little to do with health testing.

See *Pukka's Promise: The Quest for Longer-Lived Dogs* (Kerasote, 2014) for a brilliant account of the factors impacting dog longevity.

Remember, contrary to popular myth, the pick of the litter is often the "middle" puppy rather than the largest, smallest, most active, or least active puppy. Here are some tips to help you select a puppy from a litter:

- Choose the puppy that all members of your family like and one who likes everyone in your family.
- Observe the puppies interacting with each other and with their mother for at least two hours to evaluate current behavior, elimination, and chew habits already in practice.
- Choose the puppy who can hold their own ground without pushing the other puppies around.

PREPARING YOUR HOME FOR YOUR NEW DOG

The first week at home will be the most crucial week in your dog's life. Allow sufficient time for your dog to *decompress*, bond with you and become familiar with the neighborhood. The time needed will vary significantly dependent upon your dog's unique needs. Don't rush. Set up your *Doggy Enrichment Land*™ with all of your puppy's wants and needs in mind. Doggy Enrichment Land, a containment set-up giving your puppy plenty of room for activities and pleasure can be used for many training needs, such as housetraining, safe greeting protocols, dog and baby/toddler separation, and separation anxiety treatment. Doggy Enrichment Land should never feel like a punishment to your dog but rather like a sanctuary and place where special, high value items are available. Your dog is learning about the world and developing habits each and every hour.

Items You Will Need

- Baby gates and x-pen
- Crates (cloth for your bed or metal) for overnight housetraining and emergencies after decompression. Crate training must be conditioned slowly and carefully to be certain the crate is not experienced as punishment.
- Enrichment items such as bully sticks, licking mat feeders, puzzle feeders, snuffle mats, plush squeaky toys, tennis balls, and a lure toy for play and exercise
- Mat or throw rug
- Orthopedic bed

7

HOW TO FIND A GOOD DOG TRAINER— BUYER BE WARY

With the overwhelming variety of dog training methods and "training collars" advertised, it is often frustrating for pet parents to find a good trainer. The safest and most effective methods are based on force-free/pain-free/fear-free scientific principles. The consequences of using other methods include a high risk of psychological and medical injury, which are entirely unnecessary. No truly competent trainer recommends inflicting pain, fear, dominance or intimidation, shock, prong or choke collars.

The highly regarded and influential American Veterinary Society of Animal Behavior (2021b) takes an outspoken and principled stand on equipment and techniques that should be avoided in dog training. They report,

An appropriate trainer should avoid any use of training tools that involve pain (choke chains, prong collars, or electronic shock collars), intimidation (squirt bottles, shaker noise cans, compressed air cans, shouting, staring, or forceful manipulations such as "alpha rolls" or "dominance downs"), physical correction techniques (leash jerking, physical force), or flooding ("exposure"). The learner must always feel safe and have the ability to "opt out" of training sessions. (p. 2)

Good Training Tools and Tools to Avoid

Renowned veterinary behaviorist and editor of the *Journal of Veterinary Behavior*, Dr. Karen Overall, DVM, PhD, provides an outline in her article aptly titled, "Good trainers: How to identify one" (Overall et al., 2006). This easy-to-use reference guide was developed for pet parents, dog trainers, veterinarians, shelters, rescues, groomers, and other pet-related professionals. Pet parents can trust the quality of the trainer they are considering if that trainer adheres to the following guidelines as quoted from Overall below:

*"**Good Training Tools:** Safe and effective.*
a) *Small bite-sized treats*
b) *Leashes*
c) *Flat collars*
d) *Harnesses*
e) *Praise*
f) *Toys*

__Tools to Avoid:__ Cause anxiety, fear and may cause aggression.
a) *Shock collars/ electric collars / e-collars/ static collar*
b) *Prong collars*
c) *"Correction" collars*
d) *Choke collars, choke chains (sometimes euphemistically referred to as training collars)*

__Problematic Tools:__
a) *Flexible retractable leash*

What is Positive Training?

a) *Based on a reward structure that encourages the dog to want to work more with you. Only reward based, there is no punishment or "correction."*

b) *Having the dog pay attention to something that is coupled with the reward [best standards of training techniques include capturing, luring, and shaping.]*

c) *Punishment inhibits desired learning.*

d) *Punishment does not tell the pet what to do.*

e) *Punishment makes animals more reactive so it **increases aggression and arousal** [emphasis added]. Any animal that was already aggressive will become worse when punished.*

f) *Punishment increases the risk of physical and psychological injury. (Overall, et al., 2006)*

Dogs handled with choke chains and prong collars often have laryngeal, esophageal, thyroidal, and tracheal damage. Recurrent laryngeal nerve damage or paralysis may be detected by a change in bark (Overall et al., 2006).

HARNESSES AND LEASHES

Safety, comfort, and stress reduction are the most important criteria when selecting equipment used for training. The use of equipment causing stress or pain, such as choke, prong, or electronic shock collars is antithetical to *Do No Harm* training and is harmful to dogs. These devices are at odds with pet parents developing positive relationships with their dogs and may cause aggression or worsen aggression (Overall, 2006). Additionally, medical research shows stress to the neck causes injuries that include spinal cervical injury, burst capillaries in the eyeballs, foreleg nerve damage, impaired breathing, and damage that affects the function of the esophagus and trachea. A regular flat collar is recommended to hold identification tags only. Do not attach a leash to a flat collar—pressure from pulling on a flat collar may cause medical injuries as well. Make leash-walking fun and relaxing. Recommended equipment includes:

- **Harness.** An X or Y shaped harness across the breast has the least impact on movement and mobility and provides the most comfort for your dog. A front, back, or double-clip harness is recommended for all dogs and puppies, including those dogs that have developed a habit of pulling on the leash during the walk. A harness that attaches to the leash at the breastplate is fine to start, although some trainers prefer the back-clip. There are benefits and drawbacks to each. Small dogs that do not pull may prefer a step-in harness.

- **Flat collar.** Use for identification tags.
- **Leash.** Use a leash that is four or six feet in length. When you begin training, a short leash may be helpful for dogs that are difficult to walk. However, using a long (long line), very loose leash for training helps if your dog is reactive.

USING FOOD AS A REWARD

If we could not go to the grocery store and bring home bags of groceries or open the refrigerator, we would be asking, "Who's got the food? What can I do for the people who have the food?" The easiest, scientifically endorsed dog training and socialization methods involve food. Animal behavior icons from Skinner to Pavlov and progressive zoos worldwide manage very large and potentially dangerous animals by using the power of food wisely.

If you have ever taken a Psychology 101 course you may recall that food is a primary reinforcer. Dogs love and need food for survival, making food a very powerful training tool. Do not believe anyone who tells you it is a bad idea to use food to train your dog! In *The Secret History of Kindness: Learning from How Dogs Learn*, author Melissa Holbrook Pierson says, "Withholding every possible chance to learn all they are capable of, and so to feel that native joy, is mean, in the original sense of the word: miserly stingy" (2015, p. 255). Jean Donaldson has this to say about trainers who are adamantly self-righteous about withholding the pleasure of food, "The sad objective of these trainers seems to be to reach the end of the dog's life having dispensed as few rewards as possible. It's difficult to explain why an animal trainer would strive to be as stingy as possible, given the evidence of how powerful and safe positive reinforcement is" (Donaldson as cited in Pierson, 2015, p. 255).

Positive reinforcement training is an effective training method, in part, because of hand-fed treats. Using food judiciously quickly motivates a dog to learn new behaviors. Do not worry; food rewards may be decreased after a behavior is well learned and replaced with *real-life reinforcement* of value to your dog. You may also use play as a reward if your dog is more motivated by play. Use a graduated treat system for training, saving the highest value treats for the most difficult emotional issues.

- **Treats.** High value treats such as air-dried and freeze-dried meats and organs, organic and nitrite-free hot dogs, string cheese, or a homemade mixture of favorite treats cut to pea-size may be used for training. Although trainers commonly call food, "treats" or even "cookies," typically they are referring to healthy high-grade species-specific food.
- **Treat bag.** Whether you opt for a plastic baggie in your pocket, a fanny pack, or a fashionable, convenient treat bag, carrying treats on your walks and during training sessions is recommended. Having easily accessible treats makes a great difference in your ability to get your dog's attention in high-distraction environments and speeds up learning. A treat bag also keeps your hands free.

8

HOW TO FIND A GOOD VETERINARIAN AND GROOMER

Aside from choosing a force-free trainer, selecting a compassionate veterinarian and a gentle groomer are two of the most important decisions you will make for your dog. Veterinary and grooming visits are often the first regularly predictable interactions a dog will have with people and other dogs outside of the home and continue throughout a lifetime. The experiences at the veterinarian and groomer, and how your dog perceives each experience, has serious and long-lasting effects. Gentle veterinary and grooming care may prevent instilling fear, anxiety, escape avoidance behavior, aggression, or triggering tonic immobility in your dog.

Being restrained and manipulated by a stranger may be very frightening to your dog. Rushing through veterinary and grooming visits to get the task over with as quickly as possible is likely to backfire for you, your dog, and the practitioner in the long run, making future visits more frightening for your dog and more difficult for all.

If you have a wonderfully competent, kind, and gentle veterinarian or groomer who understands your dog's emotional and medical needs, bravo! These practitioners may be rather difficult to find, however, their numbers are growing exponentially: they are the wave of the future.

GENTLE VETERINARY CARE

Veterinary visits may have a profound impact on your dog both medically and emotionally. The very first veterinary experience often sets the stage for how your dog responds to veterinary visits thereafter—either positively or negatively.

So many pet parents feel helpless not knowing how they can make veterinary visits more pleasant for their dogs. If your dog is afraid of visiting the veterinarian, start practicing at home and begin a dialogue with your practitioner about force-free visits, or to find a veterinarian with a more dog-centered practice. If not handled with care, fearful or aggressive behavioral effects from fear at the veterinary clinic may be long lasting and resistant to change, causing unnecessary heartache for all. Slowly and carefully familiarize your dog to the veterinary procedures and veterinary equipment.

Veterinarians and technicians may not understand dog body language or displays of stress. When possible, ask to accompany your dog during basic or stressful procedures, if you remain upbeat and supportive, rather than leaving your dog with a stranger for what may be a painful event. Your presence can help your dog feel more secure, if you have practiced at home and at the clinic before the need arises. According to the founder of the Canine Research Studies social media group, Rebekah Hudson, "To me, clinics that take dogs to the back without their pet parents for routine blood draws and vaccinations is a sign that we need to make improvements in the veterinary clinic and in the education of dog parents. We need more collaboration between veterinary staff, force-free trainers and owners" (Hudson, 2019a, para. 15).

Hiring a gentle, mobile veterinarian for basic care may be less stressful for both you and your dog, particularly if your dog already has an intense fear of the veterinary clinic. At-home visits allow your dog the familiar environment of home, while removing the possible stress of being near other animals who may also be experiencing fear. At-home visits also keep your dog away from any risk of exposure to animals who may be ill or unvaccinated.

Vaccinations and Socialization Go Together

Most pet parents are now aware of the necessity of providing dog-dog socialization opportunities for their puppies. Nevertheless, *when,* and *how* to do it is still seriously misunderstood. Dog-dog aggression is widespread, often contributing to behavior problems. Many veterinarians, breeders, and pet store owners still advise new pet parents to refrain from socializing their new puppy with other dogs until the age of four to six months of age to avoid the potential for exposure to illnesses in unvaccinated puppies and dogs.

However, Dr. Karen Overall, Veterinarian, Diplomat of the American College of Veterinary Behavior (ACVB) PhD, CAAB, explains, "Worldwide, it's exceptional that veterinary specialists in behavior are on faculty at veterinary schools, and yet the single biggest killer of pet dogs is behavior problems. People need to realize that vets do not know that much about problematic behavior, or maybe even normal behavior. The single biggest reason people relinquish animals to a shelter is a behavioral problem."

Veterinary experts in animal behavior caution that the risk of developing behavioral problems—especially aggression—*outweighs* the risk of developing disease in otherwise healthy puppies. This knowledge is fundamental because behavioral issues are generally the primary factor in relinquishing dogs to shelters and ultimately if these dogs are not adopted, they are often euthanized. Shelters have the difficult, if not impossible, task of trying to find good homes for dogs who cannot get along with other dogs. As early as 2004, renowned veterinarian, RK Anderson, published an open letter to his veterinary colleagues titled "Puppy Vaccination and Early Socialization Should Go Together". Dr. Lynn Honeckman, DVM, states, "There is a very small window of opportunity during which it is our job to teach our puppies that the world is a safe place" (personal communication).

Socialize AND Protect Your Puppy

The American Veterinary Society of Animal Behavior (AVSAB) "Position Statement on Puppy Socialization" advises socialization in the first three months of life, before puppies are fully vaccinated, as the *standard of care*. It states that, "Because the first three months are the period when sociability outweighs fear, this is the primary window of opportunity for puppies to adapt to new people, animals, and experiences" (2008, para. 2). Socializing with littermates or in-house dogs is **not** sufficient. Dr. Lee Harris, DVM, a veterinarian who studies canine behavior, wisely counsels, "Common sense needs to be exerted about providing well-chosen socialization" (personal communication, 2012). The Pet Professional Guild (2012) offers a terrific one-page socialization guide with a checklist on one side and a "how-to" on the other side.

Work closely with your veterinarian to keep your puppy current on her vaccinations or titer testing but remain proactive about socialization requirements. Discuss the current scientific literature and create a medically safe early socialization plan with your vet and a private trainer or puppy class instructor or ask your positive reinforcement behavioral consultant for a socialization-savvy veterinary referral.

How to Choose a Veterinarian

Choosing a compassionate veterinarian who practices gentle handling and restraint is one of the most critical decisions you will ever make for your dog. Find a *pet-centered* clinic with a veterinarian where your dog comes first. Force-free handling and Fear Free® visits should go hand-in-glove. Cooperative veterinary care is a team effort. When pet parents feel comfortable with the guidance given by their gentle veterinarian, they are more likely to practice maintenance care at home between visits.

- Find a veterinarian who prioritizes compassionate care and minimizes stress instead of maximizing restraint.
- Find a veterinarian who will take the time to bond with your dog, and who uses treats liberally.
- Find a veterinarian who has studied dog behavior and who is sensitive to your dog's psychological need for a sense of security as well as their biological needs.
- Find a veterinarian who is knowledgeable in recognizing signs of anxiety and responds appropriately to comfort and calm your dog.
- Find one who will examine your dog in your lap or on the floor, if practical.
- Rather than using nylon muzzles or restraints, a force-free veterinarian might use an air muzzle, anti-anxiety, or sedative medication. An air muzzle is a ball that resembles a deep diver's helmet with an opening in the front so that your dog can release body heat by perspiration through the tongue, rather than a tightly fitting piece of nylon cloth that frightens your dog, and impedes the ability to breathe.
- Find a veterinarian who uses reward-based training methods making the experience as positive as possible for your dog.
- Find a veterinarian who stays up to date on safety and health trends through continuing education and training.
- Choose someone who is not only competent, but who is friendly and shares information willingly. Chat with any prospective veterinarians and ask pertinent questions about their practices.
- Find out if any animals have been injured or died under the veterinarian or clinic's care. Check with the International Association of Better Business Bureaus (IABBB) the network hub for the United States, Canada, and Mexico, to see if any complaints have been filed against the business.
- Request references from other pet parents.
- Find gentle veterinarians in your area using the zip code search on the Pet Professional Guild website, petprofessionalguild.com (2020a). If you cannot locate a gentle veterinarian, find one who is willing to working with a force-free trainer to learn low-stress handling and restraint, dog body language, and positive reinforcement behavior modification techniques.
- Consider in-home mobile providers.

Home Practice

Here are some handling tips that you can practice at home to make visits to the veterinarian less stressful for you, your dog, and your veterinarian. At home, reward intermittently with treats throughout the exercises listed below, to help your dog overcome the fear of handling, high places, and also rewarding calmness.

- Condition your dog to riding in the car so that travel is a pleasant experience.
- For small dogs and puppies, start early to desensitize your dog with a familiar dog carrier. For large dogs, desensitize your dog to accept containment in a securable car crate or a crash tested harness. The containment should be associated with high value treats. Early and careful conditioning to a crate is advised for use in case of injury, emergency, or for other travel needs.
- Desensitize your dog to wearing a muzzle, and an Elizabethan collar from an early age in case of emergency, injury, or if your dog bites. View the step-by-step instructional video, "Teaching a Dog to Wear a Muzzle (Muzzle Training)" expertly demonstrated by Chirag Patel (2010).
- Practice placing your dog onto a safe, raised, table-like surface. Use a rubber mat, such as a yoga mat, for secure grip. Avoid falls by securing your dog.
- Examine the entire body with your hands, checking for tumor growth and lumps.
- Examine your dog from nose to tail, looking for irritations of the skin, rashes, minor cuts, etc.
- Examine your dog's paws between each toe (Witmer, 2014). Your dog will acclimate to footpad examinations for foreign objects, foxtails, and nail trims. Regular nail trimming is *a must* for proper bone growth and stability. Nail trimming is not simply cosmetic.
- Examine your dog's ears. Lift the earflap and take a good look inside while your dog sits quietly. Check for unusual odor or inflamed skin. Head shaking may mean your dog has an ear infection. If your dog rubs his head against objects, he may be trying to scratch infected ears, or relieve dental pain.
- Examine your dog's mouth. Lift the lips and examine teeth and inside the mouth. This will not only aid in veterinary exams but will desensitize your dog to people touching your dog's mouth. Foul breath may indicate that your dog has decayed and painful teeth.
- Examine the stomach area. Examine gently as if looking for fleas: palpate the stomach area. *Do Not* alpha roll your dog for this examination.
- Massage the sacral joint where the spine meets the tail and lift the tail to desensitize your dog to the anal exam. Dragging the butt across the floor can mean anal gland impaction or worms, requiring a visit to your trusted veterinarian . . . or perhaps it just means your dog needs a baby wipe!
- Practice squeezing your dog's skin between two fingers to simulate injections. Use a retracted pen to simulate the pressure of an injection. Treat generously and calmly praise immediately. Simulate, then treat and repeat.

Your First Veterinary Appointment

Create positive memories from the very first visit for a check-up or vaccination. Visit the clinic more than once *before* taking your dog in for an exam, or vaccination visit. The purpose of the preliminary visits is to provide the opportunity to deliver treats, for a weigh-in, and to play with the technicians, administrators, and veterinarians in the hospital without any stressful experience.

- Try arranging appointments during the quietest business hours for the clinic.
- Bring your dog's favorite and familiar objects and toys with you, which will help your dog feel less fearful.
- Do not hurry. Relax. Your calm demeanor will help set the emotional stage for your dog.
- Do not wait in the reception area room with your dog. Wait in the car or have your dog wait in the car, if safe, until it is your turn to go into the exam room.
- Use a species-specific, *dogs-only* exam room so your dog is not triggered by the smell of cats or prey animals.
- Go into the treatment room with your dog first and wait if this prevents seeing other dogs and people in the reception area. Although, if the veterinarian and technicians enter the room first, your dog may react more calmly than to someone coming into "their" room. Know your dog.
- Ask the staff to avoid direct eye contact as much as possible especially if your dog is fearful.
- Both you and your veterinarian should provide your dog's favorite high value treats liberally throughout a visit. Bring your dog to the veterinarian a bit hungry.
- Ask to stay with your dog if you remain calm during basic procedures.
- Stroke and talk to your pet during exams.
- Be sure your dog is on a non-slip surface.
- Let your dog sniff the instruments.
- Ask your veterinarian to allow your dog to initiate interaction, that is, to give consent when ready, not vice-versa if trained.
- Allow your dog to *show* readiness for procedures. Do not force. Choice and consent are the progressive concepts in veterinary cooperative care.
- If your dog has fear, anxiety, or aggression issues, let your veterinarian know you want to work with them to help calm your dog, or possibly use a muzzle on your muzzle-preconditioned dog.
- Request the use of oral vaccinations whenever possible such as the Bordetella transmucosal vaccine rather than the intranasal or injectable forms.
- Ask your veterinarian to use topical pain management to reduce sensitivity.
- Use anti-anxiety drugs for those dogs who need them. You may try natural products such as Composure TM.

(Learn more in Chapter 1, Gentle Veterinary Care.)

GENTLE GROOMING CARE

Grooming is one of the most challenging dog-related professions due to the potential for accidents, and physical and psychological injury. Even the most competent, experienced, responsible, gentle groomer is not entirely immune from accidents and injuring pets. The best protection for your dog against both physical and psychological trauma during grooming is to properly research potential groomers, and to take responsibility to adequately prepare your dog for grooming, or to employ a mobile groomer who can remain under your direct supervision.

It is best to begin regular grooming sessions at home when your dog is young. Wait until your puppy is 4 months old and fully vaccinated before you visit a groomer. If your puppy needs grooming before then, do it yourself at home or hire a mobile groomer. The very first grooming experience generally sets the stage for how your dog responds to grooming for a lifetime—either positively or negatively. Visit the groomer more than once *before* taking your dog in for the first groom just delivering treats and playing with the office personnel and groomers, creating positive memories from the first day. Make the first session an abbreviated visit for bonding with office personnel, bathers, and groomer, acclimation, and lots of love and treats. Slowly and carefully begin familiarizing your dog with the grooming process and grooming equipment. If your dog already has a fear of grooming, hiring a gentle mobile groomer may be the least stressful choice for both you and your dog. This eliminates the stress of being near other animals who may be aggressive or experiencing fear themselves. Mobile grooming is often faster and less stressful in many ways for your dog. Pet parents can easily stay with their dog or check in periodically and unexpectedly.

If your dog has fear, aggression, or anxiety issues, let your groomer know that you will accept a less than perfect groom and that you place your dog's emotional well-being ahead of cosmetic appearances. Never force grooming that is not tolerated well. Dogs should not be whimpering, shaking, or snapping during grooming. Our dogs can learn to accept and even enjoy grooming with the right gentle grooming professional in a calm environment. Pet parents need to do their part in advocating for their dog by learning about grooming, finding a gentle groomer, classically conditioning their dog before and between grooming visits, and gently grooming their dog at home between visits.

How to Choose a Groomer and Salon

Choosing a compassionate groomer who practices gentle handling and restraint is one of the most important decisions you will make for your dog. Pet parents need to be proactive about the treatment their dog receives while in a groomer's care. As with veterinarians and trainers, seek groomers who are force-free, competent, accountable, and who practice transparency in advertising. Research the facility *and* the practitioner.

Sadly, the grooming industry is unregulated. Groomers, like trainers, have no formal educational requirements. Groomers are encouraged to educate themselves about using *Do No Harm* grooming protocols and equipment. Finding a gentle groomer may be a challenging task, but it is well worth the search. Find a gentle groomer who considers your dog's well-being rather than expediency first.

- Find a salon *prioritizing* compassionate care, minimizing stress instead of maximizing restraint.
- Search for a professional who takes the time to bond with your dog, and who uses treats liberally.
- Find a groomer who uses reward-based training methods to make the experience as positive as possible for your dog.
- Find a groomer who recognizes signs of anxiety and responds appropriately to comfort and calm your dog.
- Find a groomer who graduated from a training program and belongs to a professional grooming trade organization. Although groomers are not required to be licensed members in organizations such as the National Dog Groomers Association, membership often indicates continuing education and on-the-job apprenticeships.
- Be certain your groomer carries liability insurance.

- Choose a veteran groomer with years of experience. An experienced groomer is more likely to be confident and competent, and willing to admit to their limitations.
- Choose a groomer who is up to date on safety and health trends through continuing education and training.
- Find a groomer who is well versed in handling pesticides, allergic reactions, proper handling techniques, and monitoring animal behavior.
- Find out if any animals have been injured or died under the groomer or salon care. Check with the International Association of Better Business Bureaus (IABBB) the network hub for the United States, Canada, and Mexico, to see if any complaints have been filed against the business.
- Request references from other clients.
- Find gentle groomers in your area using the Pet Professional Guild website, petprofessionalguild.com (2020a). If you cannot find a gentle practitioner, find one who is willing to work with a force-free trainer to learn low-stress handling and restraint, dog body language, and positive reinforcement behavior modification techniques.
- Consider in-home mobile groomers. This can eliminate a great deal of stress and you will be close at hand to check in periodically to be certain your instructions are being followed and your dog is doing well.
- Choose someone who is not only competent, but who is friendly and willing to share information. Chat with them and ask questions.

Cooperative grooming care is a team effort, so it is imperative pet parents feel comfortable asking for guidance to properly maintain their dog between visits. This is the responsibility of the pet parent to their dog and to their gentle groomer.

Home Practice

Grooming can be a wonderful bonding experience for the pet and the pet parent. Your dog can acclimate to being handled in ways your dog is not normally handled, making professional grooming easier for your dog. A force-free trainer can teach you ways of habituating your new puppy to grooming noises, gentle restraint, and handling.

A force-free trainer will introduce grooming desensitization steps for the adolescent and adult dog including guidance on *consent* in grooming husbandry. Here are some things that you can practice at home to make trips to the groomer less stressful for your dog.

- Condition your dog to riding in the car so that travel is a pleasant experience.
- Desensitize your small dog or puppy to being transported in a carrier that is familiar, well-loved, and has been associated with treats. Early and gentle

conditioning to a carrier or crate is recommended for use in case of injury, emergency, or for other travel needs. Desensitize your large dog to accept containment in a securable crate or crash-tested harness. The containment should be associated with high value treats.

- Desensitize your dog to wearing a muzzle or an Elizabethan collar from an early age for emergencies, or if your dog bites. There is a step-by-step habituation and desensitization instructional video, expertly taught by Chirag Patel (2010) to illustrate how to do it causing the least amount of stress to your dog.
- Brush your dog every day or two. Mist your dog with a few drops of leave-in conditioner manufactured for dogs, to make brushing easier.
- Reward intermittently and generously with treats throughout practice to help your dog overcome the fear of high places, handling, and to reward calmness.
- Practice placing your dog onto a safe, raised table-like surface. Use a rubber mat, such as a yoga mat, for secure grip. Secure your pet to avoid falls. Keep your dog leashed so the grooming process is not prolonged, which can increase anxiety.
- Desensitize your dog to the sound of the blow dryer, sound of clippers, and to the clicking sound of a nail trimmer (North Shore Animal League, 2015).
- Acclimate your dog to soap and warm baths at home before going to the groomer. Avoid shampooing your dog's head.
- Clean your dog's face every day with a warm washcloth without soap, to help prevent tear staining.
- Dogs with loose facial skin, such as Shar Pei, Boston Terriers, Bulldogs and Pugs need special care to prevent dirt and bacteria from causing irritation or infection. Clean the folds with a damp cotton swab and dry thoroughly between the folds.
- Examine your dog's paws between each toe. This will help your dog to acclimate to paw-restraint for nail trims. Dogs should be comfortable with having their paws held and manipulated for up to 60 seconds. Remember, regular nail trimming is a must for proper bone growth and stability.
- Examine your dog's ears. Lift the earflap and take a good look inside the ear while your dog sits quietly. Check for unusual odor or inflamed skin. Having the hair plucked out of the ears is an unpleasant experience.
- Examine your dog's mouth. Lift the lips and examine teeth and inside the mouth. This will desensitize your dog to people touching your dog's mouth. Make sure your dog has proper dental care. Proper dental care is so often overlooked!
- Massage the sacral joint where the spine meets the tail and lift the tail to desensitize your dog to handling.
- Teach your dog how to give consent, how to ask for a break, and how to ask you to stop. Choice and consent are the wave of the future in modern cooperative care.

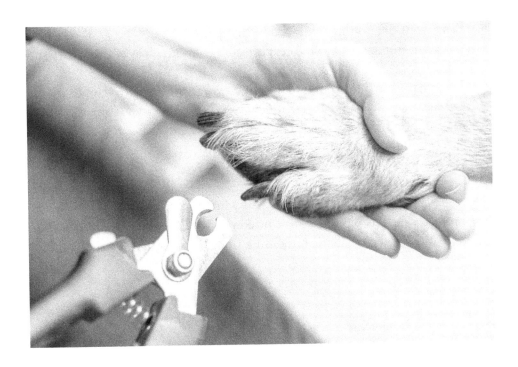

Your First Grooming Appointment

Remain calm and supportive and stay with your dog during grooming, if possible. Both you and the groomer should provide high value treats liberally throughout the visit. Stroke and talk with your pet during grooming, if possible. Bring your dog's favorite and familiar objects and toys. This will help your dog feel less fearful. Make sure your groomer is patient and kind while you observe a groom. A good groomer will show you how to groom correctly at home using the right techniques and tools to help you carry on their best practices between visits.

- Try to arrange appointments during the quietest hours at the salon.
- Make sure your dog has ample opportunity to eliminate before going inside.
- Do not wait with your dog in the waiting room. Wait in the car or have your pet wait in the car, if safe, until it is your turn to go in for grooming.
- Request a *dogs-only* grooming room, if possible, so your dog is not triggered by the smell of cats or prey animals.
- Have the groomer in the room before you and your dog enter.
- Let your dog sniff the instruments.
- Ask your groomer to allow your dog to initiate interaction when ready, not vice-versa.
- Allow your dog to *show* you readiness for grooming. **Do not force.**
- Find a groomer who will groom your dog in your lap or on the floor if possible.
- Be sure your dog is on a non-slip surface.

- Bring your dog to the groomer a bit hungry.
- Ask your groomer to avoid direct eye contact as much as possible if your dog is fearful.
- If you have a small dog that may be aggressive, ask your groomer to use an air muzzle, that is, a ball that resembles a deep diver's helmet with an opening in the front, rather than a tightly fitting piece of cloth that frightens your dog and can impedes the ability to breath. Alternatively, use a basket muzzle.
- Do not hurry.

There are anti-anxiety drugs for those pets who need it. You may try natural anti-anxiety products such as Composure™ or confer with your veterinary behaviorist. (Learn more in Chapter 1, Gentle Grooming Care.)

9

SOCIALIZATION

The most important thing your dog will ever learn

Like humans, dogs are social creatures. Today pet parents know the importance of socializing their dogs, but they are unsure how to do so safely and effectively. *Socialize early, slowly, and carefully.* It is vital your puppy experiences each interaction as entirely positive. Behavior modification techniques that include habituation and systematic desensitization and counterconditioning (D&CC) will help you and your dog learn safe ways of socializing and exercising. Start carefully supervised socialization as early as possible. Early socialization is absolutely necessary to avoid problems such as fearfulness and/or aggression later in your dog's life. Socialization training opportunities in public should be practiced frequently and regularly throughout your dog's life. Socialize! Socialize! Socialize!

Carefully expose your puppy or dog to 100 new things in the first 100 days starting on *day one* for a happy, confident adolescent and adult dog. Introduce your puppy to three new dog lovers every day! A puppy's critical socialization period is between 4 and 12 weeks of age; however, now is the time to help your dog of any age learn to accept the whole world gracefully without fear or reactivity.

Gentle daily handling and massage will benefit both you and your dog. It will strengthen your bond with your puppy or new-to-you dog and keep your dog from becoming sensitive to touch. Nevertheless, always let your dog decide when to be touched and for how long.

AVOIDING PROBLEMS AND HEARTACHE

Preparing your dog to live peaceably and happily in a people and dog-filled environment makes sense. Plan for the lifetime of happiness you desire with your dog. Socialize early with planned, orchestrated, incremental exposures to each of the commonly known dog *triggers*. People, other dogs, moving objects, loud noises, and novel situations need socialization:

People

Socialize your dog to all kinds of people, especially your veterinarian, groomer, men, children, and strangers. People wearing hats, sunglasses, using canes, wheelchairs, deep-voiced, and any type of person your dog may encounter later in life, particularly those that may tend to startle your dog when experienced for the first time. Invite dog lovers to your home for a low-arousal puppy party! However, don't pass the puppy around: let the puppy approach the guests on the puppy's own terms, while guests use encouragement with treats. Dr. Ian Dunbar, veterinarian, Animal Behavior PhD, and pioneer in puppy training tells us that safe socialization during the first few weeks at home is of "extreme urgency." Indeed, Dunbar has launched the SIRIUS Puppy Raising Initiative explaining socialization imperatives for puppies in the short *critical period* of social development (between 4 and 12 weeks of age). "Puppies must be safely socialized to people; otherwise, during adolescence they will likely become wary and fearful and may be aggressive towards people" (Dunbar, 2012, para. 2).

Other Dogs

Socialize your dog to all kinds of dogs that are well behaved. All breeds, all sizes, all colors, all ages, both sexes—neutered, spayed, and au natural, only *if dog- friendly.* Your puppy or dog must learn how to respect the boundaries set by other dogs and to set boundaries as early in life as possible. If practical, arrange playgroups with dogs you know are dog-friendly and vaccinated. A propensity toward aggression with stranger-dogs is likely without careful, proper socialization during the critical sensitive period. Inadequate early socialization early often results in aggression, which is resistant to treatment, dogfights, embarrassing and stressful barking/lunging walks, heartache, pet abandonment, and in some cases, death.

Moving Objects and Loud Noises

Socialize/habituate your dog to skateboards, joggers, bicycles, loud trucks, motorcycles, cats, rabbits, lizards, and cows! Thunder and fireworks are particularly frightening to dogs. While using video recordings and replicating the conditions are possible, recommended treatments providing a "bolt hole," comfort, and possibly anti-anxiety medication are advised.

Situations

Socialize, that is, habituate your puppy to riding in the car, shopping in malls, visiting pet stores, calmly settling at coffee shops, riding in an elevator, and anything else you expect your dog may encounter during a lifetime.

If your puppy or dog appears frightened, increase your distance from the feared object. Comfort your dog. By introducing new things *slowly and confidently,* you will avoid frightening your dog and encourage calm acceptance. The best socialization approach is introducing new or potentially frightening things in graduating *baby steps.*

What Happens to Dogs Not Socialized Early?

After the 4 to 12-week sensitive period window closes, the friendly, socializing puppy open to accepting the wide and wonderful world enters into a fear-acquiring developmental period.

DOG-DOG PLAY RULES AND MANNERS

Play between dogs should be a two-way street. Play should typically go back and forth, with one dog pursuing the other and then a role reversal. If one dog is always being chased, or hiding, it is highly unlikely this dog is having fun and intervention is necessary. Role reversal also means one dog on top, then the other dog on top. Do not allow chase games with a large dog pursuing a puppy or small dog. The *50:50 Rule* stipulates that both players have the same chance of winning (Aldis, 1975).

Here are some essential tips for the assessment and supervision of play:

- Look for wiggling body language, happy faces, and play bows from both dogs. Bouncy exaggerated rocking-horse type movements are a sign the dogs are having fun.
- Determine whether your dog wants to run back and play with another dog by giving a *consent test.* Separate the dogs, remove your dog some distance away, then observe whether your dog wants to run back and play with the other dog or not.

- Dogs should be self-imposing breaks from play to rest or get a small drink. Breaks may include sniffing. If one dog wants a break the other dog shows respect by not persisting in perpetual play inducements. If your dog comes and lies down near you, take the lead, and protect your dog from further interaction until your dog desires another round of play. Sniffing may be in order.
- Puppies and adult dogs must be monitored very carefully as should small dogs vs. large dogs. Not all adult dogs like puppies.
- Large adult dogs should change levels, that is *voluntarily self-handicap,* and let the puppy or smaller dog "win" regularly during role reversals. These behaviors balance inequalities in size, strength, and health. If role-reversals or self-handicapping are not occurring, do not allow your puppy or small dog continued interaction with an adult or much larger dog who may show aggression or cause physical or emotional injury.
- One dog may be either the victim or the bully in different contexts. Roles may also change when playing with different play partners.
- Dogs should take turns happily chasing each other where neither dog is a bully or a target, so play goes back and forth.
- With puppies, adult dogs should be willing to let the puppy win now and again and should *always* back off if the puppy squeals.
- You should not hear a puppy or dog squealing during play except if the dog is accidentally frightened or tackled too roughly.
- Adult dogs should be willing to get down to the puppy's or small dog's level, that is, *handicapping,* so that the puppy can have fun too.
- Make sure all puppies and dogs have areas to escape play if stressed or tired.

Contrary to some widely held opinions, well-socialized adult dogs are generally quite tolerant of puppies and do not actively, or frequently correct puppies with neck grabs, shakes or *any* type of aggressive behavior. If play becomes too rough the adult dog typically simply walks away, effectively ending the fun, therein, teaching the puppy what is appropriate and what is not. (See Chapter 9, Dog-Dog Play Rules.)

DOG PARK AND DOG BEACH SAFETY TIPS

Who can resist getting your dog and family outdoors to catch the surf, soak up some rays, and exercise together? Dog parks and dog beaches are wonderful places for exercise and play; however, they also come with some built-in dangers. Make the right decisions at the right time for your dog. Dog play and dog parks should be safe, fun and a source of enjoyment for both you and your dog. Watch your dog's behavior and body language carefully. Pat Miller, Training Editor for the *Whole Dog Journal*, tells us that at least half of the problems seen at the dog parks stem from inappropriate human behavior. It is the pet parent's responsibility to observe and monitor their dog's interactions at all times. Talking distractedly on a cell phone or with other pet parents is not fair to your dog or to the other dogs who are playing. Do not bring food or treats into a dog park or dog beach area.

Look for parks with separate large and small dog areas. Large, boisterous dogs may accidentally injure small dogs during play. For beginners, avoid crowds by finding a nice quiet area away from the entrance and other areas of greatest activity to avoid crowds. Some very progressive private parks have four separate areas: one area for small active dogs, one for small quiet dogs, one for large active dogs, and one for large quiet dogs. Most dog parks have signage with instructions. Attorney, Kenneth M. Phillips, owner, and author of *Dog Bite Law* (2020), warns pet parents about possible legal problems that include inappropriate dogs visiting dog parks resulting in dog fights, bites, and injuries. Canine business-owners who bring multiple dogs to a park at one time can pose unfair dangers to the average dog. Visitors who fail to clean up after their pet risk possible disease transmission. Understand that when you enter a dog park or beach, you do so at your dog's peril. You waive your rights and assume all risks if your dog is injured.

Dogs are, after all, cognitively comparable to 2 or 3-year-old children for their entire lives. They simply cannot be trusted in making good decisions by our standards on any regular basis. Plus, dogs often play by their own rules. Protect and keep your dog safe, and provide great exercise and fun by following these dog beach and dog park adventure guidelines:

- Do not overwhelm your dog. If your dog is a dog park or socialization beginner, arrive at quiet times of the day allowing your dog time to acclimate to the new environment and to feel safe there, keeping your visits short.
- Arrive first so your dog can greet one stranger dog at a time.
- Move away from the entry gate as soon as possible. The entrance is where all the other dogs rush to meet newcomers at a dog park.
- Start games with one dog, then two, then four, then more, and monitor how your dog is doing with each increasing level of intensity.
- Educate yourself on the symptoms of heatstroke, especially if you have a senior dog or a dog with a short upper respiratory tract, such as the Pug, Boston Terrier, or Pekingese. The first signs of heatstroke are increased panting, and gums or tongue that is dry, sticky and bright pink, reddish or purple. If your dog begins to vomit, become unsteady, or pass bloody diarrhea, take your dog to the veterinary emergency hospital immediately.
- Forgo dog parks or beaches when temperatures are extreme with heat, cold, or ice. Exercise early in the morning or later in the evening during summer.
- Provide small amounts of fresh water to avoid bloat/gastric torsion associated with exercise and gulping water. Offer fresh water that is cool, *not* ice cold.

- Offer frequent breaks with shady rest. Your dog will not know when to stop when they are aroused.
- Evaporation has a cooling effect. Pour a little cool, *not cold*, water down your dog's back and/or rub a bit on the tummy.
- Use baby sunscreen on noses, thin-skinned, and light-coated dogs, and upright ears—all those pink spots.
- Dogs should not wear gear, collars, or harnesses that are unsafe for group play.
- Young children should not be allowed to run or play in dog parks. Children playing with their own dog in a high-intensity environment may be at risk of injury. Other dogs may join in—aroused dogs are frequently unpredictable. Do not bring babies, strollers, prams, toddlers, or young grade school kids into a busy dog park. Nancy Kerns, Chief Editor of the *Whole Dog Journal*, tells us, "A small child who gets knocked down and starts to scream is like a magnet to some dogs. It gives me shivers" (Kerns, 2012).
- Children, the elderly, young puppies, senior dogs, and small dogs mixed in with a group of big rowdy dogs may be at risk of being hurt even quite accidentally. Supervise older children at all times.
- Train a reliable recall for better dog park off-leash reliability.

10

ENRICHMENT AND GRAZING GAMES™

Provide enrichment for your dog with ongoing training, chew-items, games, toys, and jobs for your dog to improve quality of life and enhance your relationship with your dog. Meet your dog's social enrichment needs with regular walks, outings, and activities. Learn dog body language to easily determine if your dog really wants to be touched or petted or meet someone new. If safe, consider dog sports, providing the opportunity for bonding, novelty, and to increase confidence. Try offering your dog more choices in terms of a variety of meals and treats, let them lead on a walk, provide alternative spots for sleeping, and let them choose whether they prefer to be inside or outside when possible and safe. (See Chapter 4, Novelty/Enrichment.)

Sniffing is the portal to scent identification. Chemical markers in scent identification are processed by the vomeronasal organ in your dog. A large part of the dog brain is devoted to processing olfactory information similar to our primary processing of visual information. Providing scent-filled activities, fondly called "sniffaris," and games, tracking and nose work, are enriching and a unique way of playing with a dog who may not be interested in other forms of play.

Sensory enrichment gardens have been used in animal shelters to de-stress and make dogs happier and healthier, while providing a space for exploration and exercise. Sensory gardens have become very popular when considering enrichment for all dogs (Shippen, 2016). A variety of scents your dog can self-select, such as ornamental grasses, different textures, a bed of hay, tiered levels, digging pits, a fountain or a kiddie pool, trails, hollow logs, and bird feeders can make a world of difference at home as well. Sensory gardens are also mentally stimulating building confidence in your dog.

"LIVING IN A HUMAN WORLD"

April Bove-Rothwell, former gorilla trainer and enrichment expert for the San Diego Zoo and Safari Park, and *Do No Harm* intern graduate, wrote this salient piece, adapted from her *BARKS from the Guild* trade magazine article (2016, July).

The overall goal of enrichment is to increase the behavioral repertoire of an animal. Enrichment goes far beyond just encouraging natural behaviors; it has the power to modify behavior when carefully planned and executed. Specific goals may include increasing natural behaviors like food foraging in order to increase activity. Observing and evaluating your dog's response to enrichment is crucial to assess if it is meeting the goals of a behavior modification program.

Environmental enrichment is an effective behavior modification tool that is often overlooked. Providing a stimulating environment enhances the physical and psychological well-being of an animal by allowing them to express the range of behaviors typical of their species. Environmental enrichment may significantly alleviate boredom or stress, as well as prevent or modify maladaptive behaviors caused by boredom, stress, or fear. It both passes time and expends energy.

Enrichment allows dogs to express natural behaviors appropriately with games and enrichment devices instead of the undesirable behaviors, such as incessant barking or chewing inappropriate items.

Environmental enrichment can be categorized by each of the five senses: sight, hearing, smell, taste, and touch. An enrichment program should aim to utilize all of the senses in various combinations.

Food is a very popular method of enrichment. Presenting food in a variety of feeders, locations and times throughout the day is very enriching. A dog's diet can be easily presented in a variety of ways (whole, chopped, frozen, blended), hidden in different locations, or scattered to promote foraging.

Tactile enrichment provides dogs with different surfaces or substrates with which to interact. Puzzle feeders are a tactile enrichment that increase foraging time and enhance problem-solving behaviors.

Changing the locations and times dogs spend in different areas of the home adds variety to a dog's day. Exploring areas where other dogs have been allows dogs to smell objects used by others. They may also benefit from increased visual access to other dogs but need to be able to retreat if desired.

Enrichment works because it influences behavior, even when we are not present. In-home environments may become predictable and boring, especially when there are behavior problems that make it difficult to bring the dog outside. A variety of enrichment items should be provided and can include interactive food-based toys like stuffed Kongs®, sand boxes with hidden toys for digging, games like hide and seek (with you or their toys), nose work with items like scented boxes, and tug toys to encourage play behavior.

Enrichment gives dogs choice and control, which tends to increase overall welfare and the likelihood of thriving. Enrichment, along with positive training, helps dogs cope with the unnatural human world we thrust upon them and increases their physical and mental well-being, so they can live happy lives. (Bove-Rothwell, July 2016, p. 54–56)

SCAVENGING CHANGES EMOTIONS AND BEHAVIOR

Using your dog's allotment of daily food calories helps your dog overcome emotional difficulties. Food enhances emotional associations and dispels fear. Food can effectively focus, redirect, distract, and calm a hyperactive, fearful, or noise-phobic dog, and safely treat all types of aggression. Dogs are born scavengers. By setting up grazing opportunities, your dog is given an enjoyable job keeping your dog out of trouble. Here are some of my favorite Grazing Games™ (Michaels, 2017a) that address underlying emotional drives and leads to a change in behavior.

- **Scatter breakfast and/or dinner.** There's no need to feed every meal from a bowl. Eating out of a bowl is something humans, not dogs, prefer to do. Scatter breakfast out on the patio, walkway, or pesticide and chemical-free lawn. Your dog will find every last piece of premium-quality kibble while you surf the web or drink your morning brew.
- **Use food to change emotions.** Desensitize and countercondition fear of the car, a location, noise, person, or of other dogs by scattering high value food, paired with a low-intensity version of the feared stimulus, if safe.

- **Environmental enhancement.** Grazing makes almost any environment more engaging and feel safer.
- **Separation anxiety/housetraining.** Pet parents often mistake separation anxiety fear for a housetraining problem. If you suspect your dog may be afraid to go outside without you, scatter kibble for grazing in the yard but avoid the dog's elimination area. Make certain there is no real threat to your dog's safety outdoors.
- **Greeting protocol—Redirecting doorbell barking.** Upon hearing the doorbell, redirect your dog from running to the front door and barking, to running to the back door and out into the yard where you routinely scatter treats all over the patio, walkways, or lawn at the sound of the doorbell. Practice using a recording of your doorbell or knock on the door. While your dog is busy, answer the door. Let your dog inside when calm.
- **Housetraining accidents.** Scatter high value dry food over thoroughly cleaned urination and defecation areas to speed housetraining. Dogs typically will not want to eliminate where they eat.
- **Marking.** Scatter treats over thoroughly cleaned previously marked areas to help eliminate marking. Dogs often do not like to eat where they have marked with urine. Scatter treats on and around any new or novel item, such as a new rug, brought into the home to pre-empt marking.
- **Playpen/Crate training.** Scatter food over the floor of the playpen, x-pen or crate to ensure that these containments are attractive to your dog and to help decrease fearfulness.

THE SENSORY GARDEN

A newly popular anti-stress, anti-anxiety enrichment activity for your dog involves dog-friendly landscaping and creating a sensory garden. A sensory garden allows your dog to use all of the senses—smelling, seeing, touching, hearing, and tasting within a safe environment created with your dog in mind. A sensory garden encourages exploration and exercise.

Here are some ideas that make a sensory garden fun and engaging for your dog.

- **Digging pits.** Create a digging pit using a contained area filled with sand. Bury a high value raw meaty bone, for example, for your dog to find.
- **Streams, fountains, kiddie pools.** Some pet parents create elaborate environments for their dogs by planning relandscaping designs with both the humans and the dogs in mind. However, just adding a plastic kiddie swimming pool can bring your dog a great deal of joy.
- **Trails.** Cut a running path around the perimeter of your secured property, run the trail with your dog and you may find your dog doing zoomies on the trail without you!
- **Tiered levels.** Use hay bales or hollow logs to allow your dog to get a better view of the lay of the land. Dogs love to perch on high.
- **Bird feeders.** If you have dogs who may be stressed by visiting birds, hang bird feeding stations up high so that your dog can watch, putting the safety of the birds first.
- **Sniffer patch.** And last but not least, fill the sensory garden with safe, dog-friendly plants your dog can enjoy such as bamboo, chamomile, rosemary, mint, barley grass, lavender, and dandelion. Be sure to check every currently extant and newly planted tree and plant for toxicity to dogs.

11

DOG BODY LANGUAGE—OBSERVE AND "LISTEN" FIRST

D o you ever get the feeling that your dog is talking to you? You are right. If you wonder what is going on in your dog's head, and long to communicate interactively, here is a surefire way of connecting. Reading body language sharpens your ability to understand what your dog is feeling and communicating. Learn to read what your dog is saying to you and learn to speak to your dog in a language your dog can understand. A wonderful and endearing characteristic of dogs is that dogs are truly honest and authentic about showing their feelings—they do not lie. Dogs wear their feelings on their sleeves!

How Dogs Communicate

Dogs communicate with us primarily through

- Actions
- Body language
- Vocalizations

Body language is the communicative bridge between you and your dog. Start by *listening* rather than doing. Listen first, *before doing* anything to understand your dog's state of mind, whether fearful or happy. Your dog's body language is broadcasting clear giveaways to their feelings. Hone your observational skills to decode your dog's messages. Do not ignore those messages. Respond with clear hand signals for effective communication. Dr. Lynn Honeckman, veterinary behavior expert explains, "We can learn to read the body language of dogs displaying happiness, curiosity, anxiety, fear and hostility. Even learning the basics of interpreting a dog displaying 'approachable' versus 'stay away' body language can be of the greatest benefit" (personal communication, 2015).

What to Look For

Behaviors, such as hiding, freezing, or trying to move away in the opposite direction lets you know something is seriously wrong and change is needed. Change the situation so your dog can relax and learn. Here's what to look for:

- **Tails.** A wagging tail does not necessarily indicate a dog is happy (Personne, 2015). A relaxed flag-waving tail often means "I love you" but a raised twitching tail or a tail held horizontal to the ground is most likely a warning and may be an aggressive display. Fearful dogs often display a low tail or tail tucked between the legs (Collins, 2007). The difficulty reading the "tail language" of a dog with a surgically cropped or stubby tail may put both you and other dogs trying to read the dog's body language at a serious disadvantage.
- **Ears.** Floppy ears generally indicate calm, while erect ears mean "I'm on alert". Your dog may be deciding how to react. Flattened ears are indications of fear telling you your dog is afraid.
- **Body posture.** Body posture is another emotion indicator. Forward leaning with a stiff body are warnings to stop whatever you are doing and to slowly back off. If your dog "freezes" over the food bowl, or fixates on another dog, a bite may follow.
- **Vocalizations.** Whining, growling, or barking indicates your dog is aroused and uncomfortable. Your dog is literally talking to you. Whines often mean,

"I'm scared, help me" or "I want something" whereas a growl is a warning. Barks have many different meanings, depending on the context.

- **Listening for doggy disorders.** Following you from room to room, attempts at escape to follow you, housetraining regression, or destructive behavior are some classic symptoms of separation/attachment problems. (See Chapter 22, Separation Anxiety.) Your dog is not a happy camper. Fears must be treated with very slow acclimation and exposure to the troubling stimulus. Use baby step desensitization for confidence building. Dogs with human aggression or serious dog/dog aggression problems need professional help. (See Chapter 17, Aggression.)
- **You "talking back" with rewards.** When your dog does something that you would like to see more of, such as sitting or making eye-contact on leash, *capture* it by immediately providing a treat. Rewarded behaviors are repeated. Reward what you like regularly and frequently to get more and more of what you want. Use *luring* with a treat to get a jump-start on a new behavior. You may opt to use a clicker for *marking* a behavior immediately before providing the reward.

Developing a good relationship with your dog is a two-way street. Stay positive. Do not correct—redirect. Punishment and old school dominance training methods produce anxiety in your dog and can cause aggression or make a troubling behavior even worse. Looking at the world from your dog's point of view will help you understand and respond appropriately so you can both be happy.

FLOODING AND TONIC IMMOBILITY

Behavioral body language is the single most unmistakable indicator of dog emotions. Flooding with a frightening stimulus leads to attempts at running away, hiding, or to a *shutdown*. These responses are your dog shouting, "PLEASE STOP, I'M SCARED." Victoria Stilwell, star of Animal Planet's *It's Me or the Dog*, explains what happens in situations where your dog is *flooded* with aversive stimulus and cannot escape. "In the majority of cases, flooding only makes a dog more anxious and forces the dog to adopt different coping mechanisms such as fighting or shutting down— where the dog becomes almost numb to the environment and behaves in a way that is truly out of character—an instinct that keeps him safe and ensures survival" (Stilwell, 2020. para. 4).

"Training collars" are designed for handler convenience or employing dominance tactics causing pain or choking the dog. These types of harmful tools are used as handler short-cuts or restraint. Anger, frustration, egotistical "showing off," or fearfulness on the part of the handler can result in harsh treatment where the dog experiences paralyzing fear. To the untrained eye, the dog may appear to be in a state of calm acceptance. In reality, misused equipment, intimidation, or restraint may cause a condition called *tonic immobility*, wherein fear is *mistaken and mislabeled* as "good behavior." Tonic immobility is a condition of unresponsiveness occurring during significant stress. Tonic immobility may occur at a training facility, lesson, or class, at home, or in any situation where a dog is frightened. Charging ahead to get a frightening task "over with" such as grooming or a veterinary visit can easily backfire, resulting in fear, aggression, anxiety, escape and avoidance behavior, or tonic immobility.

Tonic immobility can resemble shock and is characterized by a cessation of voluntary activity and may occur in any situation where your dog is seriously frightened. In the wild, tonic immobility occurs in response to an extreme threat such as being captured by a perceived predator. It sometimes resembles a posture suggestive of death but still maintaining an awareness of the environment (Fragkaki et al., 2016).

PART 3

GOOD MANNERS AND
BASIC TRAINING

FORCE-FREE TRAINING FUNDAMENTALS

This handbook guides you in teaching your dog the behaviors you prefer. These preferred behaviors will be the behaviors your dog will naturally repeat to get the things your dog wants. Look for opportunities to say, "Yes!" Pay close attention to behaviors and actively identify and reward the behaviors your dog already does that you find desirable.

- Consistently reinforced by you, these behaviors will be repeated and become routine automatic responses, and moreover, eventually becoming habits! Here are a couple of rules to help get you started.
- Consistently reward desirable behaviors to let your dog know, "That's great."
- Practice each manners/obedience behavior 3–4 times a day for 3–4 minutes each session.

Training is a Two-sided Coin

Side 1. Behaviors That Are Rewarded Increase in Frequency and Will be Repeated

Reward the behaviors you want repeated. When a dog repeats a behavior, your dog is telling you the behavior was successful in the past to get what was wanted. Determine the relative value of each reward to your dog so you can adjust the delivery of reinforcement more judiciously. The more challenging the behaviors, the higher the reward value required. Changing emotional responses are generally the most challenging of all. Dogs may respond to a variety of reinforcements such as

- Treats, i.e., healthy high value food
- Food, such as biologically species appropriate kibble
- Chew-items
- Real-life rewards, such as going outside to play
- Walks
- Tugging on toys
- Playing
- Attention
- Affection
- Lying on the couch
- Belly rubs
- Massage

Side 2. Behaviors That Are Not Rewarded Decrease in Frequency and May Disappear

- Do not inadvertently, that is, accidentally or unconsciously reward the behaviors you do not want.
- Use these non-aversive techniques for undesirable behavior:
  1. Prevent or manage undesirable or dangerous behavior
  2. Ignore undesirable behavior
  3. Teach an alternate behavior to the undesirable behavior.

If Your Dog Has Difficulty Learning a Behavior, Most Likely

- Your technique needs improvement. Your dog does not understand what you want and is unable to read your signals.
- You are going too fast. Effective, dog-friendly training requires taking *baby steps*. One of the most common setbacks in training occurs because a pet parent is pushing ahead before their dog is ready to move forward.
- Your treats are not of high value to your dog. Increase the appetitive value of the food reward.

Raising a new puppy can be a lot of work and you may be lacking sleep. If you find yourself getting frustrated with your new puppy, take a break but do not take it out on your puppy. Simply walk away for a few minutes and take a few deep breaths or take your puppy on a walk for some fresh air. You should both be having a good time!

Note: So that we may become a more dog-friendly culture, force-free training has modified some of the traditional training language in an effort to change the way a pet parent thinks and feels about their relationship with their dog. Language is important because it affects the way we think and feel. Teaching good manners is now replacing the rather old-fashioned idea of teaching obedience for pet dogs. The use the of the word "command" is no longer used because to give a command suggests that you are giving a military-style order to your dog. In force-free training, the word *cue* (as in verbal cue), *signal* (as in hand signal), or *ask* is used when describing your request of your dog.

12

HOUSETRAINING

If you are reading this before you get your puppy—good for you! If possible, have everything prepared before your puppy comes home. Strive to set up your puppy for success at home from day one. Start off on the right paw and get a copy of the puppy primer by Dr. Ian Dunbar, *Before and After You Get Your Puppy* (2004). If you have added a new puppy or new adult dog to your household who was never reliably housetrained or who has regressed back to making mistakes, it is time to institute or revisit housetraining protocols.

Using a Plan Your Dog Can Easily Understand

Use a housetraining plan your dog understands. From day one, the key words are *containment,* both short-term and long-term, and *reward opportunities.* Confinement in a carefully conditioned crate for night-time and in a small area during the day with an indoor sod tray or puppy pad is recommended until your pup earns more space in your home (See Chapter 22, Doggy Enrichment Land.) Frequent opportunities for elimination with food rewards will have your dog looking forward to getting on the leash to go to the chosen spot in your yard, eliminating for a yummy treat. The number one rule and the basis of force-free training is rewarding for the desired behavior rather than punishing for an undesired behavior. Plan to speed housetraining by devoting at least a long weekend to housetraining protocols. Being consistent about housetraining makes it easy for your puppy or new dog to understand the routine.

Make certain your puppy or dog has a veterinary wellness check if there is a sudden regression of house soiling or if you have continuing difficulty housetraining after following the protocols below. Rule out possible medical conditions, such as kidney disease or a urinary tract infection, which may be interfering with housetraining.

The Top 10 Do's and Don'ts for Successful Housetraining (Michaels, 2017b)

Here's how to set up your puppy or new rescue for success:

1. **Do carefully condition your puppy or dog to use a metal crate or to a cloth crate on your bed** with enough room to stretch out comfortably. When your puppy cries at night, get up and take your puppy to the elimination spot—either a sod tray or puppy pad near the door, or outside. **Do not allow your puppy to eliminate in the crate.**

2. **Do limit your dog's access to the house during the day** unless your dog has recently eliminated. Contain your dog using a playpen with a sod tray or puppy pad when you are housetraining and when you are away from home. You may have a container of sod delivered weekly to your home, or "do it yourself" purchasing sod from a nursery and using a low-lipped kitty litter tray. An extra bedroom or the kitchen with a baby gate will also do nicely. This containment should feel like a Doggy Enrichment Land where your dog has everything needed for sustenance, elimination, and contentment.

   Puppy pads are useful mainly for urination training, although some small dogs who live in condominiums also learn to defecate on puppy pads. Dogs naturally prefer a soil substrate for elimination. If your dog has been trained to eliminate on any other substrate, such as cement or puppy pads, retraining to eliminate on soil may be needed. Over time, as your puppy becomes housetrained, enlarge your dog's space. If your dog has an accident, decrease space, but please be kind and expect occasional errors at the start. If your dog pees in his bed area, elevate the bed in the x-pen. Dogs do not like to eliminate where they sleep! **Do not allow your dog to roam around your home** until your dog earns more space in the home—one room at a time.

3. **Do give your puppy a high value treat**, then praise exuberantly each time your dog completes elimination in a proper location. Dr. Dunbar recommends giving three treats when elimination is complete. Use very high value treats for these successful events to make a powerful positive association in your dog's memory and on learning. This is so worth celebrating! **Do not ignore the successes.**

4. **Do remember your puppy is a puppy and will not have full bladder control** until 16–20 weeks of age. **Do forgive mistakes. Do not be impatient.**

5. **Do provide many elimination opportunities**, at least once per hour for puppies, once every 2–3 hours for adult dogs, and also

   - Immediately upon rising in the morning
   - Thirty minutes after your dog eats or drinks
   - As soon as you walk into your home from work or other absences. Walk directly outdoors with your dog on-leash for a potty break *before* greeting your dog
   - After playing with your dog
   - After otherwise exercising with your dog
   - Before bed
   - Whenever you think your dog looks worried, is casting about, goes to hide or you think your dog might be getting ready to eliminate.

Do not think that because your puppy can "hold it" through the night that your puppy can "hold it" during the day. That is an unrealistic expectation on your part and not true for your dog any more than it's true for you.

6. **Do use a non-startling, non-punishing interrupt sound,** such as calling your puppy's name if your puppy makes a mistake while you are watching. Completely ignore the mistake itself but turn the mistake into a correct response by bringing the puppy or rescue dog to the desired elimination area. Then as soon as your dog completes elimination in the proper area, provide a reward. If your puppy makes a mistake while you are not watching, just clean it up and do not allow your puppy out of your sight or without an available "toilet" again! **Do not yell or stick your dog's nose into an elimination error.** Reprimanding or sticking your dog's nose in urination or defecation does *not* teach your dog where to eliminate and may encourage coprophagia—stool eating (Horowitz, 2021). If you punish and frighten, your dog learns not to eliminate while you are watching and may hide somewhere to eliminate, such as behind the couch to escape your facial scowl and reprimands.

7. **Do take your dog out on a leash.** Allow your dog to choose a favorite elimination spot. Use the location each time. Allow no more than the length of a 6-foot leash for your puppy or grown dog to decide on an elimination spot while you stand stationary. You may pace just a few short feet in one direction and then the other.

   Allow just 5 minutes of elimination opportunity. If your puppy or new dog does not eliminate, go back inside and confine your dog since your puppy's opportunity window is over for right now. After 1 hour, try again for another 5 minutes.

   While your puppy is eliminating and relaxing the elimination muscles, let your dog know that he or she is on the right track by speaking a verbal cue in a very calm voice. I use, "Go Potty, Go Potty," paired with elimination. Reward profusely! "Go Potty" can later become the *trigger* for elimination.

   If your dog will not eliminate in your yard for some reason, try having another dog eliminate in your yard so your dog is likely to *mark* it with urine. Get a puppy pad scented with a scent trigger bull's-eye and place it where you would like the elimination spot established. **Do not let your dog outdoors to eliminate alone.** Your dog may become easily distracted and find something fun to do outside, then come back and eliminate in the house. This won't be your dog's fault but says more about a faulty technique. By letting your dog outdoors alone during training you lose a valuable opportunity for rewarding and reinforcing good housetraining habits.

8. **Do feed on a routine schedule** to track your dog's elimination needs. You may also remove uneaten food after approximately 30 minutes. Take note of your dog's eating and elimination schedule. **Do not allow your puppy to feed**

freely all day from the food bowl while housetraining. **Note:** Puppies should be fed three times per day and should have water available to them at all times.

9. **Do clean up soiled areas thoroughly.** Use a urine blacklight identifying every area in your home where your pet or another pet eliminated. If you do not remove your dog's scent completely from a floor or carpet your puppy will consider that area a toilet. However, if a mistake does occur, you must clean up thoroughly. Your dog can smell his scent long after you can!

- **Hard surfaces.** Use an enzymatic, live bacteria cleaner or diluted bleach, if safe, for urine removal. Test for possible floor damage first. Then, allow self-drying time and rinse with water thoroughly. Scent and stain removers alone will typically not remove residual urine molecules that your dog detects.

- **Carpet, rugs, and upholstery.** Removing scent from carpeting is notoriously difficult. Urine leaks through carpeting onto the carpet pad and into the wood flooring underneath if the floor is not vinyl sealed. If this happens in your home, housetraining may be significantly slowed or seemingly unachievable . . . but it is *not* your dog's fault. Injecting a live enzyme pet odor remover with a syringe or replacing the item is recommended.

  Do not use household cleaners. They often contain ammonia and may make things worse by triggering your dog to eliminate in your home.

  Do not let your pup watch you cleaning up a mistake. Your dog may associate the waving of paper towels with playing.

10. **After the cleaning solution dries and has been rinsed thoroughly, place high value scattered food or your dog's food bowl on a previously soiled area.** Turn what was a rest/toilet area into a dinner table. Dogs do not normally want or choose to eliminate where they eat!

Frequent Mistakes?

If your puppy is making frequent "mistakes" after three weeks of training and she is at least 12–20 weeks old—remember, it is not the puppy's fault. Somehow, you are not communicating effectively in a language your dog can easily and clearly understand. Chances are

- Your technique is not quite right, or
- Your family members are not being consistent with the plan, or
- Your dog is sick and needs to see a veterinarian

Supervise your partially house-trained puppy at all times. Your dog's location options are:

- In the Doggy Enrichment Land or similar set-up with an appropriate elimination spot available
- Supervised indoor play directly after elimination
- Outside with you
- On a leash and harness with you
- In a crate for night time training, after a decompression, bonding adjustment period

Every time you miss a sniffing or circling signal telling you elimination is about to occur, you increase the amount of time needed to housetrain.

If safe, installing a doggy door leading out to a secure area where you can supervise your dog is the most practical and kindest way of ensuring reliable housetraining. Your dog will thank you.

Above all, be patient with your puppy or dog. Your dog has much to learn about the new rules of living in a house but will learn quickly if you use the most effective techniques and if you are consistent, speaking to your dog in a language your dog can easily understand.

Urine Marking Management Tips

- Remove low-lying vertical objects.
- Identify marked items and clean marked areas thoroughly with a live enzymatic cleaner.
- Then, make the marked areas "feeding station/dinner tables" by scattering food on the ground.
- Supervise when your dog is in previously marked areas so that you may intervene if necessary.

13

NO BITE! AND CHEWING

PUPPY AND ADULT DOG MOUTHING—TEACHING "KISS-KISS"

The following techniques are effective not only for puppy biting but for mouthy adolescent and adult dogs, including wolfdogs, not openly displaying aggression. Teach your puppy or a mouthy adult dog that when teeth touch human skin, everything fun stops for an instant. The fun begins again when you dog is calm and/or practicing a behavior that is incompatible with puppy biting.

157

Decreasing Arousal

- Decrease the intensity of your play. For example, if your dog is on your lap, calmly place your dog on the floor at once. Teach the association between the "bitey" behavior and ending up on the floor!
- Decrease the duration of your play. Puppies and dogs get tired and get sloppy when arousal ramps up: there is a bridge between increased arousal and biting. *You* take a time-out for 3 minutes or until your dog calms down. This is not as punishment but a cooling-out break to decrease arousal. Begin calm play again as if nothing happened or give your puppy a nap break.
- Redirect the biting behavior using chew toys. Positively reinforce your dog for chewing on appropriate items.
- Do not "yelp" at your dog. This is popular, but bad advice. Yelping like a puppy increases rather than decreases arousal and can frighten your dog. Your dog knows that you are not a dog!

"Kiss-Kiss"

Redirect puppy biting and adult dog mouthiness by teaching an alternative behavior that is *incompatible with biting,* such as licking your hand. Your puppy cannot do two things at the same time. "Kiss-Kiss" gives your puppy or mouthy dog the opportunity to use the mouth and interact with you but in a manner that is appropriate from your point of view.

- Place a high value treat in your fisted hand
- Offer your hand. When your dog licks your fist, open your fist instantly so your dog can eat the treat/reward from the palm of your hand
- Once well-learned, get additional licks before you release the treat
- Say the words "Kiss-Kiss" *as* your dog licks your fist
- Cue the newly learned alternate behavior of licking if and when your dog becomes mouthy

Fun Stops **Method**

- "Mark" any teeth-touching to human skin with a sound, such as "Aw," voiced in a disappointed, not an angry tone of voice. An angry "No" excites your dog even further or frightens your dog. The goal is to lower arousal. There is never a need to use fear to get the compliance you desire if you are practicing good technique.
- At the same time, remove all attention and reinforcement. Retract hands, turn both body and face away, and lean away, removing eye contact. Everything fun stops when teeth touch skin.
- Freeze for 3 seconds before calmly interacting with your dog again.
- Be certain the sound you make ("Aw"), is paired with the removal of attention. This will curtail the "bitey" behavior.

Use the technique below for puppies or dogs that continue mouthiness during everyday play:

1. Tether your dog to a doorknob. Kneel just near enough to your dog so that you can reach your puppy's head, but your puppy cannot reach you.
2. Follow the steps in the *fun stops* method above, but get up, turn around and walk a few steps away the instant your dog's teeth touch your skin.

Use a bitter spray on clothes if absolutely necessary after testing on the fabric. Do not apply to hands. You must maintain a consistently positive associations with people's hands. Hands are good—they deliver treats. Your hands reach out to your dog and should always be associated with welcoming.

CHEW THIS, NOT THAT!

Most dogs and certainly all puppies crave chewing. Chewing is a natural canine behavior with many benefits for your dog and you. Quality chew items such as interactive food toys, bully sticks, or durable bones provide appropriate activity and decrease stress. Chew toys ought to be either 100% indestructible or 100% digestible.

Dogs need "occupational therapy," says Dr. Ian Dunbar, DVM, animal behaviorist and puppy guru. If you do not give your dog something to do, your dog will find something to do and that something may be something you may not like.

Although dogs are genetically hard-wired to chew, some dogs like chewing more than others. Encourage your puppy or dog to be a happy, busy, life-long chewer who enjoys chewing appropriate items rather than chewing on your valuables. Habits develop early and quickly, so start training your dog on the first day home regardless of your dog's age.

The Joy of Chewing

Chewing is a species-specific, stress-relieving natural canine activity and often soothes teething pain. Favorite chew toys often act as pacifiers. Chewing is also a great outlet for pent-up energy. Chewing on a great bone can exhaust your dog because it's such great exercise for the mouth, jaws, and forelimbs as well. Chewing stimulates healthy blood flow to the gums too and can help clean teeth. Lucky for you, chewing also helps distract and redirect your dog away from engaging in unwanted activities.

Chew Toy Management and Training Tips

- Puppy-proof your home and keep wires and cords out of reach or covered, or better yet, go wireless.
- Remove access to valuable items.

- Design a dog zone sanctuary, that is, a Doggy Enrichment Land using a playpen, exercise pen, or baby-gated area for your dog so you can run errands and sleep.
- Provide a doggy toy box and rotate three or four different favorite chew items every other day.
- If your supervised dog gets off track, redirect to a toy/chew box. Reinforce your dog with praise for playing with those chew toys.
- Use a bitter non-toxic taste aversive gel for items that cannot be protected from chewing, such as staircase bannisters.

What to Chew

Provide interactive chew toys stuffed with high value foods. Try kibble soaked in beef broth. You may want to feed one half of your dog's daily calories in chew toys or interactive food toys until your dog is chew toy trained. Long-lasting chewables include bully sticks and recreational bones that are not consumed, such as marrow bones, and knuckle bones. Go "wild" with caviar buffalo jerky, duck, and air-dried pork strips. Choose Made in the USA labels for high quality control standards. Interactive food toys, snuffle mats, and licking mats are some of the latest new favorite grazing items on the market. (See Chapter 10, Enrichment and Grazing Games.)

14

TRAINING TECHNIQUES

When your dog does not know what to do, your dog will likely choose the behaviors that you have rewarded in the past (Miller, 2004). Reinforcing desirable behaviors helps dogs develop habits that will create a better fit with our human lifestyle. Desirable behaviors frequently repeated become habits. Dogs love training the *Do No Harm Dog Training* way.

IMPORTANT CONCEPTS IN TRAINING

Laying the foundation by understanding and applying the basic principles below are essential to successful force-free training. Creating controlled environments, using food, and working in small increments leads to favorable outcomes.

- **Distraction.** Begin training in a location with few distractions, making training easy for your dog. A calm, quiet home environment enhances your dog's ability to focus on you and on the lesson. Home is typically the best place to begin for the fastest results.

- **Use food.** Begin training sessions when your dog is a little bit hungry. Use small bits of high value food rewards. (See Chapter 7, Using Food as a Reward.)

- **The *Three D's*—Raising criteria.** Slowly and incrementally continue increasing the level of difficulty of a skill or emotional response as long as your dog is clearly progressing. When your dog is responding reliably, increase the difficulty of *Duration*, *Distance*, and *Distraction* in small steps.

- **Baby steps.** Divide the behavior into small increments so that you and your dog achieve success at whatever speed or level of difficulty that works for your dog. If your dog is having trouble learning a skill, shape the behavior by finding creative ways to break the desired behavior into smaller and smaller steps.

- **Verbal cues.** After a behavior is well learned and reliable with a hand signal, you may add verbal cues *before* the hand signal. Teach your dog a verbal cue, such as "Sit" or "Down," by saying the word first, followed immediately by the hand signal. Dogs want to find the shortest distance between A (your signal) and B (getting the treat). Your dog will quickly figure out that whenever the word "Sit" is spoken, it is always followed by the respective hand signal, therein, your dog learns to sit to the sound of the word "Sit" alone. Remember, dogs can separate meaning and intonation. Both the word meaning that is already recognized, and the intonation are strongly associated with the auditory reward center, so ask politely.

- **Help your dog be successful.** If your dog seems confused, go back to what your dog already does well. Slowly progress to a higher level of difficulty when your dog is ready.

- **Make training fun.** If you become frustrated, end the training session with something your dog does well. Do not train with your dog if you are upset. Training should be fun for both you and your dog!

- **Trick training.** You may want to continue adding new behaviors to your dog's repertoire. Many dogs love performing tricks and teaching your dog a new trick is a great way for the two of you to bond and have fun. Your dog will be both physically and mentally challenged each time your dog learns something new. Perhaps you like the way she cocks her head or the way she wiggles. Capture spontaneous behavior with a high value treat or a click/treat. Teach *Ring Around the Rosie* (weaving through your legs) or "Sit Pretty." Tricks are a great way to hone your training skills as well! (Ray & Harding, 2005).

Below find some popular *Do No Harm* training methods: *capturing, luring, shaping* and using the Premack Principle. More than likely, you are already using the Premack Principle training technique, such as asking your dog to "Sit" before you open the front door. The amount of time and energy you spend training and the number of *trials to criterion*—how many repetitions are required to reach reliability, will depend in part on the techniques you use. You may find a fair and unbiased, well-referenced analysis that examines the benefits and drawbacks to both lure and free-shaped training in, "Are 'Free-Shaped' Dogs Better Problem Solvers?" (LeBlanc, 2015).

Capturing Behavior

Capturing a behavior occurs when you recognize and *mark* a desirable, spontaneously performed behavior with a high value treat: that is, a behavior your dog already naturally performs without any input from you. A mark is a sound, such as a clicker, or the word "Good" indicating the behavior will be reinforced by you. Capturing behavior may be used to train all basic manners skills and quirky behaviors that may otherwise be difficult to train, such as a tilt of the head. This sequence may be used for almost any behavior you like.

For example, if you would like your feisty dog to lie down more often:

- When you notice your dog lies down for any reason, click/treat, or say "Good" and treat immediately.
- You may label the behavior by saying the word, "Down" as your dog begins to lie down.

If you want to capture "Down" more quickly, limit the space your dog has to find alternate behavior options. For example, take your dog into a small room, such as a bathroom with a rug. Distract yourself—hop online or read a book and just wait until your dog lies down. When your dog begins to lie down, say "Down." When your dog completes the *down* with belly on the floor, immediately toss a reward just far enough away so your dog must stand up to fetch it. Your dog will get faster and faster at offering a "Down" once your dog realizes how to play the training game with you. However, capturing may be time-consuming for some behaviors because you need to wait until your dog performs the behavior you like without receiving much direction from you.

LURING BEHAVIOR WITH FOOD

Lure/reward training is one the fastest and least complicated training techniques to teach basic manners skills and behavior modification. According to puppy guru and pioneer in positive reinforcement dog training, Dr. Ian Dunbar, DVM, PhD:

> For behavior modification and temperament training, food/lure reward training should be mandatory. There is extreme urgency to prevent and resolve behavior problems. Simple behavior problems such as housesoiling, destructive chewing, and excessive barking, kill dogs. Similarly, biting, fighting, and fearful dogs are hardly happy, or safe to be around, and so there is simply no time to mess around with time-consuming techniques. We must resolve the dogs' problems, relieve their chronic, yet acute, stress levels, and improve their quality of life using the most time-efficient methods available. (Dunbar, 2007, para. 1)

Typically, the best choice for both the lure and the reward is food. Interactive toys, such as a tug toy may be used as a possible alternate lure/reward for dogs who are more responsive to them, as seen in herding or working breeds. A complete sequence is

- Lure with a treat and a hand-luring movement—the hand signal
- Reward with the lure
- Once learned, a verbal cue/request may precede the hand signal as your dog begins to anticipate the hand signal after the verbal cue is heard repeatedly. This is how dogs learn words!

After 6 repetitions or so, if your technique is polished, the food lure is no longer necessary, and the dog will respond to the hand-luring movement (hand signal). Food lures should not be used for more than half a dozen trials; however, if your dog is having trouble learning a skill or performing it reliably, an alternating lure/no lure sequence may be used to get behavior back on track.

SHAPING BEHAVIOR

Shaping is a powerful and practical training tool. Shaping is a process of teaching a new behavior by first reinforcing behaviors resembling the desired behavior, systematically moving toward the goal behavior one small step at a time. Shaping teaches new forms of behaviors building upon older forms of behavior. A dog is rewarded for *successive approximations* of the end-goal behavior and sometimes given a jackpot of rewards when the end-goal behavior is achieved. A sample using shaping to train is provided in the chapter that teaches "Down." (See Chapter 16, Basic Skills.)

The Steps in Shaping

Here are the steps to shape a behavior:

1. Identify the end-goal desired behavior you would like to teach.
2. Identify a response that can easily be used to begin the shaping sequence.
3. Reward the response.
4. Incrementally require closer approximations to the end-goal behavior, reinforcing each step until the goal is reached.
5. Establish each step firmly with repetitions before moving on to the next approximation.
6. If your dog "gets lost," immediately go back to the easier, previous well-known step.

For example, if you want to teach your dog to lie down on a new rug, use the steps in shaping by rewarding your dog for walking in the direction of the rug, stepping one foot on the rug, then four feet on the rug, sitting on the rug, and then lying down on the new rug.

THE PREMACK PRINCIPLE

Understanding how to use the Premack Principle in force-free training can help boost your success rate with some of the most difficult problems you may face with your dog. The most common everyday example of the Premack Principle is, "If you eat your vegetables, then you may have dessert."

Professor David Premack's first publication (1959) was a new theory of reinforcement. It argued that the *more probable* response in any pair of responses could reinforce the *less probable* response. Most likely, you are already using the Premack Principle if you ask your dog to sit for a treat. A hungry dog has a higher probability (HP) of eating a treat, and a lower probability (LP) of sitting: the opportunity to eat is dependent upon sitting, resulting in the reinforcement of the lower probability behavior by the higher probability behavior.

Anything your dog really, really wants, may be used as the higher probability behavior, and serve as the reward, such as when your dog tells you in no uncertain terms

- "I too like cheese"
- "Please open the door already"
- "I want to go for a ride"
- "Play fetch with me"
- "Let's lie on the couch"
- "I need to sniff the hydrant"
- "I was born to chase squirrels!"

These requests help you identify the types of reward/reinforcement that your dog truly values.

The Premack Principle is commonly used when your dog wants real-life reinforcement. First ask for what *you* want, and then give your dog what your dog wants as a reward. Ask for the low probability (LP) behavior first (what you want) and then provide the high probability (HP) behavior (what your dog wants), which serves as the reward. One behavior reinforces another behavior. Here are some terrific examples provided by members of the *Do No Harm Dog Training* group.

How to Use the Premack Principle

- If your dog **sits** when asked (LP), then your dog gets a treat (HP).
- If your dog **sits and waits** at the open door (LP), then your dog gets released to run outside in the backyard as the reward (HP).
- If your dog keeps a **loose leash** (LP), then your dog gets to sniff something as the reward (HP).
- If your dog **comes** when called (LP), then your dog gets released back to whatever your dog was doing as the reward (HP).

- If your dog cooperates with **nail trims** (LP), then you deliver high value treats intermittently as the reward (HP).
- If your dog **drops** the tug toy or ball when asked to, "Drop" (LP), then your dog gets to play tug or fetch with you again as the reward (HP).
- If your dog **looks at you** when your dog sees a reactive trigger (LP), then you provide more distance or a high value treat as the reward (HP).
- If your dog **ignores the triggers** (LP), then your dog gets "throw downs" of treats to graze as the reward (HP).
- If your dog **eats the treats instead of chasing birds** (LP), then your dog gets to calmly watch birds as a reward (HP).
- If your dog **settles** on the indoor mat when you bring the mat outdoors (LP), then, your dog gets to "Go Play" outdoors as the reward (HP).

(See Chapter 5, Premack Principle.)

15

TRAINER "SECRETS"

The end goal of basic manners training is to experience ease and harmony in everyday life with your dog. One possible concern about training with treats is that you may believe your dog will continue requiring treats for learning and performing each behavior. However, this should not be a problem. Smart, competent trainers are experts in preventing treat dependence. Although we train new behaviors on a *continuous schedule of reinforcement*—one trick, one treat, the schedule changes once a behavior is learned. For some behaviors providing food on a steady or intermittent basis, such as for a reliable recall (Come), is the best practice in maintaining happy voluntary compliance. Food is like money to your dog, and who works for free? Nobody. Operant behaviors are all tricks as far as your dog is concerned. However, some dogs, especially the working and sporting breeds frequently prefer a tug toy to a piece of food.

Use real-life reinforcement, learn how to remove the lure, and discover how linking behaviors can enhance progress, gradually replacing some food rewards with other types of rewards. Begin giving random rewards of affection or praise for a job well done as part of your dog's daily routines. Use these trainer secrets:

REAL-LIFE REWARD REINFORCEMENT

Your dog wants to experience the joys of life just as we humans do. Identify and make use of one of the most powerful rewards: real-life reinforcement. Many dogs prefer play, such as a quick game of tug, over food. Here are some real-life reinforcement ideas to practice with your dog:

- **Fetching.** "Sit/Wait" . . . Throw the ball. The real-life reward is chasing the ball again after waiting.

169

- **Eating.** "Sit/Wait . . . Okay" before meals. The real-life reward is eating breakfast and dinner.
- **Going for a walk.** "Stand/Wait . . . Okay" while putting on your dog's harness and attaching the leash. The real-life reward is going for a walk.
- **Going outdoors.** "Sit/Wait . . . Okay" at each doorway. The real-life reward is going out the door.
- **Going for a ride in the car.** "Sit/Wait . . . Okay" before your dog gets into the car. The real-life reward is going for a ride.
- **Getting out of the car.** "Wait . . . Okay" before your dog gets out of the car. The real-life reward is getting out of the car and going somewhere with you.
- **Crossing the street.** "Sit . . . Okay" at the curb on a walk. The real-life reward is crossing the street and continuing the walk.
- **Running and playing.** "Come" and/or Name Response. The real-life reward can be a tug on a favorite toy or "Okay, Go Play" in the yard.

What My Dog Really Likes That I Can Use as a Real-life Reward Instead of Food

Make a list of the items and activities your dog finds rewarding. You can easily modify behavior because you already possess access to the resources your dog wants, including the following real-life rewards you have identified.

1.
2.
3.
4.
5.
6.

REMOVING THE LURE

This is the step where many pet parents make mistakes and falter, and then say that their dog will only perform for treats when food is used as a lure in training. Once the new behavior is learned, stop using the treat as a lure. Instead, use the next treat for a reward. Here's how: as soon as your dog can perform a behavior by following the treat with the nose (luring), remove the treat from that hand for the next trial. Now, ask for the behavior using the same lure hand-movement you were using. Then after you get the behavior, give the treat from the other hand. You have just taught a hand signal while removing the food lure.

LINKING BEHAVIORS

Link two or more well-learned behaviors together in a sequence, then reward. Agility competitions link a series of behaviors together and often provide a tug on a favorite toy at the end of the course as the reward. First, link two behaviors, then three, and then four.

Here are some examples of linking:

- **Playing fetch.** "Get It" . . . "Come " . . . "Drop It". . ."Sit." Offer a treat or real-life reward such as quickly throwing the ball again.
- **Eating.** "Sit . . . "Down" . . . "Wait" . . . "Okay." Offer the real-life reward of breakfast.

ALTERNATE REWARD REINFORCEMENT

Replace some of the treats by gradually substituting with other rewards such as affection, massage, a toy, or an exuberant "good" for desirable behavior, if your dog responds strongly to praise and enthusiasm. Continue rewarding with food selectively throughout your dog's life.

RANDOM REWARD REINFORCEMENT

When your dog is learning a new behavior, reward (reinforce) every time the desired response is given. Continue treating after each correct response until your dog performs the behavior consistently when asked. A well-learned behavior will become a reliable response. Reliability in dog training generally means achieving an average success rate of eight out of ten times while keeping in mind that dogs are not robots. As soon as the behavior is well learned, begin treating randomly as *random reinforcement* is the most powerful type of reinforcement schedule. Your dog will continue offering the learned behaviors as long as you continue providing sufficient intermittent rewards. Here is an example of a sequence of phasing in random rewards:

- Sit—Treat
- Sit—Treat
- Sit—Praise
- Sit—Treat
- Sit—Scratch on the chest

Build on this schedule until your dog gets a food reward one out of five times on average. Increase the difficulty of the task as long as your dog is happy and continues performing for you. Always substitute real-life reinforcement if there are no treats available.

Note: Continue rewarding your recall/ "Come" cue as often as possible throughout your dog's life, particularly when your dog is not near you and distracted. Maintaining a reliable recall under challenging conditions may be the most difficult behavior for your dog to perform reliably.

CLICKER TRAINING OPTION

Clickers are most commonly used to teach new, complex, novel, and/or shaped behaviors. Not all trainers, clients, or pet parents want to use a clicker, but it can be a very useful tool when used in moderation.

The clicker serves as a *bridge*, that is, a *secondary reinforcement* between your dog's behavior and the reward. The sound of the clicker is an audible marker indicating a reward has been earned. You click at the same instant the desired behavior is performed. The click means, "That is right, a treat is coming!"

Learn the Clicker Rules

- **Think of *click/treat* as one word.** That is, if you click, you must give a reward. A click is your promise to your dog that a reward is coming. If you make occasional clicking errors, do not worry, it will not adversely affect training as long as you treat after each click.
- **One click = one reward.** However, provide multiple treats (a *throw down*) for completion of a shaped behavior, or after your dog learns a more difficult behavior.
- **Do not allow anyone else to use your clicker** unless they understand and follow the clicker rules.

Learn the Sequence of Events

Understanding the *sequence of events* in clicker training is necessary to the process. You must take the steps below in the following order:

1. **Get the behavior you want.** Use luring, capturing, or shaping when approximating toward the goal of the desired behavior.
2. **Click.** Mark the correctly completed or the shaped approximation behavior instantly with a click followed by a treat. You may substitute a word, such as "Good" or a click of your tongue as a marker if you do not want to use a clicker, or if your dog is afraid of the clicker sound.
3. **Reward.** Reinforce your dog immediately with a small, high value treat.

Tips

Now that you know the rules and the sequence of events, here are some salient tips to help make clicker training work efficiently for you and your dog:

- **Use a soft clicker.** If your dog is sensitive, be careful not to frighten your dog with the sound of the clicker. A soft-sounding clicker is always preferred. Dogs have very sensitive ears.
- **Do not point.** Do not point the clicker at your dog like a remote control. Instead, hold the clicker by your side, in a pocket, or even behind your back.
- **Accurate clicker timing.** Clicking on time (not too late) is important for communicating the precise instant of a desired behavior and indicating a reward is coming. A click marks the exact behavior that will be rewarded. A click is like a snapshot communicating to your pet what they need to do with their body and muscles to get the treat/reward.

- **Treat timing.** Timing the delivery of the treat/reward/reinforcement is not as important as your clicker timing. A couple seconds of delay should not decrease the power of the *click/treat association.*
- **Rate of reinforcement.** Teach a *maintain* behavior, such as increasing the duration for Sit, by increasing the number of treats and the speed that you deliver them as long as your dog continues to Sit. Click/treat to end the maintained behavior.

16

BASIC SKILLS

GREETINGS AND JUMPING

Greeting You and Visitors

Greetings may well determine the course of the relationships between you, your dog, and your guests. Protect all of those involved in greeting by ensuring all greetings go well. Your dog may be quite aroused and uncomfortable and does not know how to behave when you permit a "rush to the door." Do not ask your dog to decide which of your friends feel safe. That decision is your responsibility. Dogs are not famous for making reliably good decisions. Your dog will thank you for not having the weighty responsibility of guarding the doorway.

Greeting You and Other Family Members. Delay Greetings to Calm

Delay your own greeting until your dog is calm so your greeting does not escalate the adrenaline spike your dog experiences the minute you arrive home. Walk into your home and go about your routine calmly. Greet your dog with calming affection rather than exuberant excitement. Smile and say, "Hello." Calmly let your dog go outdoors to eliminate. Later, play! Many dogs stop jumping and display decreased symptoms of separation issues when this technique alone is consistently employed, but it can be the hardest behavior for pet parents to change!

Greeting Guests. Contain to Calm

Start by managing your dog's environment to get things under control. If your dog jumps on guests, growls, or shows any stress or aggression, confine your dog as a safety measure for your guests. Do not give your dog the opportunity to jump on or bark at your incoming guests. Give your dog time and space to calm down in a safe place and to accept the arrival of guests in the home before attempting to let your dog greet your guests. Confine your dog to an exercise pen (x-pen), the yard behind a sliding glass door, a guest room, or your kitchen with a retractable gate until your dog is able to greet visitors calmly. Then, bring your dog out on a leash and allow calm greetings to unfold naturally. Have guests toss high value treats to your dog, if safe, to speed and ease the process of acclimation and create a bond between your dog and strangers entering your home. Do not be concerned that this newly learned behavior will stop your dog from guarding your home from intruders. It won't. Guarding is a genetically driven canid territorial predisposition.

No Jump

First, review the techniques above to calm your dog. Squirting water guns, shaking cans of marbles near your dog's sensitive ears, and reprimands do not produce lasting results. Stepping on toes, kneeing the chest, electric shock, or yanking a chain are simply not acceptable options. These outdated methods can backfire, causing aggression and may well alter the joyful relationship pet parents want with their dog.

What is a pet parent to do? Whether your dog has been jumping up on you for years, or you have a new puppy in training, try the dog-friendly techniques below to help your dog learn how to get what is wanted using behavior you find desirable. Give your dog something to do, that is, teach a substitute behavior to replace jumping known as **redirecting** unwanted behavior. Learn new ways to give your dog what your dog wants when you get what you want. Preempt jumping by teaching your dog an alternative behavior which is easier and simpler in the long run. If you practice consistently, your dog will receive the attention your dog wants for appropriate greeting.

If your dog is about to leap into your arms uninvited:

1. Treat, praise, and give calm affection for *four on the floor.* The instant your dog has all four paws on the floor, provide a high value treat. If your dog jumps up, stand up straight. These repetitions lead to a "light bulb moment." If you are patient and your technique is good, your dog will figure it out. Withdraw interaction such as, touch, words, and eye contact for jumping. From your dog's point of view jumping now pushes your "Go away" button, whereas sitting pushes your "Treat/pet" button!

2. Ask your dog to "Sit," then calmly and immediately, treat and praise. Give the hand signal for the well-rehearsed Sit your dog already knows from practice in low-arousal training situations with you. Your dog cannot sit and jump at the same time. If jumping continues, turn, and walk away from your dog, and practice "Sit" more frequently in less emotionally charged situations.

3. Direct your dog to run directly to the dog "cookie jar" instead of jumping on you. As soon as your dog sees you, consistently walk directly to the "cookie jar" and ask for a "Sit." Toss the treats in a spray. Make this the new routine for greeting.

4. If your dog comes rushing at you from a distance, teach an alternate behavior to jumping that allows your dog to expend energy. Teach your dog to target your hand by holding your palm down at the height of your dog's nose and a few inches *away* from your body. When your dog's nose touches your hand, reward as long your dog performs the nose-touch, and does not jump. Happy wiggles are encouraged! If jumping continues, use a baby gate as a barrier which can be helpful to practice homecomings without jumping.

5. Take time-outs to relax. Lastly, if your dog jumps up on you or your guests regularly, and you have not trained an alternative behavior yet, set your dog up in a nice area with a chew toy, or time *yourself* out by leaving. Time-outs allow your dog time to happily calm down so you can try again next time, however, time-outs are not to be used as a punishment.

If you touch or make exciting sounds, even screeching in pain when your dog jumps up on you, your arousal inadvertently teaches that jumping is fun. If you occasionally greet your dog with affection when your dog jumps on you but occasionally get upset when your dog jumps, you are sending confusing mixed messages. Help your dog understand your desires by sending consistent, calm, and clear messages in a language your dog can understand.

SIT

Two great ways to easily teach Sit are *capturing* and *luring*. (Learn more about capturing, luring, and shaping in Chapter 14, Training Techniques.)

- **Capturing Sit.** Capture Sit and provide a reward. Reward sitting whenever your dog sits as a normal part of daily activities!
- **Luring Sit.** Use food first as a lure and then as a reward. Hand signals are easier to understand than words because dogs are experts at reading body

language but not so great at spoken languages. Remove the food lure as soon as possible and transition to food as a reward as soon as you can get a reliable Sit. If you do not remove the food lure promptly, your dog may not learn the behavior but will just follow the treat with the nose and Sit only when you have a treat near the nose. This can be easily avoided by following these steps:

1. Start with your dog facing you on-leash in a quiet location with a minimum of distractions.
2. Show your dog a small, high value treat (the lure) at nose level, and slowly raise it slightly above and then just behind your dog's head.
3. As your dog's eyes follow the path of the treat, your dog's rear will move towards the floor.
4. Mark the Sit with the word "Good" the instant your dog's rear end rests on the floor, and reward immediately with the treat.
5. As soon as your dog is successful at Sit when following the food lure, it is time to remove the food lure from your hand and use the hand movement alone you have used for Sit, this time without luring your dog with a treat.
6. Morph and shape your hand signal by bending your arm at the elbow from your side up to your shoulder, palm facing toward your face, and move your hand upward. Shape the Sit hand signal to your standing position bit by bit. This is the traditional hand signal for Sit.
7. Click/treat or "Good"/treat immediately after a Sit is performed.
8. Release your dog saying, "Okay," or another release word of your choice such as "Free." If your dog does not stand up from the Sit after saying your release word, take a step back and call your dog to you. Reward for coming when called!
9. When your dog Sits reliably with the hand signal, you may teach the word cue "Sit" by saying, "Sit!", *then* immediately giving the Sit hand signal.
10. Practice rewarding Sit at least 5 times per day with the hand signal for a few days, and periodically after that.

DOWN AND SETTLE DOWN

Shaping a Down

A behavior can be taught in tiny steps by clicking with a clicker, or otherwise marking, for *successive approximations* of the end behavior you want to see. In other words, you are rewarding small, incremental steps on the path to the goal behavior. *Shaping* is an excellent opportunity to use a clicker effectively. Click/treat or "Good"/treat for each approximation which is closer to the end-goal behavior than the last performance.

Down

1. Teach and ask your dog to "Sit" first.
2. Squat or kneel in front of your dog.
3. Shape a body language signal in the form of the letter "L" by placing the treat at your dog's nose level, and then slowly bring your hand to the ground in a straight vertical line down to your dog's toes. Now, slowly draw your hand horizontally across the floor toward yourself, luring your dog forward with the treat. The goal is that your dog reaches one foot forward at a time while the rest of the body remains on the floor—click/treat!
4. Lure your dog to move the other foot forward—click/treat.
5. Continue luring until your dog is in a crouching position—click/treat.
6. When the belly touches the ground—click/treat.
7. Remove the treat lure at the very earliest possible trial.
8. Gradually stand up by using incremental small steps.
9. Use the Down hand signal, which is the reverse of the Sit signal: your arm moves down, palm facing down, with a sweeping motion in front of your body.
10. After the behavior is well learned, you may add the verbal cue "Down" immediately *before* giving the hand signal. In time, your dog will respond to the verbal cue, "Down."

The most common problem for dogs learning Down is the dog's rear end rising upwards during shaping: if the rear end pops up, do not reward with a treat but begin again with Step 1. Proceed slowly mastering each successive approximation before moving to the next level of difficulty. Polish your technique. If your dog does not understand what you are trying to teach, it is your responsibility to make the steps smaller, thus communicating more clearly to your dog.

Here's a hot tip for training small dogs and relieving your aching back: train Down for your small dog on a raised surface such as the couch which may be more comfortable for you and easier on your back.

"Relax" Down

Your dog is not truly relaxed in the standard *sphinx* Down position, so your dog may tend to pop back up. Observe your dog at rest and train a "Relax" cue to your dog's favored resting hip, right or left side. Be consistent with cueing and reinforcing to the naturally favored hip. Try this:

- Ask your dog to "Down" using the hand signal and/or verbal cue.
- Use a treat to lure your dog's nose back and around toward the opposite side of your dog's favored hip. Shape the movement bit by bit.
- Click/treat the instant your dog rests on the favored hip.
- Repeat again and again.
- Remove the treat lure at the *very earliest* possible trial and begin using the lure as the reward after your dog performs the desired behavior.

Settle Down

Teach your dog to relax by using your dog's own naturally occurring behavior, capturing and rewarding a Settle Down. The goal is that relaxing becomes an *automatic behavior* when you sit down or make the Settle Down request. An automatic behavior is also called a *default behavior* in force-free dog training. Settle Down is highly effective for use in desensitization and counterconditioning when teaching emotional and behavioral modification in the face of triggers such as other dogs and wildlife when appropriate thresholds are established. Follow these steps:

- Sit with your dog on leash beginning in a low distraction environment. Allow just enough leash, approximately four feet, for your dog to sit and lie down on a warm, soft surface, such as a mat or a rug.
- Do not interact with your dog. Do not look, touch, or talk.
- Wait patiently for your dog to sit.
- When your dog sits or lies down, immediately reward with a high value treat.
- Wait for your dog to lie down. When your dog lies down, drop a few treats between your dog's paws.
- "Sneak" treats between your dog's paws when your dog is not looking. Learning is accelerated if your dog does not observe you placing the treats between the paws.
- Continue providing rewards intermittently as long as your dog remains in the down position.
- After the behavior is well-learned, you may add the "Settle Down" cue, such as pointing and saying, "Settle Down" in a kind tone.
- Practice capturing and rewarding Settle Down 3 times per day.

WAIT/STAY

Wait/Stay is one of the most useful tricks your dog will ever learn. Wait means "do nothing." Teach your dog Wait/Stay in the Down position first, which is typically more relaxing. This is easier than teaching Sit/Wait or Stand/Wait first: these iterations may be added later. You want each and every attempt at Wait to be successful.

Wait

Ask your dog to

1. "Sit," then "Down."
2. Give the Wait hand signal: that is, make a fireworks burst type movement with your palm facing toward your dog's face. Say the word "Wait" at the same instant. Your dog is already doing the behavior of waiting. All you do now is increase the level of difficulty.
3. Increase **Duration** first, then **Distance, Distractions,** and **Disappearing. separately**—The *3 Ds* plus one. Increase Duration first to 20 seconds, bit by bit without moving.
4. Always repeat the hand signal and verbal cue when you increase the level of difficulty.

5. If you think your dog is about to get up, give the Wait hand signal and verbal cue, intermittently. Repeating the signal is perfectly acceptable and helpful when raising criterion. However, you need not give reminders often.

6. Watch your dog as you move just one foot distance away (Distance). Now return to your dog and reward. Your dog will know you are watching and be less likely to get up.

7. Always come back to your dog, rather than calling your dog to "Come" to you. At this stage in training, if you call, your dog will anticipate your call rather than relaxing into the Wait. After the behavior is well learned you may call your dog to you, perhaps one out of three times.

8. Always release your dog by giving the verbal cue, "Okay" or the release cue of your choice.

9. After Wait is well learned in the down position, graduate to Wait in the sitting and standing positions.

10. Practice in various positions, such as standing to the side of your dog or away from your dog.

11. Practice in real-life situations including at doorways, before getting into the car, and at curbs on walks before crossing the street.

12. Practice 5 times per day.

Stay

Stay is not necessarily a different behavior from Wait, but rather a difference in duration. Wait is defined as a few seconds or a short period of stillness, whereas Stay means a longer period of perhaps a few minutes. A puppy may need to mature a bit to learn a long stay. Use a bully stick or other favorite chew item when practicing longer Stays.

There are very few situations, if any, where it is necessary to put your unleashed dog in a long Stay. It is kinder and safer to keep your dog on a leash. Using Stay to show off to others or dominate your dog must not be the focus. Teach behavior for practical purposes to make life with your dog happier for both of you.

COME

Dogs perform best on the reward system. Always reward when your dog comes to you. Make coming to you, known as *recall*, fun and rewarding, one small step at a time. Each time your dog Comes to you when you call your dog's name, reward your dog with a high value treat. You may substitute some meal calories for training calories. Using food in training helps your dog learn quickly. Practice regularly and frequently. It's imperative to involve the whole family to assure consistency in training.

Name Response

Name Response is one of the most useful skills you can teach your dog. Name Response is the first piece of teaching "Come." That is, getting your dog's attention focused on you with a head turn first.

Playing the Name Response Game

1. Make a game of this training exercise having everyone in the family call your dog, one person at a time, in a round-robin circle. Mix it up.
2. Click/treat or "Good"/treat when your dog turns her head toward you.
3. Graduate to hiding then calling your dog's name, and let your dog find you! Watch the glee on your dog's face as your dog learns to respond and comes running to you.
4. Practice Name Response at least 10 times per day.

Lightning Recall aka "Come" Long Distance

Start with easy Comes. Begin training inside your home and progress slowly, week by week, to more challenging environments. Start by using a big hand signal from just 3 feet away.

Come. Foundational Training

1. Call your dog's name from a short distance.
2. When your dog turns the head toward you, give the "Come" verbal cue. The point at which your dog *makes the decision* to come toward you is a point at which a click or verbal marker teaches that turning toward you when called will earn a reward.
3. Treat as soon as your dog reaches you from a very short distance, graduating step-wise over time to longer distances.
4. Add Sit to the routine when your dog is ready to link Sit with Name Response and Come. This often happens quickly if you have taught a solid Sit.
5. Increase distance, vary distractions, and vary locations in small increments.
6. Later, work outdoors in an enclosed area or with a 20, 35, or 50-foot leash until recall is reliable.
7. Always reward when your dog comes back to check in with you *without* being called.
8. Once learned, use recall throughout the day to cement it.
9. Do not bounce back and forth between a sugary-sweet, singsong, "Come, Blinky," and a frustrated, commanding, "Blinky, Come!" Your dog won't trust that coming to you is a wise idea.
10. Never punish when your dog answers your call to "Come." Do not clip nails or medicate after calling your dog to you. Do not scold your dog for being slow to Come. Do not leave the dog park immediately. First, reward for coming;

play a minute, and then do what your dog dislikes, if necessary. Recall multiple times throughout a park visit, so recall does not always mean leaving the park. Otherwise, your dog will learn that "Come" means something unhappy happens after heeding your call, so your dog may run the other way when you call!

11. Practice Come and reward in four 3 minute sessions per day.

Maintain realistic expectations for your dog. Some breeds naturally wander farther than others. If you train your dog to "Come" followed by dinner, your dog's ears will perk up when your dog hears those words in other contexts, too! Watch a video of wolfdog Smokey learning Lightning Recall (Michaels, 2015b).

Arm Signal Training

Practice Come indoors first, then in your yard. Add distance and distractions incrementally (baby stepping), building to more challenging locations and situations.

1. Call your dog's name.
2. Squat down to your dog's eye level so you will be in your dog's line of vision when your dog hears your call and looks up.
3. Give the Come, arms-wide-open signal, using a big up-down, up-down sweeping gesture your dog can see from a distance. I prefer the arms-wide-open signal that looks as if you are flagging a race car for a pit stop or bringing in an airplane. You want your dog to be able to easily see and recognize the signal from afar.
4. Reinforce and keep your dog on track by saying "Good, good, good" *while* your dog is in the process of coming to you.
5. Click/treat or "Good"/treat enthusiastically and liberally every time your dog Comes whenever you are able to do so. Once well learned, you can use the verbal signal "Go Play" as a reward in your regular practice trials as well.
6. Later add the voice cue, "Come" *as* your dog is coming toward you. After your dog has learned to come to your arms-wide-open arm signal alone, add the word "Come" *while* your dog is in the act of coming to you. You are *pairing* the behavior of coming to you with the word "Come." This is how your dog will learn the meaning of the word.
7. Practice the backyard to indoors Come regularly. Walk directly to the refrigerator to get a little piece of string cheese and make this part of your routine!
8. Practice long distance Come at least 3 times per day.

A truly reliable recall with many distractions in the environment, such as at the dog park, requires time, practice, and consistent reinforcement with high value rewards at lower levels of intensity.

Whistle Training Lightning Recall

Learning Come outdoors is the hardest request for your dog to respond to consistently, particularly with high distractions. Having a long distance outdoor Come cue is very important. Practice so your dog responds quickly and enthusiastically to your call. One of the most popular ways of teaching a Lightning Recall is using a whistle as the signal cue. Standing directly in front of your dog, blow the whistle softly and follow up immediately with a treat. Repeat, repeat, repeat. Next, slowly increase distance and add distractions in small steps, as long as your dog continues to respond reliably. Whistle training is an excellent way to train a lightning recall if and when you reach a safe leash-free recall level.

LEASH-WALKING

Safety, comfort, and stress reduction are the most important criteria when selecting equipment used for training leash-walking skills. The use of equipment causing stress or pain, such as choke, prong, or electronic shock collars, is antithetical to *Do No Harm* training and is harmful to dogs. These devices are at odds with the positive relationships pet parents are developing with their dogs. Studies show these devices **cause, rather than cure** aggression, and otherwise worsen behavior. Additionally, medical research shows that pressure on the neck may cause injuries that include cervical spine injury, burst capillaries in the eyeballs, foreleg nerve damage, and damage that affects the function of the esophagus and trachea, causing breathing impairment (Overall et al., 2006). A standard flat collar is acceptable to hold identification tags but not as the attachment point for the leash.

Wear your treat bag or carry a pocketful of high value treats such as cheese bits or hot dogs while teaching leash-walking so your dog develops a habit of focusing and connecting with you while on leash.

Most right-handed pet parents walk their dogs on their left side, leaving their right hand free to open doors, greet others, or carry a package. Professionals typically walk dogs on their left side. However, choose whichever side you are most comfortable with and be consistent. Ideally, choose the side to walk your dog that everyone in your family agrees upon.

Leash-Walking Equipment

The easiest way of achieving successful leash-walking begins by starting down the right path with the right equipment early in your dog's life: however, loose-leash walking may be learned at any age. The following equipment is recommended:

Harness

A front, back, or double-clip harness is recommended for all dogs and puppies, including dogs who have developed a habit of pulling on the leash during the walk. An X, Y, or H style harness provides the best mobility, prevents chafing, and allows free movement of the limbs and proper gait. Some trainers prefer the back clip on these styles because of possible mobility and gait issues. Small dogs that do not pull may prefer a step-in harness. Most veterinarians strongly recommend a harness rather than a collar for all brachycephalic breeds with a short muzzle. These dogs are already susceptible to upper respiratory breathing issues, so they breathe easier without the added pressure of a collar around the neck, as do all dogs.

Leash

A four or six-foot leash is recommended for leash-walking contingent upon your dog's skill and the situation. The longer leash provides your dog the freedom to make choices and is often preferred for training loose-leash walking. The shorter leash is recommended for dogs who bark and lunge on leash for safer control, if necessary, to prevent hazards.

Leash-Walking Skills

Basic Principles

To improve loose-leash walking skills, practice training off-leash *indoors* first, teaching your dog to walk close to you. Below find two of the basic principles for successful loose leash-walking:

1. **No pulling, no thank you.** Do not go where your dog pulls you! Instead, when your dog pulls, stop walking. Change direction the instant you feel pressure from your dog on the leash: stop, plant your feet, and pivot, making a 180-degree turn in place and begin walking again, while saying "Let's Go" (see below). Click/treat when your dog is at the correct location after catching up to you. If you allow your dog to pull you, you are inadvertently reinforcing pulling during walks and your dog responds by pulling harder. Your consistency in not following your pulling dog is very important.

2. **Maintain a connection between yourself and your dog while out on walks.** Dogs often become environmentally fixated when there is so much to see, hear, and smell. Actively maintain your bond with your dog while out on walks. You are taking a walk together.

"Let's Go"

Walk from the stationary position. Use the term *"Let's Go"* signaling your dog that something different is going to happen on the walk. "Let's Go" means, "I am leaving, and you are coming with me!" Practice "Let's Go" whenever you move from a stopped position while on walks. "Let's Go" is the green light. It also has the effect of a turn signal before making a change in direction. If you use this phrase often, your dog learns what it means, while sniffing and it is time to go, when you are planning to cross the street, or when leaving another dog and continuing your journey. It is so exciting when you and your dog work as a team!

Name Response on Leash

Use Name Response when you want to get your dog's attention immediately for any reason while leash-walking. Call your dog's name while on leash. Teach your dog to look at you for further instruction, as a check-in behavior while on walks, and to redirect fixation on other dogs, distractions, or stressors.

1. Call your dog's name.
2. The instant your dog makes eye contact with you, mark it with a click/treat, a "Good"/treat, or simply a treat.

Automatic Eye Contact

Reward your dog generously in some way for both looking at you automatically without being asked and for looking at you when you use Name Response. Start *marking and rewarding* whenever your dog freely offers eye contact while walking on leash without calling your dog's name. You can click/treat or just treat. Turning toward you when called and making eye contact without being asked are highly desirable behaviors your dog can do while leash-walking and keeping a connection with you. The goal is having your dog check in with you frequently.

Slow Walking

You want your dog to learn that walking slowly and calmly with you is rewarding. Walking at the slow pace of a human generally must be taught to dogs. It is not natural for a healthy, young dog to walk slowly: if it were up to your dog, your dog would be zigzagging and circling everywhere you go. The slower the better to start. Do not let your dog rush you. You should decide speed, direction, "sniff-sniff" breaks, and when and where to stop, although going on walks letting your dog choose the route is one type of valuable enrichment of choice and can be fun for you too. Try it!

Hand Targeting Heel

Many interesting, complex, agility, and service dog behaviors begin using a *target*. The purpose of hand-targeting for leash-walking is a technique of using your hand as a target for your dog to follow. That is, teach your dog to follow and touch your open hand with the nose while you are both in the leash-walking position. The presentation of your hand is both the hand signal *and* the target to be touched.

1. Begin by practicing off-leash at home with no distractions.
2. Stand in standard leash-walking position with your dog at your side and your dog's head near your leg or knee or a slight bit behind you.
3. Hold your left hand down at your side if you are right-handed.
4. Teach your dog to touch your palm with the nose. The first step may be simply a glance at your hand. You may wiggle your hand until your dog touches the palm of your hand with the nose. Or rub your hand with a little bit of food to lure your dog to touch the palm of your hand. Click/treat or "Good"/treat any movement toward your hand.
5. Add the word "Touch" as your dog touches the palm of your hand with the nose.
6. Take one step forward, say "Touch," and mark the touch the instant your dog touches the palm of your hand with the nose. Reward.

Hand targeting is useful for teaching many other behaviors. Present your hand with your palm facing outward. Then add distance, change direction, change hands, and add distractions. Other practical uses for hand targeting in addition to leash training include

- Speeding up or slowing down while leash-walking
- Coming to your hand
- Standing in back of you
- Getting on or off the couch
- Ringing the bells as a request to go outside: place your open, target hand behind the bells

PART 4

WHEN THINGS GO WRONG

17

AGGRESSION PREVENTION, ASSESSMENT, AND TREATMENT

Laying a foundation for success with emotional and behavioral modification means having realistic expectations of your dog particularly with children and other dogs. Although you rightly consider your dogs to be family members, at the same time, dogs in reality are a unique and distinctly different species. Understanding what drives, motivates and may frighten your dogs is your responsibility and is the first step toward becoming a good pet parent and trainer. If your dog has an aggression issue of any kind, be sure your dog gets a wellness check from your veterinarian to rule out any underlying medical conditions, previous injury, or other causes adversely affecting behavior or causing pain.

Your dog speaks to you through body language—ear and tail carriage, posture, behavior, and vocalizations. Your dog may be experiencing an overload of stress and telling you with body language and behavior. If so, avoid any potentially dangerous situations while you begin a scientifically endorsed behavior modification program. In their "Position Statement on Puppy Socialization", the American Veterinary Society of Animal Behavior (AVSAB) advises, "Classes and at-home training should be based on positive reinforcement with frequent rewards, praise, petting, play and/or treats. Positive and consistent training is associated with fewer behavioral problems and greater obedience than methods that involve punishment and/or encourage human dominance" (The Process of Socialization, 2008, para. 3).

Meeting Needs

Use The Hierarchy of Dog Needs pyramid when identifying behaviors indicating that your dog may be experiencing unmet needs. For example, if the need for secure attachment, trusting humans, or play are under-met behavior problems will inevitably arise. Address these needs using the force-free methods listed in The Hierarchy of Dog

195

Needs. Make certain your dog is getting sufficient exercise, proper nutrition, social interaction, mental stimulation, and novelty on a daily basis. If these basic needs are not met, stress increases.

Prevention

The best way to prevent aggression is practicing a program of careful, frequent, and regular socialization from a young age, if possible, especially during the sensitive period of socialization, 4–12 weeks of age. In addition, prevent traumatic experiences by carefully managing socialization. Avoid *flooding*. Assess your dog's experience at the veterinarian and groomer as possible contributing factors to aggression. Get in-home care or be the first appointment of the day. Bring treats. (See Chapter 9, Socialization.)

Decreasing Stress

Stress is an underlying cause of aggression. "Stress matters," says Diane Garrod, developer of the first, systematic, canine stress release protocol, *Stress Release For Dogs: The Canine Emotional Detox*. She tells us:

> What is occurring in the dog's body is important to understanding why releasing stress is so important. Stress can cause a dog to aggress and cause a dog to exhibit a number of other behaviors, such as licking, over-barking and hyperactivity. Stress might be looked at as the equivalent to human burn out. Hans Selye, considered by many as the father of the study of stress (Selye, 1936), said that a direct relationship exists between chronic stress and excessive wear and tear throughout the body. (Garrod, 2021)

In over 600 case studies, Garrod found that releasing stress results in longer-lasting behavioral change first, faster progress, helps with better retention, and guides the practitioner in individualizing emotional and behavioral modification protocols.

Management and Avoidance

Safety first is always the most important rule when it comes to aggression. Management is the first step in any aggression treatment program. Additionally, management can always fail, so it is not enough, but rather the place to begin getting behavior under control. Avoidance can be a good management tool, but it does not treat the underlying drives and motivations of aggression or lead to any long-term or permanent change.

Basic Skills

When addressing aggression, teaching just a few basic manners skills is optimal. However, the foundational skills below should be rock solid. Get these behaviors reliably learned and you can avoid a great deal of trouble. Learn alternative behaviors to reactivity:

- "Let's Go." Teach this verbal cue to initiate an immediate 180° U-turn to walk away and stay *under threshold.*
- Name response.
- Automatic eye-contact with a head turn, also known as checking in with you.

(See Chapter 16, Basic Skills.)

Proper Equipment

Be sure to use only dog-friendly leash-walking equipment. Muzzle train if your dog continues posing any threat to people or other dogs and for use in emergencies

GREETING PROTOCOLS

Greetings often determine the course of the relationships between your guests and your dog. Dogs are not famous for making reliably good decisions. That is your responsibility! Protect your guests and your dog so that greetings go well:

- First, allow your dog to calm down in a secured area to acclimate to visitors being in the home *before* attempting greetings. This alone will help your dog and your visitors as well.
- Do not answer the door with your dog when your dog may be uncomfortable and does not really know how to behave.
- Your dog should not have the responsibility to decide which of your friends, and certainly not which dogs feel safe, and which do not.
- Provide your dog with high value treats such as cheese or healthy hot dogs, that you initially feed in the secure space when guests arrive. Later, if safe and practical, have your guests toss your dog treats. You must protect your guests by not giving your dog access to them, unless and until:

  1. Your dog appears entirely comfortable with them.
  2. You have advised and instructed your cooperative guests about how to interact with your dog.

INTRODUCING A NEW DOG INTO YOUR HOME

Never bring a new dog into your home and just "see how it goes" (Richmond, 2004/2019). This all-too-common mistake can set up your dogs for a lifetime of squabbling or worse. Your resident dog is well established as the only child. Abruptly adding another dog or a puppy into the household as a visitor, a foster, or a newly adopted dog can easily lead to territorial aggression. Serious resource guarding between the dogs may erupt if your resident dog feels that an intruder has just invaded the home. Ideally, introduce each dog to the other's scent and allow each dog to acclimate to the other's scent before you house the dogs together. Follow these cardinal rules:

1. Smell, No See

Set up separate, secure areas for each dog. The dogs should not be allowed any eye contact whatsoever. Switch their scent articles such as old-t-shirts, blankets, and toys to the other dog's area. You may also use Nicole Wilde's "rag wipe" technique. Wipe a rag around dog A's anus near the main scent glands, then wipe that same rag around dog B's shoulders and rear. Now do the same with dog B (Wilde, 2018). This mixes their scents for recognition of familiarity. Then, switch living spaces and yard time, giving each a chance to leave scent without seeing the other dog. Later, let your new dog roam around the house and yard leaving scent. Now, allow your resident dog to do the same thing. Repeat this again and again daily until you see little to no reaction to other dog's scent by either dog, especially your resident dog. This process may take days or weeks. Patiently using this process right from the start, while carefully observing body language, can save yourself and your dogs, years of heartache, angst, and trouble. If you have advance notice, place the cloth in a self-sealing plastic bag and freeze to preserve the scent, then deliver to the other dog's current residence, packed in ice.

2. See, No Touch

Take your leashed dogs out for a parallel walk, walking side-by-side, with handlers on the inside. The configuration should be from left to right: Dog A, Human A, Human B, Dog B. This technique introduces your dogs on neutral territory with a positively reinforcing activity, so your resident dog is less likely to consider your new dog a territorial intruder. A different individual must handle each dog. The technique of parallel walking includes plenty of time for sniffing, then gradually moving them closer together as long as both dogs are clearly under the threshold of reactivity. Now, allow the dogs to sniff each other for just a few short seconds, separate and continue the walk, with high value reinforcement being provided to each dog by the handlers.

3. Structured Interactions

Allow the dogs to meet on neutral property, such as a friend's yard, leash-free, or dragging their leashes with a high level of supervision and intervention, if needed.

If meeting on leash, let the dogs sniff and greet each other very briefly—a few short seconds, then break. Rest and then repeat until you feel confident both dogs are comfortable with each other.

4. Free Access

If all has gone well, allow the dogs to have free access to one another as long as they continue socializing properly without incident.

ASSESSMENT

Act Now

There really is no such thing as a "nip." Even an air snap is considered a "bite", albeit the lowest on Dr. Dunbar's *Bite Scale: An assessment of the severity of bites based on evaluation of wound pathology* (Dunbar, 2007–2020). However, an air snap is nonetheless a bite-display of warning. If you see displays of aggression in your dog, do not wait to address the problem. Aggression is not something your dog will outgrow. The longer you wait, the more difficult, or perhaps impossible, modifying aggressive behavior will become. Once the momentum for aggression has begun, it is likely to snowball with an increasing risk of a person or another dog getting bit. Conversely, it is more likely to decrease or disappear if addressed promptly and competently.

Aggression may be categorized as either defensive or offensive, although the lines are not always clear. Many dogs will go on the offensive out of fear to protect themselves from a perceived threat. However, understanding what is driving the aggression may be helpful:

- **Defensive fear-based aggression.** The bark-lunge seeks to keep frightening people or dogs further away, called *distance increasing behavior.*
- **Offensive-based aggression.** The bark-lunge seeks to inflict injury going out of the way to attack another, called *distance decreasing behavior.*

Identify the Type of Aggression Problem, such as

- On-leash aggression
- Off-leash aggression
- Territorial aggression
- Fence-barrier aggression
- Resource guarding aggression
- Sibling rivalry aggression, also known as multi-dog household fighting

Assessing Severity

When assessing the severity of aggression, you will need to examine the bite factors below using the resources provided:

- Context, that is, understand the nature of the triggering antecedent
- Ameliorating and exacerbating factors
- Predictability
- Warning displays, or lack of warning displays
- The duration of time between a warning and a bite
- *The Dog Bite Scale: An assessment of the severity of bites based on evaluation of wound pathology,* by Dr. Ian Dunbar, DVM, PhD (2007).
- *Dog-dog Bite Hierarchy,* by Cara Shannon (2020).

Once all of the people who interact with the dog are on the same page with force-free training, the dog can better predict human behavior and as a result people can better predict the dog's behavior. Remember, not all dogs care for other dogs and we should not expect them to be social butterflies. It is just not fair. After all, sociability in people varies widely between individuals too.

RED FLAGS

Attempts to escape a situation or person, by moving away, or walking away are indications your dog is feeling threatened and is politely asking for the perceived threat to end. Change what *you* are doing before you trigger or exacerbate the propensity for aggression. Below find some behavioral signs that can alert you that trouble may be coming. Do not ignore these behaviors, body language, or vocalization communications and warnings:

Aggressive Behavior
- Biting
- Lunging at people
- Lunging at other dogs
- Fighting on-leash, or off-leash
- Guarding food, toys, people, space, or other
- Stalking

Aggressive Body Language Warnings
- Raised hackles (hair on the back and neck), also known as *piloerection*
- Body stillness, freezing/rigid body
- Head down, and body erect standing tall

- Hard stare, fixation
- Raised lip
- Puckered muzzle
- Show of teeth
- Ears pricked forward, or ears flat back
- Tail flared, held straight out, or held high, vibrating, or fast wagging

Aggressive Vocalization Warnings

- Barking
- Growling
- Snarling
- Distress whining

Refusal to Take Treats When Reacting

Refusal to take treats is a very good indication your dog is *over-threshold* and more distance, and less intensity are needed to stay *under-threshold*.

There are no guarantees with behavior; however, working with a competent force-free trainer in managing or mitigating aggression can be a wise first step. If aggression has progressed, is repetitive, or if there have been any bites, your dog needs the attention of a behavior professional trained in force-free aggression treatment. Contact your force-free aggression specialist or your veterinary behaviorist for individualized and customized treatment plans. Search the Pet Professional Guild behavioral consultant guide by zip code (2020a).

WHAT BEHAVIOR CONSULTANTS SHOULD PROVIDE IN AGGRESSION CASES

A complete background, history, and an incident report are recommended for dogs who have bitten a person or another dog. A thorough assessment will include examining each bite and the circumstances surrounding it, understanding the triggers, and the ameliorating and exacerbating features of the bite incident. A professional emotional and behavioral modification treatment package should include these elements:

- A health assessment request, and medical clearance by a trusted/*Do No Harm* veterinarian
- Background/history and incident report analysis. See the Assessment Intake for Behavior Consultants below.
- Safety and greeting templates. Aggressive dogs should be secured away from visitors to the home. The trainer and guests must be protected by not allowing a dog access to guests until a treatment plan with an aggression behavior specialist is developed.
- Both human and/or dog-dog bite scale assessment examining severity and bite style based upon wound pathology, frequency of incidents and bite/release factors.
- A thorough explanation of the factors contributing to aggressive behavior: Genetic, improper or insufficient socialization during the critical sensitive period, or traumatic experiences from the dog's perspective. Other common causes of aggression include a failure in meeting a dog's real needs, and using training methods other than those in The Hierarchy of Dog Needs, such as shock, prong, or choke collars that have been shown to *cause rather than to cure* aggression.
- Understanding liability. Each state, and most counties have their own liability laws and regulations for dangerous and vicious dogs. For example, California has a strict liability statute. The statute states that a dog's owner can be held liable for injuries caused by a dog bite "regardless of the former viciousness of the dog or the owner's knowledge of such viciousness" (California Legislative Information Civil Code, 2020).
- Dog body language communication and analysis of vocalizations (See Chapter 11, Dog Body Language.)
- Desensitization and counterconditioning techniques aiding in both emotional counterconditioning and behavior-substitution learning for the dog

Assessment Intake Questionnaire for Behavior Consultations

Instructions for Clients

The Assessment Questionnaire is divided into six sections. Please complete all of the sections that pertain to issues you would like to address with your dog(s) and provide concise, yet complete, behavior information. Thank you.

1. Background Information
2. Aggression with Humans (including Resource Guarding)
3. Aggression with Other Dogs—Dog-Dog Aggression
4. Separation Anxiety and Fearfulness
5. Annoyance Problems, such as: Barking, Marking, Pulling on Leash and other
6. Training Goals

1. Background Information

Name	Address
Home Phone	Cell Phone
Email 1	Email 2
• What is your primary reason for contacting a behavior consultant/trainer? • Secondary reasons?	
How did you find us?	

Household Composition - People

Name, Gender, Age	Name, Gender, Age
Name, Gender, Age	Name, Gender, Age
Name, Gender, Age	Name, Gender, Age
Circle the regular visitors that your dog interacts with, such as: • Friends • Employees • Housekeepers • Personal Assistants • Landscapers Please describe any specific difficulties with visitors.	

Household Dogs

Name 1		Breed	Age	Male or Female Neutered/Spayed
Name 2		Breed	Age	Male or Female Neutered/Spayed

- Age when your dog joined your family?
- If chosen from a litter, why did you choose this puppy?
- If chosen from a rescue or shelter, why did you choose this dog?

Health

- When was the last time the dog with the primary behavior problem had a complete veterinary wellness exam?
- Has your dog had a complete veterinary wellness exam after the onset of the problem behavior?

Does your dog have any medical conditions that may impact training? Circle the ones that apply. • Hearing Loss • Vision Loss • Hip dysplasia • Arthritis • Other

- Is your dog taking any medication?
- Please provide the name of the medication and dosage, or over the counter (OTC) product

Food Allergies?

May I have your permission to discuss your dog's case and progress with your veterinarian? Yes/No

Veterinarian Name	Address
Phone	Email Address

Training History

Circle all that apply   • Classes   • Private   • Boot Camp

- How successful was the training?
- What did you like about the training?
- What did you dislike about the training?

How do you define "correction?"
In what ways have you corrected or disciplined your dog for unwanted behaviors?
Which basic manners skills does your dog already possess?
Which basic manners and obedience skills would you like your dog to learn, if any?
• Has your dog been boarded? • Describe any emotional or behavioral changes you may have noticed upon your dog's return home, if any. • How long was your dog boarded? At what facility?

Diet

Brand of food. Please have food-packaging labels available for evaluation.
Daily Supplements.
Daily Feeding Schedule: • Once   • Twice   • Three times
Eating Behavior. Choose one: • Normal   • Picky   • Gulping

Exercise

How would you describe your dog's energy? • High   • Medium   • Low
Which leash-walking items do you currently use? • Harness   • Flat Collar   • Head Halter   • Martingale Collar • Shock Collar   • Prong Collar   • Choke Collar   • Retractable Leash Describe you and your dog's typical on-leash walking experience
What type of regular exercise does your dog get? • Walks   • Backyard   • Fetch • Dog Park or Beach   • Playing with Household Dogs   • Other
How much time per day does your dog spend outside? • Supervised   • Alone

Socialization Skills

People. On a 1–5 scale with 1 being the worst, and 5 being the best, please rate your dog's socialization skills with people.
How does your dog greet strangers coming into your home? Is it a problem?
Children. If you have an infant or toddler in the home, please describe • Your dog's behavior toward the child • Your child's behavior and feelings toward the dog • What role do you play as supervisor, facilitator, or intervener? • Describe what behavior has occurred with the children that concerns you.
Other dogs. On a 1–5 scale with 1 being the worst, and 5 being the best, please rate your dog's socialization with Strange/New Dogs _____ and Household Dogs _____
Have there been any dramatic changes to your dog's home or surrounding environment recently, such as: • Construction • Move • Death • Birth • Other Describe your dog's reaction to these changes.

Your Dog's Favorite Things

List your dog's favorite things, such as: • Treats   • Affection   • Belly Rubs   • Toys   • Other

Your Dog's Day

Describe a typical weekday
Describe a typical weekend
Does your dog have a special place to relax, away from an otherwise noisy environment?
What does your dog do there, such as: • Sleep • Guard • Watch Birds • Chew

2. Aggression with Humans

(Aggression with Other Dogs is addressed separately in Section 3.)

Complete this section if your dog has aggression problems with you, other family members, strangers, children, men, guests, other people, or reactivity (barking and lunging) at moving objects such as: skateboards, bicycles, joggers, trucks, motorcycles, cars, other.

Does your dog have a bite or "nip" history to people? Yes/No • How many bites?
How long has your dog been showing aggression? How long has your dog been… Circle those that apply: • Biting • Snapping • Growling • Posturing • Guarding • Stalking • How old was your dog when the first bite to a person occurred?
How does your dog feel about being touched? • Are there areas of your dog's body that are sensitive to your touch, such as: • Paws • Ears • Mouth • Tail • Other
Did your dog have any traumatic puppyhood experiences that you know of?
Does the aggressive behavior limit you or your dog's daily activities? How so?
Does your dog bark/lunge at people while on leash? • Under what circumstances?
Does your dog grab onto you or other people with the mouth? • Do you feel teeth when playing, hand-feeding, or in other interactions?
Does your dog "guard" from the inside of your home, such as… Circle those that apply: • Sitting at the window to bark at passers-by • Guarding the perimeter of your fenced yard?
Does your dog guard the entryway to your home, or fail to calm when guests enter your home?
Do you play chase games with your dog?
Do you or a family member play tug, or wrestle with your dog?

Bite Incidents. Please answer the following questions to the best of your knowledge detailing *bite incidents*. A bite incident is considered any interaction or altercation where your dog uses its mouth to inflict injury. Please provide one bite incident report for

    A. The most Recent bite to a person
    B. The most Severe bite to a person
    C. The Chronic, ongoing nature of the human aggression
    D. Resource guarding items from people

A. The Most Recent Bite to a Person

When was the most recent incident?
Who did your dog bite?
What is the approximate age of that person?
Where did the incident take place? Was it in your home, the sidewalk in front of your home, elsewhere?
Did your dog give a warning before biting, such as… Circle all those that apply: • Attempt to Escape • Air Snap • Prolonged Growl • Short Growl • Body Language Displays • Other
Did your dog make contact with the person's skin or clothing, tear the clothing, or break the skin? Circle all those that apply.
What part of the person's body did your dog bite?
What type of clothing or shoes, if any, covered that body part?
What was the proximity of the body part to your dog's mouth? That is, did your dog jump up, or move or to reach the body part, or was the body part directly near the dog's mouth?
Did the person require medical treatment?
If yes, what type of treatment was necessary? • Emergency Room • Sutures/Stapling • Surgery • Other
Was a hospital stay required?
Circle the best way to describe the bite • Air-snap • Bruising no Puncture • Scratching • Tearing. • Lacerations • Puncture and Release • Puncture and Hold • Puncture and Thrash • Multiple Punctures
Did the dog shake the victim?
Circle the best description of the bruising around the bite • Light Gray • Medium Gray • Dark Gray • Deep Purple/Black
In your estimate, what percentage of the dog's sharp canine teeth entered the body • Less than 15% • 15–30% • 30–50% • More than 50%
What were the circumstances surrounding the bite, that is • What was happening *before* the bite? • What did your dog do *after* the bite? • What did *you* do with your dog after the bite?

Why do you think your dog bit the person?
List your previous attempts to address aggression and resource guarding of people and/or treatment or diagnosis from other animal professionals.

B. The Most Severe Bite to a Person

When was the most serious incident?
Who did your dog bite?
What is the approximate age of that person?
Where did the incident take place? In your home, the sidewalk in front of your home, elsewhere?
Did your dog give a warning before biting, such as… Circle all those that apply: • Attempt to escape   • Prolonged growl   • Short Growl   • Air Snap   • Body Language Display   • Other
Did your dog make contact with the person's skin or clothing, tear the clothing, or break the skin?
What part of the person's body did your dog bite?
What type of clothing or shoes covered that body part, if any?
What was the proximity of the body part to your dog's mouth? That is, did your dog jump-up, or move to reach a body part, or was the body part directly near the dog's mouth?
Did the person require medical treatment?
If yes, what type of treatment was necessary?   • Emergency Room   • Sutures/Stapling   • Surgery   • Other
Was a hospital stay required?
Circle the best way to describe the bite   • Air-snap   • Bruising no Puncture   • Scratching   • Tearing   • Lacerations   • Puncture and Release   • Puncture and Hold   • Puncture and Thrash   • Multiple Punctures
Did the dog shake the victim?
Circle the best description of the bruising around the bite   • Light Gray   • Medium Gray   • Dark Gray   • Deep Purple/Black

In your estimate, what percentage of the dog's sharp teeth entered the body
• Less than 15%   • 15–30%   • 30–50%   • More than 50%

What were the circumstances surrounding the bite, that is:
• What was happening *before* the bite?
• What did your dog do *after* the bite?
• What did *you* do with your dog after your dog bit the person?

Why do you think your dog bit?

C. Describe the Chronic Nature of the Human Aggression

D. Resource Guarding Items with Humans

1. Does your dog guard resources from people such as:
   • Food Bowl   • Rawhides   • Toys   • Bed   • You   • Other People
   • Other items or locations

Circle the best answers.

2. List the other items that your dog guards from people
3. Describe specifically what happens if you try to take a high value item from your dog? Circle all the options that apply: • Nothing.   • Snarl
   • Growl   • Air-Snap   • Bite

3. Aggression with Other Dogs. Dog-Dog Aggression

Please answer the following questions to the best of your knowledge for *bite incidents*. A bite incident is considered any interaction or altercation where your dog uses its mouth to inflict injury. Please provide one bite incident report for

  A. The most Recent bite incident to another dog
  B. The most Severe bite incident to another dog
  C. The Chronic, ongoing nature of aggression to other dogs
  D. Resource guarding items with other dogs

A. The Most Recent Bite to Another Dog

When was the most recent incident?
Which body parts were bitten?
Did your dog give a warning before biting, such as… Circle all that apply: • Attempt to Escape • Prolonged Growl • Short Growl • Air-Snap • Body Language Display • Other
How many times has your dog been involved in dogfights?
How many of these fights resulted in a veterinary visit due to injuries?
How severe were the injuries to each animal?
Is there "sibling rivalry" in your multi-dog home between pets?
Why do you think your dog bit?
Your previous attempts to address the problem and any diagnosis from other animal professionals.

B. Most Severe Bite to Another Dog

When was the most severe incident?
Which body parts were bitten?
Did your dog give a warning before biting, such as… Circle all that apply: • Attempt to Escape • Prolonged Growl • Short Growl • Air-Snap • Body Language Display • Other
Did this fight result in a veterinary visit due to injuries?
How severe were the injuries to each animal?
Why do you think your dog bit?

C. Describe the Chronic Nature of the Aggression to Other Dogs

D. Resource Guarding Items with Other Dogs

> Does your dog guard resources from other dogs, such as… Circle all that apply:
> 1. • Food Bowl • Rawhides • Toys • Bed • You • Other People • Other items or locations
> 2. List the items that your dog guards from in-house dogs or other/stranger dogs
> 3. Describe specifically what happens if one dog tries to take a high value item from the other dog, such as… Circle all that apply: • Nothing • Snarl • Growl • Air-Snap • Bite

4. Separation Anxiety and Fearfulness

Separation Anxiety

> Please describe your dog's specific behaviors
> 1. As you prepare to leave the house
> 2. After you leave the house, if known
> 3. Upon your return

> Which of the following apply to your dog when you are gone? Circle all that apply.
> • Self-inflicted injuries or mutilation, such as wounds from biting paws or flank
> • Attempts to escape the home
> • Housetraining regression
> • Destructive behavior
> • Barking, crying, whining
> • Staring out the window awaiting your return
> • Other

> Please describe how bonded you are to your dog, that is:
> • How many hours per day do you spend together, on average?
> • How many hours spent apart, on average?
> • Are you crating your dog for Separation Anxiety?

> Does your dog sleep in bed with you?

> Please describe your emotions and behavior toward your dog when you
> 1. Say "Goodbye" as you leave the house
> 2. Greet your dog as you arrive home

What limitations does separation anxiety cause to you or other family members? List your previous attempts to address the problem and any diagnosis from other animal professionals.

Fearfulness

Circle all that apply. Please describe any fearful behaviors, body language, vocalizations or circumstances that appear to be a problem

- Attempts to run away
- Attempts to hide
- Displays of submission or appeasement such as:
  - Tail between the legs
  - Excessive licking
  - Crouching or crawling
  - Rolling over to expose the tummy area when in fearful situations such as a *tap-out/go away* request
- Other

5. Annoyance Problems

Please describe each problem you would like to address with training and treatment. Circle all that apply.
- Housetraining
- Barking
- Jumping
- Mounting
- Puppy Biting or Mouthing
- Marking
- Pulling on Leash
- Basic Manners
- Other/Explain

6. Training Goals

Describe your family's goals and expectations.
Are there social dynamics within the family that may impact consistency in training?
Describe your and other family members' willingness to participate in training.
Describe your willingness to keep your pet.

The statements contained in the Assessment Form above are true to the best of my knowledge.

Names of Client/Pet Parents (Please Print) _____

Signatures of Client/Pet Parents _____

Date _____

Functional Analysis

Procedures called functional analysis and behavioral diagnostics are now on the cutting edge of treatment in pet dog behavior modification. In *How Dogs Learn*, functional analysis is defined as the "process of analyzing the interaction between the environment and behavior" to develop an efficient treatment plan for the dog (Burch & Bailey, 1999, p. 94).

In research, case studies are single-subject designs, often used in applied settings such as dog training. On the other hand, laboratory research, uses a sample population of many subjects comparing the subjects and/or groups to each other. In determining whether a treatment is effective in a single-subject examination and in research investigators compare the data before the treatment to the data after the treatment in the same dog(s) in what is referred to as an ABA design:

A = Before Treatment
B = Treatment
A = After Treatment

Functional analysis looks at the cause of the behavior, not just the behavior itself. Developing a treatment plan requires understanding the function of the behavior, i.e., the purpose of both the *antecedents* and the *consequences* that are driving the dog's behavior. We ask two questions:

1. **What is motivating the behavior?** For example, is the dog seeking to communicate a need, such as the need to eliminate or a need to escape? Is the dog seeking reinforcement such as water, food, or chew toys? Is the dog seeking attention? Is the dog seeking sensory reinforcement, such as novelty?

2. **What is maintaining the behavior?** For example, is the dog finding the behavior reinforcing by accessing food, toys, or escape? Is the dog receiving attention? Is the dog receiving sensory reinforcement, such as sniffing?

The process of conducting a functional assessment is comprised of the following steps, as explained succinctly by Niki Tudge, founder of the Pet Professional Guild (Tudge, 2015, p. 151–155.)

1. **Informant Interview**
   - Informal interview with the client
2. **Direct Observation Stage**
   - Behavior observed
   - Relationship between the variables measured
3. **Functional Analysis**
   - Detailed in simple terms
   - Antecedents
   - Behaviors
   - Consequences

4. **Contingency (If/Then) Statement.** The information gathered in 1–3 above leads to a statement that defines:
   - How the behavior is evoked and
   - How the behavior is maintained

Liability Contract Template for Behavior Consultants

LIABILITY RELEASE AND ASSUMPTION OF RISK AGREEMENT

The undersigned on behalf of any and all participants authorized or permitted to attend any lessons, agrees to defend, indemnify and hold harmless your dog trainer/behavior consultant ————————————— (hereafter referred to as the "RELEASED PARTIES" or "TRAINER") and agents from all liability and damages for any claim, loss, or injury, which may occur or may be alleged to have occurred to any person, animals, or property arising from or related to the training, consultations or lessons. The Client agrees that TRAINER, the owners, officers, employees and agents, will not be liable for any injury, death or property damage resulting from the training, counseling, or advice supplied to Client by TRAINER.

The TRAINER reserves the right to refuse training any dog that is obviously sick, abused, neglected, or overtly aggressive. Trainer cannot guarantee any individual dog's ability to learn and/or understand training cues or signals or to desensitize to fear or aggression triggers. Furthermore, the Client agrees that non-compliance with the recommendations of TRAINER constitutes non-liability to the trainer.

Acknowledgement of Risk. Client is aware of the present and continuing inherent risks of injury, death, and property damage to Client, Client's Dog(s), and persons and Dogs of third parties that are involved, and those not involved, in the activity of training, including without limitation risks due to dog bite or infectious disease. Client acknowledges that the Dog's behavior now and in the future is solely Client's responsibility. Client is voluntarily engaged in training as an activity with knowledge of the known risks and other risks that may result from Dog's participation in training, including but not limited to injury, death, or property damage from disease, stray dogs, running away, other dogs in training, other animals, or injury, death, or property damage caused by Dog to other dogs, animals or persons.

Assumption of Risk. If Dog causes property damage, or bites or injures any dog, animal or person, including but not limited to the RELEASED PARTIES, during or after the term of this Agreement, Client agrees to assume full responsibility and liability for any injury, death or property damage, and Client agrees to pay all resulting losses and damages suffered or incurred, and to defend, indemnify, and hold harmless the RELEASED PARTIES from any and all resulting claims, demands, lawsuits, losses, costs of expenses, including attorney's fees.

Release of Liability. Client releases RELEASED PARTIES from all liability to the Client, and Client's representatives, guardians, successors, assignees, heirs, children, and next of kin for all liability, claims, damage, or demands for personal injury, death, or property damage, to the Client or to the Client's Dog(s), arising from or related to this Agreement or to participation in training, whether the injury, death, or property damage occurs on or off the training site.

Knowing and Voluntary Execution. Client acknowledges that he or she has carefully read this Agreement, understands its contents, and understands that this Agreement includes an assumption of the risk of Client's Dog, and a release of the RELEASED PARTIES liability. The undersigned acknowledges that the RELEASED PARTIES are materially relying on this Agreement in allowing the Client to participate in the activity of training. Client acknowledges that TRAINER has not represented, promised, guaranteed or warranted that Dog will never bite, that Dog will not be dangerous or vicious in the future, that Dog will not exhibit other behavioral problems, or that the results of the training will last for any particular amount of time. Only a written instrument signed by both Client and TRAINER may amend this Agreement.

The statements contained in the Assessment Intake form are true to the best of my knowledge. I acknowledge that I fully understand the terms and provisions of this Waiver, Assumption of Risk and Agreement to Hold Harmless and that I am setting my hand hereto delivering the same freely and voluntarily and unconditionally. Cancellations with less than 72-hour notice may incur a Cancellation Fee of 25%.

Name of Dog(s) ——————————— M or F Breed(s) ———————————

Age ——————————— Color ———————————

Names of Clients (Please Print) ———————————————————

Signatures of Clients ———————————————————

Date ———————————————————

Your electronic signature and return of this assessment constitutes your agreement to the above clause of non-liability.

Copyright ©2022 Linda Michaels. With permission from *FAR Beyond Training*.

Veterinary Behavioral Report for Behavior Consultants

If you are working with a veterinarian who is referring clients to you, you may want to provide them with an update of your assessment, treatment, and future lesson plans for the referred dog. Here's an outline of what a report might include for your referring veterinarian.

1. **Background information**
   - Training history
2. **Description of the presenting problem**
   - Assessment tools
   - Functional assessment intake including bite incident reports
   - Specific body-area sensitivities assessment
3. **Behavior analysis**
   - What is driving the behavior?
   - What is maintaining the behavior?
4. **Intervention**
   - Fear desensitization
   - Desensitization to handling
   - Written materials provided to the client
   - Recommended reading
5. **Outcome**
6. **Prognosis**
   - Indications for co-operative care with the referring veterinarian
   - Future lessons planned

MANAGEMENT OF TRIGGERS AT HOME, AT THE VETERINARIAN, AND AT THE GROOMER

Be sure your dog is eating a biologically appropriate and nutritionally balanced diet, maintaining sufficient and friendly social interactions, mental stimulation, play and novelty enrichment on a daily basis. Refer to The Hierarchy of Dog Needs pyramid. Fear cannot be ruled out as a motivation when your dog displays offensive posturing and territoriality. Avoid exacerbating reactivity in your dog in the following ways:

- Remove guarding stations at windows, doorways, outdoor fencing, and gates. Guarding stations are areas where your dog can watch for, commonly known as "lying in wait," or anticipate people and/or dogs passing by. Eliminate guarding stations in your home and yard preventing aggression from developing and generalizing to other situations involving strangers and other dogs. All dogs are genetically hard-wired to guard the home, but some breeds are more predisposed to do so than others.

- Remove the opportunity for fence fighting aggression with neighbor dogs by using visual barriers, double-barriers, or only allowing your dog outdoors when the neighbor dogs are not outdoors.
- Remove the opportunity for aggression towards neighbors when you and your dog leave or enter your home by changing your schedule, using the back door, or otherwise rearranging the environment.
- Assess your dog's experience at the veterinarian and groomer as possible contributing factors to dog-dog reactivity. Get in-home mobile care or schedule the first appointment of the day and bring treats. (See Chapter 8, Gentle Veterinary and Grooming Care, for Desensitization Protocols.)
- Stop feeding from a bowl and use half of your dog's daily calorie ration for training alone. Use high value treats, such as healthy hot dogs, air-dried meat, cheese, boiled chicken, or whatever healthful food your dog values above all else.

Lunging, Barking, and Biting

In "Lunging, Barking, Biting, Oh My" the founder of the *Canine Research Studies* group, Rebekah Hudson, MPH, CVT, emphasizes the critical need for understanding thresholds and trigger stacking when using force-free methods for emotional and behavioral modification. Hudson stresses the importance of choosing the best leash-walking practice location which minimizes trigger stacking. Use muzzling desensitization for safety and peace of mind (Hudson, 2019b).

The amount of time it takes to see improvement in aggression varies depending on three things

- Severity of the reactivity
- Your dog's responsiveness to training
- The amount of time you devote to practicing emotional and behavioral modification protocols

Desensitization and Counterconditioning Techniques

For the aggressively behaving dog, desensitization and counterconditioning (D&CC) decreases aggression and increases acceptance of people, other dogs, moving objects, and novel situations. D&CC is the gold standard for aggression treatment.

The desensitization and counterconditioning process occurs when your dog is exposed to a fear, aggression, or hyperactive evoking object or situation at an intensity that does not evoke a response—staying below the threshold of reactivity. The goal of successfully implementing D&CC is to no longer observe a reaction to the trigger. After establishing a threshold of *no reaction*, decrease the distance or increase the intensity between the dog and the person, other dog, moving object, or situation in tiny steps, as long as your dog continues to remain calm. Over time move as close to the trigger as possible as long as your dog does not react. There is never a need to provoke a response: Indeed, you seek to prevent the opportunity to react with the old behavior. Avoid harsh methods or collars that cause pain as they may stop a behavior in the moment, but in truth they increase fear and anxiety, and may be the cause of aggression (Overall et al., 2006).

Identify Triggers. List your dog's triggers and reactions below. Examples of triggers are: Other dogs, strangers, children, men, skateboards, motorcycles, or the washer and dryer in your laundry room. Examples of behaviors and vocalizations are: Staring, then barking and lunging with hackles raised.

Successful Desensitization Depends Upon Faithful Adherence to Two Principal Rules:

Rule 1. Always stay below your dog's threshold of reaction. This means your dog does not have the emotional, behavioral reactions, or body language expressions listed in the chart below.

Rule 2. The intensity of the trigger is increased gradually in very small increments, and only if and when your dog does not have the reactions listed in the chart. Increasing the level of intensity often means decreasing the distance between your dog and the trigger, one small step at a time, while your dog continues remaining under threshold. Progress too quickly and you will see regression with your dog's reactions becoming worse, progress too slowly and you will see little improvement.

Two Types of Changes Occur with Desensitization and Counterconditioning

1. **Emotional Change**
   Classical Counterconditioning = Conditioned Emotional Response (CER), that is a new emotional reaction

2. **Behavioral Change**
   Operant Counterconditioning = Response Substitution, that is, learning a new behavior

Trigger	Behaviors and Vocalizations	Body Language
1.		
2.		
3.		

Use this chart to help you identify your dog's triggers and responses. Your dog's ability in acclimating gracefully to new or troubling stimuli will be facilitated by the positive, loving relationship you already have with your dog. If your dog cannot trust you, dispelling fears and calming over-reactivity may not be possible.

The Engage-Disengage Game, teaches the coping skill of self-interruption. The game reinforces new emotions and desirable behavior by teaching an alternate response. There are two levels: the first level reinforces the dog for engaging with the stimulus while the dog is under threshold, and the second level reinforces the dog for voluntarily turning away from the stimulus (Tong, 2020).

FRUSTRATION REACTIVITY

Frustration/hyperactivity reactivity, also known as over-enthusiasm results from allowing your dog to greet and interact with other dogs or people at will while your dog is over threshold. A strong reinforcement history is inadvertently established and continues driving the behavior.

Does your dog have the symptoms listed below? These are signs of frustration reactivity:

- **Hyperactive behavior.** Jumping up, pulling, grabbing leash, pacing on leash, lack of focus
- **Hyperactive body language.** Hyper-alert, nervous, fidgety
- **Hyperactive vocalizations.** Barking, whining, or excessive panting
- **Refusal to take treats** when aroused/excited

In the hyperactive dog, desensitization and counterconditioning decrease frustration and reactivity, and increase calmness and attentiveness.

Frustration reactivity distress occurs when your dog is not allowed to greet each dog or person on your path while moving further away increases rather than decreases your dog's frustration. With this type of reactivity, your dog wants you to *decrease* the distance rather than to increase distance from the other dog or person.

Establish the threshold at which your dog does not react by using a *rapid rate of reinforcement* with high value rewards when triggers appear. Pause—let your dog look at the other dog or person. Your dog will then look to you rather than fixating on the trigger if your distance is correct and your treats are high value to your dog. Next, begin decreasing the distance between your dog and the trigger slowly and incrementally as long as your dog stays under threshold. You may also toss treats in the opposite direction of an on-coming dog or person saying, "Find it."

REALISTIC EXPECTATIONS

Pet parents enjoy socializing with their dogs. They often and understandably want everyone to like their dog and they want their dog to like everyone including other dogs and strangers. Pet parents often feel it is a reflection on them personally if their dog is not friendly to other people and dogs. It is not. Stay safe and have fun with your dog!

Genetics, early socialization, or the lack of exposure during the critical sensitive period of social development, traumatic experiences, and health status, shape how your dog responds to people, with other dogs, moving objects such as bicycles, noises and to the environment as a whole. (See Chapter 9, Socialization, to learn how to socialize safely and effectively.)

A realistic goal may be taking your dog for a pleasant walk in the neighborhood to avoid barking and lunging incidents while you work on emotional and behavioral modification. Walks should be pleasant for both of you. If your dog shows signs of anxiety with "stranger dogs," it is all right to skip group activities and play at home instead. Use a chase lure-toy in the backyard, play up-the-stairs fetch, or place a hula-hoop in a doorway for indoor hurdles. Play *nose-games* and practice scent-work. Supervised playdates with carefully selected well-matched friends may be another alternative.

Love the dog you have. Consider the dog named Ricochet. From the moment she was born the training exercises and goal for Ricochet were to become a service dog. However, Ricochet did not complete the training because of her penchant for chasing birds. Ricochet found a new job—surfing, which made her a beloved surf dog fundraiser with a video gone viral on YouTube. Ricochet walked the red carpet to rave reviews at the American Humane Association Hero Dog Awards where she won the Emerging Hero Dog category in 2011 as a "rising star" (Fuoco, 2011).

HUMAN AGGRESSION TREATMENT

Human directed aggression is one of the most serious behavior problems a dog can develop. Aggression toward humans is a heart breaker for pet parents and often involves dogs that are otherwise perfectly delightful. There are many different types of human aggression that may be directed at people

- Territorial
- In-home with family members
- In-home with visitors
- On-leash walks
- Off-leash dog parks
- Resource guarding of food, beds, people, space, or other coveted objects

The good news is that aggression is typically context specific. This means if you change the situation or your location, the aggression is likely to decrease or disappear. (See Chapter 5, Management and Antecedent Modification.)

The "Red Zone" Dog Myth

A common myth is that dogs with aggression problems need harsh training methods and collar devices. Nothing could be further from the truth. The American Veterinary Society on Animal Behavior states in no uncertain terms (2021c), "Animals with challenging behavior disorders such as aggression should be treated with effective, compassionate, and humane methods of training, rather than with "a heavy hand". There are no exceptions to this standard." (p. 2.)

Dogs trained with the use of dominance methods are at risk for further deterioration. Academically credentialed experts in animal behavior believe dominance training and aversive collar devices are *a cause not a cure* for aggression. Aggressive dogs have already lost trust in humans if any person has hurt or threatened them. Trust needs to be slowly, carefully, and methodically reestablished. It is not an easy-fix regardless of what some "balance" trainers may tell you. If someone physically hurts or threatens a child, how likely is the child to trust people?

Training is a two-sided coin

- Stop doing the things that are making your dog worse
- Start doing the things that will make your dog better

DO NOT list for Family, Friends, and Visitors

There are some very simple but essential things to learn about what may trigger a bite because a dog feels threatened. It's surprising and disappointing how these interactions are often depicted in the mass media and misunderstood by pet parents, and many trainers. Every person who interacts with your dog should be abiding by the rules below:

- Do not allow anyone to behave threateningly or dominantly with your dog. This will heighten arousal, and is a **cause, not a cure**, for aggression.
- Do not hit, yell at, punish, or frighten a dog.
- Do not pet or touch any dog that you do not know well.
- Do not approach an aggressive dog. Your over-riding, primary goal should be to *stay safe*. If a dog is growling, barking, or lunging toward you, the dog is telling you to "Go Away!"
- Do not run away, yelp, or make sudden body movements. Back away slowly and calmly. The Be a Tree program has special suggestions for children to learn to stay safe (Doggone Safe, 2018).
- Do not stare or make direct eye contact with an aggressive dog. A direct stare is interpreted as a threat and a challenge.
- Do not pet a dog over the head as is common in our culture. A human body leaning over and above a dog with an arm reaching over the head may easily

be perceived as a threat and become a trigger to bite. Your face may be the closest and easiest place to bite. Alternatively, if a dog approaches you, if safe, calmly offer a fist at your side and allow the dog to sniff the fist. Then, if safe, pet the dog under the chin or on the breastplate with gentle strokes.

- Do not leave infants, toddlers, or young children alone with *any* dog for *any* amount of time, regardless of how friendly the dog may be otherwise.
- Do not hug or kiss a dog that is not your own.
- Do not attempt to move or stop a dog by pulling on the dog's collar or neck. Instead, call the dog to you, or toss a piece of food.
- Do not pet or touch a dog while the dog is eating food, chewing on a bone, or other item of value to the dog.
- Do not reach to remove food, toys, or other valued objects from your dog. If it is necessary to remove an object, *trade up* by offering an irresistible piece of food. (See this chapter, Resource Guarding, below.)
- Do not corner a dog to examine, give medication, clip nails, groom, or pet.
- Do not disturb a dog that is resting. Instead, call the dog over to you.

DOG-DOG AGGRESSION TREATMENT

Displays of aggression between members of the same species are common in animals. Conflicts over resources such as food, territory, mating privileges, and access to others, are well documented in the animal behavior scholarly literature. Rules of appropriate social behavior in dog society are quite different than in human society. Dog-dog aggression can be a dangerous problem for you, your dog, other dogs, and anyone who tries to break up a dog fight. We expect dogs to play-nice with new dogs in group situations and when out on neighborhood strolls. Reexamine your expectations and goals for your dog. Realistically, if your dog exhibits generalized dog-dog aggression, it is unlikely your dog will turn into a social butterfly, but with consistent training and management, you can make the world less stressful for both of you. The most common mistake pet parents and trainers make is rushing the process, causing setbacks. Your dog needs to learn to trust that you will not be walking into stressful or dangerous situations so there is no need to remain on high alert. Do not give up! Before you head off to the local dog park or dog beach there are two important questions to ask yourself: "Is it safe?" and "Is my dog really having fun?" (See Chapter 9, Dog Park Safety Tips and Chapter 3, Fair Play.)

Walks—Working Below the Threshold of Reactivity

Walks should be completely stress free, starting now. Much of the time you will keep moving during a walk, however, at times it is best to let your dog stop, sniff, and just relax on the walk. Remember to breathe deeply and do not let your nervousness "run down the leash" to your dog. Your dog will sense anxiety in a tight leash and in your voice. Talk or sing to your dog in a relaxed and confident manner. You may want to try a waist leash, so you are not tempted to pull or yank on the leash. Bouncing back and forth between happy-walking sniffaris, and barking and lunging is counterproductive.

Re-training Techniques and Protocols

- **Spider walks.** Let your dog know what to expect on walks in the immediate area surrounding your house first. Do not take long, meandering walks. Start with walking up to your corner and back home. Later, walk to the other corner and back to your dog's *home anchor.* It may take more than three weeks to slowly graduate to walking around the block or down two blocks depending on how well your dog can handle this task and how skilled you become at implementing the techniques. Do not rush it.
- **Increasing the distance.** Increase your distance from the other dog. Make a U-turn if necessary, and then walk in the opposite direction from the other dog.
- **Blocking.** Keep your dog below threshold and avoid over-stimulation by blocking your dog's access, view and/or sound of the trigger. Use cars, shrubs, or a neighbor's driveway, to visually block your dog's view of the other dog. If safe, use your body as a physical and visual barrier to block your dog's view of the other dog. Create audio barriers to block sound using your voice or soothing music. Your dog may be aroused by the sound of another dog's identification tags before your dog sees the other dog.
- **The *Open Bar/Closed Bar* technique.** Click/treat or say "Good" the instant a trigger appears. Make positive associations between your dog and the other

dog by hand feeding high value treats when the trigger appears. The goal is to make a very strong impression on your dog that *good things happen when another dog appears.* Say the word "Good" at the instant the stimulus appears and then follow with the treat. Provide treats every second (a high *rate of reinforcement*), then begin to extend the duration between treats to every 2–4 seconds when the trigger can be seen by your dog and your dog is not over threshold.

- **Getting attention.** Use name response, and "Let's Go" for U-turns or redirection. (See Chapter 16, Basic Skills).
- **Rewarding automatic eye-contact check-ins.** Reward with clicks/treats or with treats alone whenever your dog turns to you on a walk so that redirecting attention to you becomes your dog's new habit. Maintain the bond with your dog while walking.
- **Following walking.** Seek out another dog-friendly dog walking in your neighborhood as a training partner. Then, use the other dog as a trigger, but keep your dog's stress level under the threshold of reactivity. Cross the street if necessary and walk behind a friendly dog at a distance. Shorten the distance always staying under your dog's threshold of reactivity. Provide food rewards.
- **Parallel walking.** Now cross the street. Slowly and incrementally draw nearer to the dog across the street until you are walking parallel with the friendly dog. Provide food rewards.
- **Approach/retreat.** Use approach/retreat, or a zigzag approach which adds regular periods of relief from stress.
- **Use *throw downs* of treats.** At an under-threshold distance, drop treats onto the pavement, providing your dog a scavenging opportunity, which decreases stress in the presence of another dog.
- **Teach Settle Down.** Settle down may be highly effective for desensitization and counterconditioning when teaching a new emotional and behavioral modification skill in the face of triggers such as other dogs or wildlife. Start at a distance below the threshold of reactivity and systematically close the distance to the trigger as long as your dog remains under the threshold of reactivity.

How to Break Up a Dogfight

A *bite redirect* onto a handler is common when people interfere with a dog fight. Avoid taking any action that may cause the dogs to redirect their aggression onto you. Understand the risks and weigh your odds when breaking up a dog fight.

- Have an exit strategy well before you try to break up a dog fight
- Teach a lightning recall and *proactively* intervene with recall before a fight starts
- Do *not* grab a dog by the collar

- Do not put your hands or other body parts near dogs that are fighting
- Do not use the wheelbarrow technique unless you are an expert bite specialist
- Pour a soda, preferably one with fizz, over the dogs' heads
- Spray water from a spray bottle for breaking up dogfights
- Douse with water to separate dogs
- Use a water hose full force to separate dogs
- Use an air horn for breaking up dog fights only
- Use an air corrector for breaking up dog fights only
- Throw a thick blanket, sweatshirt, coat or towel over the instigating dog
- When encountering loose strays on walks, use a pop-up umbrella to frighten the dog away, and to create some space for you and your dog to escape
- Toss a spray of treats just over the stray dog's head to give you and your dog time to escape
- If safe, lift small dogs completely off the ground and immediately out of reach such as on top of a vehicle
- At home, for aggression between dogs, ring the doorbell if this does not typically increase aggression between the dogs
- Have some pots and pans on hand and loudly clang them together
- Use a baby gate and press down firmly between the dogs' muzzles
- Use an object, such as a broom handle to pry dogs apart, if safe
- For deaf dogs, stomp on the floor
- Wear a t-shirt for prevention such as one that says, "Leash your dog, owner bites!"

Bites

If your dog has bit another dog or has been in a number of dog fights, find a force-free certified behavior consultant with expertise in aggression for help in changing your dog's underlying drives, and behaviors. A complete intake evaluation will help in developing a plan of treatment based upon your dog's history. Dog bites are complex problems, and each case requires an individual approach.

SIBLING RIVALRY—MULTI-DOGS HOUSEHOLD AGGRESSION TREATMENT

One of the most difficult situations that trainers and pet parents face is sibling rivalry between your home dogs or between genetically related siblings. First, make certain both dogs' needs are being met as outlined in the Hierarchy of Dog Needs pyramid. Spend time alone with each dog individually, so bonding occurs early in the relationship, and you are better able to manage them when they are together. Medical, nutritional, security, exercise, and emotional needs must be attended to before rivalry between your dogs is likely to show any significant improvement. For minor incidents with dogs who have otherwise good social skills with each other, let them work out non-violent differences without your intervention. If your dogs scuffle a bit, give them a chance to calm down by securely separating them. Then remove the triggers and release them to play together again supervising closely and intervening if necessary.

Serious cases of sibling rivalry can be among the hardest to treat. However, steps can be taken to prevent sibling rivalry from developing from the start. If sibling rivalry is addressed early, these cases may have surprisingly good outcomes.

Prevention and Management

Prevention and management are gravely underestimated as first-line methods to resolve behavioral problems and/or to prevent problems from arising entirely. Many behavioral problems are highly predictable when dogs are put into situations where reactivity is the only perceived option from the dog's perspective. Here are some ways you can be proactive about aggression:

- Eliminate the stressors (Miller, 2010/2020).
- Rearrange the antecedents. (See Chapter 5, Force-free Training Needs.)
- Practice desensitization and counterconditioning protocols.
- Find activities your dogs can safely enjoy together, such as sniff-filled walks or car rides while separated.
- Proactively protect your smaller, weaker dog, even if your smaller dog is the instigator.
- Teach both the instigator dog and the other dog a reliable recall so that you can call them to you if you sense trouble brewing.
- Make certain your dogs have a place of sanctuary in the home where others will not intrude in case of high tension or altercations.

Set Your Dogs up for Success by Avoiding These Tense Conditions

- Feed your dogs separately to avoid competition, food swapping, and stress during feeding.
- Remove all items either one of the dogs guard.
- Keep dogs separated by creating both physical and visual barriers such as: Baby gates, separate rooms, tethers, or rotating one dog indoors and one dog outdoors.
- Later, switch their locations.
- Make certain the dogs are getting plenty of exercise.

Eliminating Stressors

The first step in diffusing sibling rivalry is identifying each of your dogs' stressors and eliminating as many as possible. Avoid *trigger stacking* your dogs' stressors which can lead to fights over resources. Identify the resource, context, and the trigger for each threat display, such as

- Food or treats, including crumbs left on the floor
- Chew items, including high value, or low-value guarded items
- Squeaky or other toys
- Locations, including the bedroom, beds, couches, and narrow hallways
- Situations, including over-arousal at greetings
- People

The No Jealousy Game

Start by sitting in the middle with each dog sitting on either side of you. Next, move back and forth between your dogs. The dogs will learn you always return to them, but they have to patiently wait their turn. Waiting their turn serves to desensitize and countercondition, that is, to change the emotional reaction to each other. With serious cases of sibling rivalry aggression, you will need three people, or to securely tether each dog where they cannot reach each other or you, and move back and forth between them.

1. Quickly but calmly, turn toward Dog A. Call Dog A's name, walk to Dog A and treat. Then return to center.
2. Quickly, but calmly, turn toward Dog B. Call Dog B's name, walk to Dog B and treat. Then return to center.
3. Turn more slowly, extending the duration incrementally between trials.
4. Repeat until both dogs relax, patiently waiting their "turn."
5. If and when safe, decrease the distance between the dogs one small step at a time until you can safely have them calmly sitting on either side of you.
6. If either dog tries to overstep the boundary, stop instantly, and begin from the start with that trial.
7. Do not rush this process. It may take weeks of practice.
8. If your attention or proximity to you has been a trigger, if and when safe, after polishing the above method, have your dogs lie on either side of you and pet them both.

Open Bar/Closed Bar

This is a different iteration of open bar/closed bar elucidated in the dog-dog aggression section. However, with sibling rivalry you carefully control the timing and exposure of the dogs to each other. Ideally, you will have two handlers for this exercise. Alternatively, put one dog securely behind a baby-gate and toss food to that dog while you feed the dog you are handling.

1. Establish a *threshold distance* where the dogs are aware of each other but not aroused or fearful.
2. Keep Dog A and handler A stationary, while Dog B is brought out by Handler B from behind a visual blocker, such as from another room or around a corner.
3. The instant the dogs notice each other, begin a rapid rate of reinforcement, feeding both of them bits of high value food for several seconds until Dog B is removed back behind the visual barrier. Start with short periods of exposure.
4. Continue repeating these steps until each dog looks at the respective handler for food at the appearance of the other dog, signaling a change in Emotion—a *Conditioned Emotional Response* (CER) (Miller, 2017a).
5. Increase the length of time the dogs are exposed to each other using the same reinforcement protocol.
6. Increase the level of distractions by having Dog B become more animated with friendly arousal, performing Sits, Downs, etc., in front of Dog A (stationary dog), using the same reinforcement protocol.
7. Later, have the dogs switch roles with Dog B and the Handler B stationary, bringing Dog A in with Handler A, using the same reinforcement protocol.
8. Now, begin to decrease the distance between the two dogs by incremental baby steps as long as they both remain under the threshold of reactivity until they can comfortably remain within 6 feet of each other.

If there was a serious fight that resulted in physical injury and/or one dog is much larger and/or stronger than the other, permanent separation or rehoming may be your only answer.

RESOURCE GUARDING

We all guard resources. Resource guarding is in part what motivates people to build and live inside of houses, and why we lock our doors: We do not let others take our belongings. We are all resource guarders evolutionarily by nature. Resource guarding is genetically adaptive to survival but is more pronounced in dogs.

When you give your dog a meal or a bone, your dog will not understand that you may need to remove it, perhaps for their own safety. Your dog cannot understand that you purchased and provided the meal and the bone and now you want it back. Your dog simply does not have the cognitive ability for processing complex thoughts on this level. Once you give your dog food or items your dog highly values, your dog considers it to be dog property. Dogs may guard food, bully sticks, bones, toys, balls, people, beds, locations, crates, shoes, toilet paper, and other miscellaneous items they find of value for one reason or another.

For dogs that guard items from humans, a program of carefully planned and executed desensitization and counterconditioning is the gold standard for treatment. The trainer and pet parent must always put safety first! Treatment begins with a neutral object presented at an intensity where your dog does not display *any* distress or reactive behavior, including body language. Distance is closed, bit-by-bit, incrementally, over the course of treatment, as long as the dog remains under the threshold of reactivity and there are no indications of stress or reactivity. Various objects are used - slowly graduating to the typically guarded item, person, or location. In the classic trade favorite, *Mine! A Practical Guide to Resource Guarding in Dogs*, author, Jean Donaldson, details step-by-step meticulous hierarchical plans addressing common types of resource guarding, and the variables affecting the intensity of guarding (Donaldson, 2002.) The course of treatment may be many weeks and should be undertaken with the guidance and under the close supervision of a qualified force-free emotional and behavioral consultant who specializes in resource guarding.

Resource Guarding Between Dogs

Resource guarding between dogs is a different type of problem. Dogs are genetically hard-wired to prevent others of their species from stealing their valuable resources. The easiest and best answer is management. Remove the guarded object and provide close supervision while practicing a proactive lightning recall. Dogs may need to be separated by barriers (Miller, 2002/2017b). (See this chapter, Sibling Rivalry.)

Handfeeding

One rarely mentioned but very important conditioning effect of force-free training is the *pairing* of your hand with receiving high value food. This pairing develops trust that your hand always delivers food, but never takes food away.

Food Bowls

Make your approach to the food bowl something your dog finds not only non-threatening, but also very positive. Your approach toward the bowl means more, not less food for your dog, and higher value food.

For puppies or dogs who do *not* already guard bowls

- Sit on the couch with your dog on one side and a bowl full of food on the other side. Hand-feed your puppy or dog, piece by piece, from the bowl.
- Start with the empty food bowl in its normal location. Begin the process of desensitization by walking over and dropping one piece of food into the empty bowl as you pass by. This is how your dog learns to trust people when they are coming near the food bowl.
- Then, put some *low value* food in the bowl, and as your dog is eating, walk by and drop a *higher value* bit of food into your dog's bowl. For example, if your dog is eating kibble, walk by and drop a piece of chicken into the bowl.

- *If safe,* slowly, and carefully pair your hand reaching toward the food bowl to deliver food. Never let your dog associate your hand with taking away a valuable item or food bowl.

Trade Up, and Drop

Trading Up

One of the standard preventive resource guarding best practices is to *trade up* with your dog if your dog is already in possession of something you need to retrieve for safety reasons, or an item that does not belong to your dog. Be certain the value of the new food or item for trade is of higher value to your dog than the item your dog is guarding—not just of higher value in your opinion!

For example, trade your dog a piece of hot dog for a tennis ball if your dog loves hot dogs more than tennis balls *and* decisively wants to trade for it. Alternatively, trade your dog a different tennis ball for the tennis ball you would like your dog to drop. Toss treats away from your dog and away from the item in possession, so your dog is walking in the opposite direction with the rear end (not the head) facing you while you safely remove an item that may be dangerous to your dog, such as a pill bottle.

Drop

Teach your dog to drop what is in the mouth by giving the verbal cue "Drop" and then tossing treats away from your dog repeatedly in practice sessions. Very slowly, increase the value of the item you ask your dog to drop for a high value treat.

Dog Property Laws

"Dog Property Laws" (Anonymous) are quite different than human property laws. If you are not aware of these dog laws, take heed. Framed in comedy here, they are funny yet uncannily true.

- If I like it, it's mine.
- If you have something and put it down, that makes it mine.
- If it's in my mouth, it's mine—please don't forget that.
- If I can take it from you, it's mine.
- If it looks remotely like mine, it's mine.
- If I saw it first . . . or last, it's mine.
- If I had it a while ago, it's mine.
- If I chew something up, all the pieces are mine.
- If I don't want it, it's yours—unless,
- I want it back, then it's mine!

If you tried several force-free dog behavior professionals and consistently followed the steps they suggested regarding aggression but are not seeing results, then re-homing your dog may be an option if it can be done safely and responsibly. Please be aware, most shelters and rescues will not take a dog with a bite history. A personal friend or force-free trainer who understands your dog's history may be a possibility but be aware that finding someone suitable may require a great deal of dedicated effort. Always address a problem with aggression at the *first sign* of trouble, rather than waiting to treat a dog and a family in crisis where conditions have already escalated and seriously worsened.

18

ALLERGIES

ALLERGIES IN DOGS SYMPTOMS

EARS

SYMPTOMS: BAD ODOR, WAXY DISCHARGE, YEAST INFECTIONS

BEHAVIOR: SCRATCHING, RUBBING, SHAKING HEAD

FACE

SYMPTOMS: RED, HAIR LOSS AROUND EARS OR MUZZLE, SWOLLEN

BEHAVIOR: LOTS OF SCRATCHING, RUBBING FACE WITH PAWS, SNEEZING

SKIN

SYMPTOMS: REDNESS, BAD ODOR, HAIR LOSS, SCALY SKIN, DRY, IRRITATED

BEHAVIOR: SCRATCHING, LICKING, TREMBLING, RUBBING ON OBJECTS

HAIRCOAT

SYMPTOMS: REDNESS, BARE SPOTS, BAD ODOR, DISCOLORED FROM LICKING OR SORES

BEHAVIOR: LICKING BODY, SCRATCHING, RUBBING ON FURNITURE

PAWS

SYMPTOMS: DISCOLORATION, INFLAMED, HOT SPOTS, DRY SKIN, RED OR BROWN BETWEEN TOES

BEHAVIOR: CHEWING AND LICKING

I n addition to whatever your trusted veterinarian may suggest, taking action with management and behavior will help your dog get through the allergy season with less stress and injury. Confer with your integrative practice veterinarian for the best medical care from both standard allopathic and more wholistic-oriented treatments. An allergy-sensitive dog often develops more than one allergy. Allergic reactions are immune system regulated resulting in itchy skin in some pets and vomiting and diarrhea in others.

Bathe your dog weekly with a gentle hypoallergenic dog shampoo, leave-in conditioners, and cool rinses. Brushing your dog's coat daily distributes natural oils that relieve itching. Avoid air fresheners and diffusers. Keeping your dog busy avoids fixation on scratching the itch! Learn the art of stuffing food enrichment toys. You can find recipes and stuffing instructions online.

There are three known common causes of allergies—the environment, fleas, and diet. Allergy to fleas and allergens in the environment are much more common in dogs than food allergies, but all have similar symptoms.

Environmental Allergens

The most common season for allergies is spring, or at the first sign of winter. When exactly do the symptoms begin with your dog? Monitor the episodes. Keep a record for your reference.

In a fair number of cases there is a hereditary factor, such as a predisposition to atopic disease. Atopic Disease (AD) is analogous to hay fever in humans triggered by pollen, mold spores, dust, and dust mite droppings. Dogs may be exposed through breathing (inhaling) or through the skin. Determine whether other dogs in the litter have atopic disease triggered by environmental factors. Before the age of three, 75% of dogs with atopic disease show symptoms.

This etiology most often affects the feet, armpits, face, groin, tummy, and ears. Pay special attention to the inside the ears. Rubbing the face against furniture is often misinterpreted as an annoyance behavior rather than an attempt to relieve the discomfort of an allergy-related medical condition.

Reducing Exposure

Put some of these preventive and protective techniques to work during your dog's allergy season. Whether you can specifically identify the allergen or not, limit possible exposure as much as possible. Here are some things you can do to help your dog avoid and heal from itching:

- Create a new space for your dog. Use an alternate elimination area, such as the front patio: Create a Doggy Enrichment Land dog zone that your dog prefers, getting some distance from the inhaled pollen and the pollen on the ground that is picked up on your dog's paws and coat. Install a grassy area to pee and poop or train your dog to eliminate on synthetic grass that you can spray with a hose to clean.
- Avoid going outdoors with your dog during times of high pollen, such as at dawn and dusk.

- Limit outdoor time during peak allergy seasons. Check the pollen forecast online. Keep your dog indoors on high pollen days.
- Your dog's head should not be out the window when riding in the car.
- Use dehumidifiers to help control mold and mites.
- Rinse paws with water or clean the paws with baby wipes each time after your dog comes indoors so your dog does not lick the paws and inhale allergens or track allergens throughout the home.
- Keep your floors as clean as possible. Use organic/hypo-allergenic cleaning products only.
- Have your dog wear socks or boots when outdoors. Remove them at the door before coming inside.
- Wipe your dog's coat with a damp cloth to remove the airborne allergens after going outdoors.
- Install air-conditioning and/or air filtration systems, to avoid reintroducing allergens back into your environment. Use a high efficiency particulate air (HEPA) filter.

FLEAS

Dogs with flea allergy dermatitis (FAD) are hypersensitive to flea saliva. However, a dog need not be invested with fleas to cause an allergic reaction. A single fleabite can cause itching for days. Here's how you can help protect your dog:

- Wash all dog beds, dog bed covers, and blankets including the couch blanket with a hypoallergenic detergent weekly.
- The heat of the clothes dryer will kill fleas at all life stages.
- Dust and vacuum often but *not* with your dog in the room. According to Dr. Patrick Mahaney in PetMD (2012, July 3), keep your home as flea-free as possible by vacuuming rugs, upholstery, and car interiors every seven days. Throw out the vacuum bag right away, disposing of it outside of the home in a sealed bag or container.
- Reduce the ability for outdoor creatures such as stray cats, rats, and raccoons to enter your yard. Keep windows and doors closed and prevent your dog from going to outdoor areas that may possibly be flea infested.
- Protect your dog against contact with dogs who may be flea carriers.

DIET

Be certain your dog is on a nutritionally balanced, biologically appropriate, premium diet to keep the immune system strong. Poor quality or biologically inappropriate food to which your dog has become sensitized is also a possible cause of allergic reactions.

- Avoid additives, coloring, and preservatives.
- Try a dietary *elimination trial* with one source of novel protein and one complex carbohydrate vegetable such as potato, plus the necessary fats, vitamins, and minerals. Choose a specifically named meat such as duck or venison, that your dog has not eaten previously or proteins that are hydrolyzed. Try duck and sweet potato, for example for at least a month. Whatever you feed, be certain that it is part of a nutritionally balanced diet.
- Most dogs are allergic to an animal protein, whereas grains are an uncommon cause of food allergies, contrary to some pet food industry promotions (Cummings Veterinary Medical Center Tufts, Clinical Nutrition Service, 2017).
- Try Balance IT® from Davis Veterinary Consulting, the guide for nutritionally balanced recipes for home cooked meals developed by a board-certified veterinary nutritionist (2004–2020).
- Include farm raised salmon or an Omega 3 supplement.
- Include probiotics.
- Check out *The Holistic Health Guide* by Dr. Doug Knueven, DVM, and sought-after speaker at veterinary conferences (2008). This book is one of the best resources on holistic health in the field. See Chapter 1, Proper Nutrition, for more information.

PREVENTING INFECTION

If the skin has been rubbed raw with sores, help prevent bacteria from causing infection by:

- Cleansing wounds with a hypoallergenic soap, made for dogs, and warm water.
- Applying an anti-bacterial ointment.
- Limiting activity if sores are on the pads of the paws.
- Having the nails clipped short and smooth so your dog causes minimal damage if scratching. Consider using nail protectors if your dog can be conditioned to tolerate them.
- Applying a bitter apple spray or gel that does not burn to prevent licking of the wounds. Test first on your own wound.
- If necessary, duct tape socks or booties so they fit snugly, but *not* to your dog's fur or skin.
- Make sure all wounds can breathe. Use mesh-type protective wear.

19

BARKING, BARKING, BARKING

Does your dog bark while running in circles, bay at the moon, bark at bugs, or scare your visitors out of their boots? Dogs do not know the difference between welcomed guests and unwelcomed intruders for the most part. Dogs are genetically hard-wired for guarding your home. Barking is as natural a vocalization for dogs as speaking is for people. From your dog's point of view, barking is happening for a reason, a very good reason. Look at the context to understand why your dog is barking. Basic barking is normal, but incessant barking indicates an unhappy dog. Get a veterinary wellness check and rule out a possible medical cause for your dog's barking.

Calming your emotionally aroused dog with food does not "reward" barking. It is not the same as operantly teaching "Speak!" Rather, you are calming the underlying emotional state that is causing your dog to bark.

WHY DOGS BARK

Barking is one of your dog's only means of communicating with you and the world, so please pay attention. There are many different motivations that may be driving or triggering the barking.

Your dog has different types of barks:

- **Alarm barks** repel real or perceived intruders, that is, territorial protective barking
- **Request/Attention barks** ask something of you, i.e., a request to get needs met, such as hunger, thirst, exercise, comfort, or security
- **Boredom barks** occur when your dog needs something to do. If you do not provide something engaging for a dog to do, barking draws attention to the lack of stimulation and frustration
- **Cognitive deficit barks** are the result of cognitive slippage or dementia often seen in senior dogs
- **Medical illness barks** are the result of pain, organic disease, parasites, allergies, or arthritis
- **Loneliness, isolation barks** indicate the natural and pleading need for interaction on a regular and frequent basis
- **Separation anxiety barks** occur when your dog experiences separation or abandonment distress. (See Chapter 22, Separation Anxiety.)
- **Aggressive barks** arise from a perceived threat, fear, or frustration. Do not ignore this. (See Chapter 17, Aggression.)
- **Play barks** express joy. Not a problem!

HOW TO DECREASE BARKING

To decrease barking, first identify why your dog is barking. Then, address each trigger separately. If you have a multiple-dog household there is generally a ringleader instigator while the other dogs will often chime in. Starting with the instigator, train each dog separately. Bring peace and quiet to your home and follow these non-aversive training tips:

- Remove the trigger through environmental management.
- Decrease the intensity of the trigger. (See Chapter 5, Antecedent Modification.)
- Teach your dog to do something other than bark when triggered. (See Chapter 5, Differential Reinforcement.)

- Decrease your dog's sensitivity to the trigger to decrease the frequency and intensity of barking. (See Chapters 5 and 17, Classical and Counterconditioning and Desensitization.)
- Provide enrichment such as food delivery toys, snuffle mats, and alternate activities such as a sensory garden, scent games, and varied exercise. Include your dog when running errands. (See Chapter 10, Enrichment and Grazing Games.)
- Hire a force-free dog walker to break up your dog's day with natural activities your dog enjoys for stress relief.

Alarm Barking

A dog who is perpetually "on patrol" experiences continual chronic stress and anxiety. Dogs should be able to fully relax in their own home and yard.

- Have visitors carry treats and/or mount a treat bag on your outside doorknob that reads, "Please feed the animals."
- Throw treats out into the backyard when the doorbell rings or someone knocks on the door, so your dog focuses on scavenging food rather than on barking.
- Alternatively, put your dog in a quiet location with a chew item until your dog calms down.
- Acknowledge the communication. For example, say, "Thank you. All is well."
- If you are home, redirect your dog to another location. For example, call your dog to you and reward.
- Give your dog plenty of exercise to relieve pent-up energy and stress.
- Desensitize your dog so the doorbell no longer means "Scary stranger is here," but proclaims, "Treat-friend is here!" You may record the sound of the doorbell, starting the process at a very low volume with high value treats. Pair the trigger with treats in quick succession: Bell/treat, bell/treat, bell/treat, bell/treat.
- Give treats for a "Down/Wait" in your dog's bed.
- If your dog stalks, sits, or lies in wait for dogs or people passing by your home, or spies on squirrels out in the yard, rearrange and manage your dog's location using a visual blocker removing the guarding opportunities.
- Provide your dog with novel stimuli, such as a food toy, to replace guarding activities.
- For recurring outdoor noises near your home, try an audio blocker such as background television. Select a happy channel, such as the cooking or shopping channel where nothing stress-inducing is aired. Alternatively, turn on the stereo or download the sound of the ocean or a fan. Recent research indicates dogs prefer reggae and soft rock music.

Request/Attention Barking

It is highly distressing to your dog if you do not respond in a timely manner to meet your dog's real needs. How would you feel if you could not get your basic needs met on your own? First, ask yourself, "What is it that my dog wants?" Is your dog barking to alert you to a need or a reasonable request that requires your attention?

- Figure out the underlying cause of the barking and how to make both of you happy.
- Provide alternative activities, if appropriate, redirecting and rewarding desirable behavior.
- Reward your dog for calm and well-mannered behavior.
- If your dog's request is unreasonable or evolves into annoyance-type barking, redirect the behavior, or as a last resort, turn and walk away.
- One of the easiest things you can do to decrease barking frustration caused by hunger is to feed your dog *before* you eat—regardless of what you may have otherwise been told.

WHAT *NOT* TO DO

Citronella bark collars, electric bark collars, debarking surgery, spray bottles, shaking cans of marbles near delicate ear structures, or shouting, have undesirable and often serious medical and emotional effects. The use of these items is punitive. Never punish your dog for growling or barking because the next time your dog may forego the bark and just bite. You want your dog to calm down, not *shut down*, or teeter on the brink of aggression.

Punishment may backfire and have these unwanted effects

- Aggression
- Fearfulness
- Damage to the relationship between you and your dog
- A strengthened negative association/relationship with whatever or whoever your dog is barking about
- Loss of hearing

20

DOGS AND BABIES

Are you planning to bring a puppy or new dog into a family with an infant or toddler? Are you concerned about protecting your newborn but still want one big, happy family? Many dogs accept a new baby into the home without any problems; however, some do not, and some need a lot of help. This chapter is designed to help you prevent common problems and encourage you to be well-prepared to care for both dog and baby.

As responsible baby and pet parents, it is your job to protect your baby from your dog, and to protect your dog from your baby. Safety first is the cardinal rule.

Many online posts show appallingly unsafe interactions between babies, young children, and the family dog. Children are the group most frequently bitten by dogs, and most often those bites are from the family dog or a well-known dog. Take the relationship between your child and your dog very seriously. Ultra-close supervision is the responsibility of the parents, not the responsibility of the dog or the toddler. Keep your child and your dog safe and prevent harassment or teasing of your dog by your naturally curious child. It is up to you, your child's parent, and your dog's pet parent, to draw clear physical boundaries and make the rules.

The relationship between your baby and your dog will change while each of them grow through their respective developmental stages. Dogs react differently to children at each stage of the dog's development, and at each stage of the child's development, and vice versa. Most parents see a change in the dog's behavior when the child begins to crawl, toddle, walk, and then run.

Get a veterinary wellness exam and rule out a possible medical condition, disease, or pain that may be an underlying cause of unwanted behavior. Be sure to update titer testing or vaccinations for your dog.

Developmental Stages in Children

Consider the age of your child before adopting or bringing a dog into your home. The pioneering psychologist, Jean Piaget, in his *Construction of Reality of the Child* (Piaget, 1954) described the stages of cognitive development in children exploring the process of thinking and intellectual development at each stage. Research on a child's normal brain development indicates that it is not until approximately the age of five that a child can process the information that the dog can hurt them, and that they can hurt the dog. Ideally, parents ought to add a dog to the family after children have reached the age of five years old. This may not fit your plan or situation, but keep these ideas in mind:

1. Younger children simply do not have the cognitive ability to understand that a dog can bite. Toddlers cannot understand how a bite would hurt and affect their own lives, how it would affect other family members, and certainly not what it could mean for the dog's life.
2. Toddlers cannot understand that they can hurt and/or frighten a dog. A child does not have the ability to understand the difference between a dog and a moving plush toy, that is, your child does not know your dog experiences fear, feels pain, and can be hurt.

Achieve safety and harmony for both your child and your dog through proper preparation and careful management until your child is old enough for a positive and safe relationship with your dog. By the time you bring your baby home, you want your dog to be

- Highly desensitized
- Well-trained
- Healthy

Learn to Read Your Dog's Body Language

Become a dog body language reading expert. You will know right away if your dog is experiencing stress around the baby. Learn the difference between how your dog looks when happy versus how your dog looks when stressed. Also, be on watch for either avoidance of, or fixation on, the baby. Listen for vocalizations of distress or warning signals, such as a growl or whining. These are your dog's only way of "speaking" to you. (See Chapter 11, Dog Body Language.)

Never Leave a Baby or Child Alone with a Dog

Make certain the dog NEVER has access to the baby without an adult present. *No dog* should be trusted with a small child . . . and *no small child* should be trusted with a dog! Any dog will bite if sufficiently provoked and any child can put herself or himself in danger by intentionally—or unintentionally—grabbing, falling, poking, hugging, or being otherwise overly enthusiastic. Your dog may not recognize your newborn as a member of the family. Keep your baby's sleeping quarters safe by making the inside of the nursery off-limits to your dog. Secure it.

WHEN YOU BECOME PREGNANT

Prepare your dog months in advance for the arrival of a baby into the home. Providing plenty of attention through reward-based training prevents additional stress and helps your dog be a "good dog" around the baby. Dogs love routines and your dog will thank you for providing some new routines to follow. Here are some guidelines to help you prevent predictable problems:

- **Transitioning.** Foster independence in your dog by slowly transitioning the primary dog care-taking duties to another family member long before you bring the baby home. Start practicing new routines for your dog. Make the arrival of the baby as seamless as possible from your dog's point of view. Alter routines before the baby comes home and give your dog time to learn and accept the new lifestyle.

- **Personality and temperament profile assessment.** What is your dog's temperament and history? Assess your dog's behavior toward infants, toddlers, strangers, and reactions to novel items, smells, and situations. Does your dog have small-animal predatory tendencies, resource-guarding behaviors, startle phobia, or fear responses? If so, call a professional for an assessment and treatment. Do not play aggressive games with your dog.
- **Management.** Create a safe sanctuary that is, a Doggy Enrichment Land *dog zone* for your dog. Separately, create a safe sanctuary *baby zone* and enriched environment for your child. For older children, put painter's tape around the dog's bed or crate to draw the boundary line. Ask the children not to cross that line. It is amazing how kids follow rules, and how they often they are willing to "correct" their siblings and their parents if a parent break the rules!

Enclosed gated areas keep the dog and your defenseless baby separated and safe, so both you and your dog can relax. Your dog needs a safe place to relax away from your child as well. Always keep your dog either with you or in a secured dog zone. Use a playpen to contain toddlers and allow your dog to roam free, if safe.

Here are some essential elements to start practicing in your dog and baby plan as soon as possible:

- *Habituate* **and desensitize your dog to new baby stimuli before you bring your baby home.** Acclimate your dog to the incoming new baby sounds, gadgets, smells, and various baby routines by role-playing activities such as diaper changing, and stroller walks with a doll before you bring your baby home. Everything associated with the baby should become the new normal routines, as opposed to sudden or anxiety-provoking novel experiences. Check out "Baby Sounds for Pets, Dogs, Cats and Other Animals", a recording of crying, grunting, bathing, happy squealing, snoring, and giggling baby sounds from Dr. Lewis Kirkham (2014).

- **Socialization.** After taking the desensitization steps above, and under close and careful supervision invite close friends with infants to visit. This will slowly and safely acclimate your dog to the presence of babies in the home. Take your people-friendly dog to observe children at play from a distance. Reward your dog with treats and soft praise for remaining calm while in the presence of small children. Your dog will develop positive associations with babies.
- **Training basic manners and skills.** Address training and behavior issues *before* the baby arrives. Practice using voice instructions with your dog to keep your hands free to care for your baby. Train-out the behaviors you do not want. You do not need to teach your dog a great many behaviors. Numerous instructions may be confusing to your dog. Focus on training both basic manners and impulse management in a distraction-free environment for optimal results. Your dog should know the following behaviors reliably well

  A. Name Response
  B. Sit
  C. Down
  D. Wait/Stay
  E. Come
  F. Calm Leash-walking

- **Evaluate the nutritional needs of your dog.** Diet affects behavior. Feed your dog a truly healthful, biologically appropriate nutritionally balanced diet. (See Chapter 1, Proper Nutrition.)

BRINGING BABY HOME

Exercise

Provide your dog with sufficient aerobic, non-aerobic and mental exercise. Try to provide running, swimming, or doggy playdates at least twice a week for active dogs. Hire a force-free dog walker if your dog needs more exercise, fun, or socializing more than you can now comfortably provide.

Introduce Your Dog to Your Baby Slowly and Gradually

Help your dog experience the arrival of the baby as a good thing. Share your attention with the dog when the baby is present. This will endear your baby to your dog and prevent "sibling" rivalry. Make the arrival of the baby to your home a *neutral event*. When coming home from the hospital, have a parent come into the house alone and calmly greet the dog first. Then put your dog on leash and ask for a "Sit" or a "Down." Have a parent come into the home with the baby and either retreat to another room and save introductions for later, or if your dog looks relaxed, walk your dog calmly and slowly toward the baby and let your dog sniff your baby's toes—not your baby's face. Ideally, your dog will not be overly interested in the baby in the future, and will treat your baby with relative indifference, which is best at this stage. You don't want your baby to be intently or primarily interested in the dog either. Do not encourage your baby's fixation on the dog but redirect attention away from the dog for the most part.

When to Seek Professional Help

Generally, dogs that display aggressive behaviors are not appropriate for families with small children. These problems need IMMEDIATE intervention. Seek professional help anytime you have concerns about

- Interactions between your dog and your child
- Interactions between your dog and other family members
- Growling or other displays of aggression
- Guarding behaviors of items or people
- Sudden changes in your dog's behavior
- Conflict between dogs in the home

Attend a Dogs and Babies seminar or arrange for a private consultation in your home with a local force-free behavior consultant who specializes in dogs and babies. Renowned baby and dog specialist, Colleen Pelar's, *Living with Kids and Dogs* (2012) may be found online. Her website is filled with helpful articles, an advice column and more. Dr. Sophia Yin published a wonderful children's picture-book booklet called, *How to Greet a Dog,* (Yin, 2011). Another wonderful resource is Family Paws Parent Education with founder Jennifer Shryock (2018). The American Veterinary Medical Association has a must-read online brochure, "Dog Bite Prevention" (n.d.).

21

FEAR

If you are wondering why your dog is not more playful with you, with other people, or with other dogs, do not be dismayed. Most dogs can learn to be less fearful and become playful and affectionate with desensitization and counterconditioning training the gold standard of treatment for fearful dogs. Sometimes we need to train a water-shy Labrador to swim. Be realistic about your expectations for your dog and seek to meet your dog's needs as the priority, not only your own, and remember in real life, classic celebrity-dog Lassie was a group of actor-dogs, each with specific, limited skills, raised by an animal trainer. Chances are, you have a real dog—who may well be suffering.

Misused equipment, intimidation or restraint may cause a condition called *tonic immobility*, wherein *fear is mistaken and mislabeled* as "good behavior." Tonic immobility is a condition of unresponsiveness occurring during significant stress. Tonic immobility may also occur at a training facility, lesson, or class, at home, or in any situation where a pet is frightened. Charging ahead to get a frightening task "over with" such as grooming or a veterinary visit can easily backfire, resulting in fear, aggression, anxiety, escape/avoidance behavior, or tonic immobility. (See Chapter 11, Flooding and Tonic Immobility.)

Use desensitization and counterconditioning techniques. Desensitization is an effective behavioral treatment that decreases your dog's fearful reaction to things your dog currently finds disturbing. The goal of desensitization is for your dog to maintain a level of calm acceptance in the face of people, other dogs, moving objects, or situations that previously or currently upset your dog.

Assessment

These are indications of fear. Does your dog exhibit any of the following?

- **Fearful behavior** includes attempts to run away or hide, displays of appeasement behaviors such as excessive licking, crouching, crawling, or rolling over to expose the tummy area when experiencing stress.
- **Fearful body language** includes ears down, tail between the legs, crouching, body stiffness, rear of body pulled back from stimuli, and *whale-eye*—when you see the whites of your dog's eyes.
- **Fearful vocalizations** include crying, howling, barking, or panting more than usual, although not thirsty.
- **Refusal to take treats** is a classic symptom of a fearful dog. If your dog typically enjoys treats, refusal to eat indicates your dog is experiencing stress in the environment or the interaction.

Noise Phobia

Symptoms of noise phobia are similar to those of otherwise fearful dogs, above, with the additional hypersensitivity to sound. In the noise-sensitive dog, desensitization and counterconditioning increases tolerance to noise and decreases reactivity to sounds that may otherwise result in chronic stress or acute stress.

WHAT DRIVES FEAR?

Fear is adaptive to survival and thus easily acquired and difficult to treat, because it is deep-seated in the brain. Most frightened dogs will run away or hide if possible. Some have an active defense reflex and attempt to attack what frightens them. Genetics, i.e., nature, may be more important than learning, however conversely, learning, i.e., nurture, may be more important than genetics in some individuals and in differing situational contexts. Personality is a combination of genetics and behavior learned through early interactive environmental experiences. A traumatic experience may also shape future behavior.

- Genetics
- Early developmental experience
- Traumatic triggering events

Genetics

Choosing your dog or puppy carefully will help cut down on the surprises that come with haphazard breeding. Your dog's temperament is, in part, an inherited collection of traits. Temperament is the first expression of personality. There are four dimensions of temperament: Novelty seeking, harm avoidance, reward dependence, and persistence (Service, 2012). Traits such as aggression and trainability were found to be shared by genetically similar dogs in a recent landmark study using data from more than 14,000 dogs described in the C-BARQ, a pet parent self-report data base (Serpell, 2020). Fearfulness showed a smaller genetic contribution in genetically similar dogs (MacLean et al., 2019).

Early Development and Early Exposure

A dog's fear of strangers or other dogs may be inherited, however, some studies show that experiences in early development and socialization may override the effect of genes. Keep in mind neglectful or aggressive mothering and relationships between siblings are also part of the socialization process that may negatively affect your dog's psychological development. The *Big Five* dimensions of personality are: Openness to experience, conscientiousness, extraversion, agreeableness, and neuroticism that includes impulse control, anxiety, and emotional stability (Service, 2012).

The critical, aka as the sensitive period of socialization occurs within a window of socialization between the 3rd and 12th week of life. The ideal period to transition a puppy into a forever home is between the 8th and 10th week of life, generally speaking. Breeders have a great deal of influence not only concerning your dog's genetics but also in the critical early stages of social development of your dog. Keep in mind that puppies often behave one way with the breeder family and household pets but behave differently with strangers once your puppy comes home. We encourage careful and proper socialization outside of the breeder's inner circle, habituation to common noises and surfaces, early chew toy training, housetraining, and proper restful sleeping conditions.

What happens or does not happen during the critical sensitive period of socialization will dramatically affect your adolescent and adult dog. Make certain your dog's socialization is a series of controlled positive experiences. Positively expose your puppy or rescue dog to 100 new things in the first 100 days, enriching the environment with gradual, gentle, controlled exposure to new people, places, things, other friendly dogs, situations, and moving objects. Take your puppy with you frequently when going out and conversely practice frequent separations. Do not overwhelm your puppy but allow plenty of downtime for sleep, decompression, and bonding setting your dog and your family up for success.

Triggering Events

Negative associations from the past or unfamiliar stimuli, known as neophobia, often generalize from one specific trigger to wider and wider categories of other dogs, people, or events. Some fears produce a state of hyper-arousal and chronic stress in your dog.

TREATMENT

Protect the physical safety and psychological security of all dogs and people. Remember, every good treatment plan begins with management. Whatever the source of your dog's fears, the gold standard of treatment is the same—desensitization and counterconditioning. Pair positive associations with slow, managed, incremental exposure of the trigger stimulus. Over-exposure to a feared stimulus, also known as *flooding,* typically further traumatizes dogs and is not something you can "undo." Avoid exposures where your dog is over the threshold of fear reactivity as communicated through behavior, vocalizations, and body language. Food may be the initial bridge to change your dog's response from one of fear to one of a positive experience. Follow these guidelines:

- Avoid getting the old response where your dog repeats and practices an undesirable behavior.
- Create new positive associations by linking a very mild version of the fear with something your dog adores. Work to get the right balance between the supported exposure and the trigger to foster an increased sense of security and safety.
- Your best guide is your dog's body behavior, vocalization, and body language. Learn to read your dog's body language, so you can recognize fear: Mouth clamped shut, ears pinned back, tail between the legs, attempting to hide, running away, growling if trapped, or air snaps.

22

SEPARATION ANXIETY

Separation Anxiety (SA) Disorder is both a devastating condition for dogs and a heart-wrenching experience for pet parents. SA is a stress-related disorder, more specifically, a fear reaction to being left alone. It is defined by emotional and physical distress brought on by the absence of an attachment figure. When left alone, dogs suffering with SA disorder experience what is akin to a panic attack in humans.

Research in the field of developmental psychology has shown that SA in dogs may be similar to an *attachment disorder* in humans. Separation anxiety indicates there is an *insecure* anxiety-driven attachment most often to a pet parent, or possibly to a canine housemate (Ainsworth & Bell, 1970). Some dogs are comforted with another person as a substitute for the primary relationship, but many are not. Generally, if a dog appears overly attached to a pet parent, getting another dog is unlikely to solve the problem.

Lamentably, "Most separation anxiety in dogs appears to be 'idiopathic' meaning we do not understand what is causing it," (Overall, 2013, p. 681). It is not well-understood why some dogs suffer from separation anxiety and others do not. Puppies from the same litter with similar puppyhood experiences have developed SA, while the other puppies from the litter have developed normally.

One or all three of the following factors may play a part in any single case of separation anxiety:

- It may reflect a dog's relationship with a pet parent
- It may result from a single traumatic event in a dog's life
- There may be a genetic predisposition to SA

Factors associated with SA include being left alone for long periods of time or, conversely, not spending enough time alone. Preventive strategies are recommended in order to avoid heartache for pet parents as well as their dogs early in the dog's life or early in the relationship (Sargisson, 2014a).

The peak intensity of problems related to separation is typically seen shortly after the pet parent's departure. In an extensive review of the literature, Sargisson (2014b) found that, on average, dogs with SA begin vocalizing 3.25 minutes after departure, and destructive behavior begins 7.13 minutes after departure. Keep in mind your dog could be suffering from a condition that is often mistaken for separation anxiety—boredom!

The good news is that SA is treatable. The solution is training dogs to enjoy time alone or at least be accepting of reasonable periods of time spent alone. Make the time your dog spends alone as pleasant as possible, baby stepping your way toward recovery. Just as you would not expect a person experiencing a severe panic attack to "Just get over it," neither can you expect a dog with SA to have symptoms resolve quickly. It may take months rather than weeks of dedicated treatment. Do not listen to misbegotten advice to let your dog "cry it out". Recovery is a process. (See Chapter 2, Attachment and Abandonment.)

Encourage your dog to become more independent by becoming a proactive pet parent and trainer helping your dog to feel more emotionally secure. Practice separation anxiety prevention by using the treatment techniques in this chapter early in your dog's development, or when adding a rescued dog to your family, and regularly thereafter. Teach your dog to enjoy being a dog and a "happy camper" even when you are not home.

The Need for Social Contact

Dogs are social creatures and need social contact much like we do. However, your dog does not have the choices afforded by social or other media, to go out on the town, or to entertain guests when desired, but depends entirely upon you to provide adequate opportunities for social interaction. Leaving your dog, a member of a social species, alone all day is without question contraindicated. Dogs should not be left alone, on average, for more than five hours at a stretch if they do not have social contact and elimination opportunities. If your dog withholds urination, longer periods may create medical problems, such as a build-up of toxins in the bloodstream resulting in kidney conditions and urinary tract infections as well as psychological distress. If your job keeps you away from home for long stretches of time, engage outside help to find a dog-friendly alternative to leaving your dog home alone all day. Here are some ideas you may want to consider:

- A force-free pet sitter with whom your dog has already closely bonded can provide daily visits, play, and walks. Arrange to receive a per visit photo or video and/or a text message to help you adjust to the separation and help relieve guilt feelings in you that may crop up.
- A well-researched doggy day care facility may be an option *if* your dog is suitable for such a high intensity environment with other dogs, and if safe.
- Take your dog to work with you when possible.

Prevention

In 2014, Sargisson (2014c) undertook an enlightening review of the scientific literature on strategies for the management and treatment of SA in dogs. She found that preventive measures include the following:

- Providing a wide range of experiences outside the home and with other people
- Having stable routines
- Making regular absences from the dog–not too long but not too short in duration part of your dog's routine
- Avoiding punishment

Typically, having a dog sleep in bed is not a problem unless the dog already has SA. If a dog does have SA, pet parents may want to reconsider their sleeping arrangements in a kind and step-wise manner. There is evidence that allowing dogs to sleep in bed contributes to SA or other behavior problems. According to attachment theory, co-sleeping practices may exacerbate SA when the attachment figure is away from the home (Thompson & Smith, 2014). Jagoe and Serpell (1996) found that dogs who sleep in bed with pet parents may respond adversely to separation and display the separation-related problems of urination and defecation, having developed an "unbalanced" attachment to that person. They may also engage in competitive resource guarding.

This research should not be used to assign blame to pet parents for letting dogs sleep in bed. Instead, it allows us to look carefully at how pet parents can change their home environment in a way that helps their dogs overcome SA.

ASSESSMENT

Dogs at Risk

There are risks factors associated with SA. In many cases, a dog habituated to continual contact with the pet parent never developed the sufficient confidence needed to be left alone. Dogs at risk of becoming *insecurely attached* to pet parents and who may be particularly susceptible to developing separation related issues are:

- **Puppies.** Puppies who never learned to be without the pet parent or to socialize with others are at risk.
- **Dogs living with a single adult**. Dogs living with a single adult are 2.5 times more likely to suffer with SA than those living with two or more people (McGreevy, 2010).
- **Dogs living with pet parents who work from home.**
- **Dogs living with pet parents who are retired.**
- **Rescued dogs.** Rescued dogs often suffer from SA as a result of being abandoned and the commonly frightening and lonely experience at a shelter: although rescue staff and volunteers do a wonderful job of rehoming dogs, avoiding SA can be an especially difficult challenge for a rescued dog. Check to be certain your rescue facility uses only force-free behavior modification methods to help avoid additional problems and suffering.
- **Boarded dogs.** Dogs may develop separation anxiety for the first time in a kennel or board and train facility when pet parents go away on vacation or business.
- **Apartment living.** Dogs who live in apartments may be more at risk than those who live in homes with yards.
- **Children.** Some research indicates that dogs who live in homes without children may be at higher risk.

- **Breed predisposition.** There may be a factor of genetically driven, breed-related predisposition to separation anxiety. Some of the breeds mentioned in research include the Australian Shepherd, Bichon Frise, Border Collie, Cavalier King Charles Spaniel, Chihuahua, German Shepherd Dog, Jack Russell Terrier, Labrador Retriever, and Vizsla.

Gathering Pertinent History Information

Answers to the below questions help a behavioral consultant determine the severity of the SA related issue or disorder for the purpose of creating a customized treatment plan for a client.

- How many hours per day on average do you spend with your dog?
- How many hours per day on average is your dog left alone?
- How old was your dog when you first noticed symptoms?
- How old is your dog now?
- Was there an event, such as a vacation spent together, or being home with you for a long period of time, that preceded your dog developing symptoms?
- Was there a change in family routines, family structure, or family location?
- Was there an event that your dog may have perceived as traumatic separation, such as boarding or kenneling, that preceded the onset of symptoms?
- Does your dog dislike spending even a short amount of time alone in your yard?

Symptoms *Before* You Leave Home

Understanding the signs of stress your dog displays anticipating your departure and identifying the chain of emotional events that occur before you leave the home provide clues for treatment. Here are some signs of anxiety your dog may experience indicating that a panic attack is likely.

- Following closely on your heels from room to room throughout the day. Not all dogs who follow closely suffer separation anxiety.
- Sadness/worried look. Dog body language and facial expressions are reflections of how your dog is feeling and your dog's state of mind.
- Panting, from stress—not from overheating or exercise.
- Pacing.
- Crying/whining. Crying is a sure sign your dog is in distress and has unmet needs.
- Other.

Symptoms *After* You Leave Home

If you do not know what your dog does after you leave the house, find out. A remote or stationary video camera is an important tool for gathering this information. Alternatively, quietly "sneak up" on your dog by peering into a window to see and hear what is going on in your absence.

If your dog has a *cluster* of two or three of the symptoms below, or one of the more severe symptoms, a diagnosis of Separation Anxiety Disorder is possible. What are your dog's typical signs of anxiety after you leave the home?

- Incessant barking or crying—but not boredom.
- Destructive behavior—but not boredom.
- Defecation or urination in the house—even though otherwise housetrained.
- Immobility, such as staring out the window or sitting at the door the while you are away.
- Chewing or scratching at windows, doors, or other exit routes.
- Other attempts at escape to find you.
- Repetitive pacing.
- Self-mutilation or excessive licking of paws or flanks resulting in wounds. These are not unusual behaviors for a dog with SA who has been locked in a crate. Consider this: if you were having a panic attack how would you react to being locked in a closet?

- Drooling.
- Wet coat or sweating from the pads of the paws, leaving footprints.
- Trembling.
- Frantic greeting although you were gone for just a short while.
- Anorexia. Not eating high value food while you are away.

SEPARATION ANXIETY TREATMENT

The most successful treatment modalities Sargisson found are counterconditioning (CC) (see the "Little Peter" experiment discussed below) and systematic desensitization (SD) (2014d). CC is a form of behavior modification used to induce a behavior that is incompatible with an undesirable behavior such as the symptoms seen in SA. CC was central to the development of systematic desensitization, a treatment for phobias in which the patient is taught relaxation techniques and exposed to progressively more anxiety-provoking stimuli. The goals of CC and SD are reducing the dog's dependence on the pet parent in a stepwise and planned manner. Sargisson notes that some studies indicate the power of SD is greater when combined with CC than when either is used alone.

An in-depth systematic review of counterconditioning (Keller et al., 2020) examined the effectiveness of counterconditioning at preventing relapse when compared with *extinction*, which is nonreinforcement of a previously reinforced behavior. A negative emotional experience (in this case anxiety) is replaced with a positive emotional experience (such as eating food) using *appetitive counterconditioning* (AC). A number of animal studies included in the review demonstrate that counterconditioning is more effective at reducing fear than mere exposure to the stimuli. Relapse to the original negative association is more likely to occur with extinction than with counterconditioning. The review also reveals that earning the reward—such as with an interactive food toy, or Grazing Games scavenging—may lead to even better outcomes than desensitization exposure alone. (See Chapter 10, Enrichment and Grazing Games.)

Sadly, separation anxiety is rarely an easy fix and may take months, not weeks. However, SA is frequently responsive to treatment if:

- A customized plan of treatment is developed
- The plan is demonstrated clearly by the behavior consultant and
- The plan is practiced consistently by the pet parent

With separation anxiety, we are treating insecurity and fear, so building confidence is key to your dog's recovery (Wilde, 2010). Building confidence in dogs is believed to be similar to building self-esteem and self-efficacy in humans. Force-free training focuses on positive reinforcement which has been shown to increase confidence.

Find a happy medium at each stage of treatment between

- Independence from the pet parent
- Proximity, that is, nearness in space and time to the pet parent

Your dog must learn to **trust** that you will return home every single time you leave home. Applying a consistent treatment plan will teach your dog that it is safe to be alone because your dog can trust that you will always return.

All emotional and behavioral modification programs are two-sided coins. Each side of the coin is equally important.

- Start doing the things that will help your dog achieve independence while you
- Stop doing the things that work against your dog's success

What Not To Do!

There are some cardinal rules to follow when implementing a program of recovery from separation anxiety and some rules about what not to do to avoid derailing progress.

- Do not punish. Punishing will never help, regardless of what may have happened in your absence, but it will make an already anxiety-stricken dog even *more* insecure and most likely worsen problems.
- Do not let your dog *cry it out*. Research now indicates that letting your dog cry it out creates more, not less insecurity and is seriously detrimental to well-being.
- Do not put your dog in a long Down/Wait and then leave. A short Down/Wait of less than two minutes may be all right, but you want your dog to be either active or relaxed while you are away, not performing obedience tricks awaiting your release.
- Do not change routines suddenly. For example, post-pandemic routines should be changed gradually in terms of mealtime, walks, and playtime to minimize stress and make the transition back to work more seamless for your dog.
- Do not leave your dog alone during the initial stages of treatment.

Doggy Enrichment Land™ Containment—The Enhanced Environment

Changing the situational context and adding novelty may enhance learning a new response during counterconditioning (Haubrich et al., 2015).

Set your dog up for success by creating a Doggy Enrichment Land containment area. Create a private sanctuary for your dog to prevent your dog from following you about the house as you practice the frequent separation techniques outlined below. A doggy playpen, x-pen, metal baby gate, doggy door that allows access to a secured balcony, or using the walls of your home are some popular options. A large gated closet with a view may work. This *safe space* must never be used as a punishment. Do not lock your dog in a crate. The use of a crate for SA treatment is generally contraindicated. Self-mutilation and injury are not uncommon for panic-stricken dogs locked in a crate. However, there is the likelihood your dog may find an *open* covered crate a "security blanket."

To start treatment, allow your dog to practice being independent in your carefully designed Doggy Enrichment Land while you are home. A separate dog zone where your dog can happily "play house" while you are in another room is emotionally beneficial for your dog in the long term.

Providing Comfort Items

You are the ultimate comfort item . . . but you may also be the trigger prolonging problematic emotional dependency. Make certain your dog does not associate the comfort items below with you leaving your home, or the high value items will become yet another predictor of your impending absence. It's important to avoid associating the presentation of food with leaving the home.

Here are some comfort items and activities you can provide for your dog in the Doggy Enrichment Land:

- **Grazing Games.** Dogs, like us, use food for both survival and enjoyment. Most dogs love, love, love food. Dogs are scavengers by nature so searching for food can help condition new emotions, changing how your dog feels about being alone. For example, scatter high value air-dried food on the floor of your Doggy Enrichment Land along with a few pieces of food hidden in a rolled-up towel if safe for your dog. Take care that pieces of food do not fall underneath the furniture where your dog cannot reach—this may cause frustration. (See Chapter 10, Grazing Games.) Don't forget to provide water!

- **Stimulate your dog.** We all need something to do. Leave your dog with something to do. Provide special treats judiciously in a planned fashion. Leave favorite chew items and long-lasting food toys in the Doggy Enrichment Land dog zone such as a chew item stuffed with wet food, a bully stick, or soup bone, if safe. Many dogs suffering from separation anxiety become anorexic in the absence of the pet parent, so begin by providing high value items at "happy times," to create a positive association with special treats. Then, offer these items during separation trials while you are home, and during no stress and low-stress periods when you are both available and unavailable to your dog in the home. (See Chapter 10, Enrichment.)

- **Room with a view.** An outdoor view and scent from an open window have a number of positive benefits providing enrichment, novelty, and positive associations that often fascinates dogs. Observing the natural world and smelling the great outdoors distracts dogs from anxiety related to the absence of the pet parent. However, take care to avoid setting up "guarding stations" in your containment area.

- **Favorite toys.** Bring out your dog's favorite safe squeaky, or plush toys that your dog now gets *only* when practicing no-stress separations or when you are away. Rotate the toys in Doggy Enrichment Land every other day.

- **Your scent.** Leave your sweaty t-shirt or dirty socks with your dog if safe! These scent-orienting items can help your dog feel that you are not so far away after all providing a measure of security.

- **Bedding.** If your dog has chewed the bed, try a zippered bed, remove the stuffing, and replace the stuffing with your old, worn, unwashed clothes. The bed will smell like you and will help prevent shredding and destructive behavior. Alternatively, try a dog cot. A warm towel right out of the dryer can help comfort, too.

- **Your voice.** Provide a food dispensing voice-toy that dispenses treats and allows you to see, speak and reward your dog via a phone app you can use from work or while you are otherwise away. Alternately, get a voice toy with a prerecorded loop of your voice saying a few pleasantries to your dog. There is a device available online that records your voice and then "talks" to your dog when your dog nudges it or "talks" once every five minutes.

- **Television and radio.** Leave the television tuned to a cooking or shopping channel where nothing emotionally disturbing ever happens! Leave the radio tuned to a station that is calming such as a reggae music, recently shown to be effective, or an easy listening soft rock music station. Keep the volume down.

Separation Trials

Practicing separation is the key to success. Make separations a part of your dog's regular routine. Start small and build confidence slowly and incrementally. Remember, patience and practice are needed for your dog to reach the level of trusting security that you will always return.

Expend anxiety-driven energy and increase endorphins by exercising your dog before leaving home. If you cannot walk or run your dog, use a lure-chase toy, for example. Also, make certain your dog has sufficient elimination opportunities before you leave.

Begin training with your dog *under the threshold or reactivity* where you are not seeing any of the anxiety symptoms listed above—before and after you leave home— then increase the duration of your absence and distance from you as long as your dog continues to stay under threshold.

- **Providing frequent separations *while you are at home*.** Begin frequent separations of very short duration behind a closed door and/or with your dog contained in the Doggy Enrichment Land-style enclosure. Too much space can cause some dogs to feel insecure. Too little space can cause some dogs to feel insecure, too. Make your dog's "room" as comfortable and happy as possible.
- **Establishing a *safety cue*.** Stand in front of your dog with your dog contained in Doggy Enrichment Land and say, "I'll Be Back." Turn around with your back to your dog, then immediately turn back to face your dog again, saying in a calm voice, "I'm Back." Practice in four two-minute sessions per day. Increase both distance and duration separately and incrementally. Once your dog trusts that you will be back, leave your dog with the familiar upbeat parting cue, "I'll be back."
- **Begin with *pass-bys*.** Allow your dog to get a comforting glimpse of you and a smile as you walk by—but do not provide interaction once you have established that it is now "alone time".
- **Closing the door.** Slowly acclimating your dog to accepting a barrier between the two of you begins the process of healing from separation anxiety. Starting with the bathroom, keep your dog on the other side of a closed door inside the home for short periods each day. If your dog tries to follow you into the bathroom, toss down grazing treats and provide a comfort item, then gently close the door. You may need to begin this process using a baby gate

or a partially closed door. Talk to your dog through the door if talking keeps symptoms from emerging. Later, slowly phase out talking.

- **Extending distance and duration in baby steps.** The desensitization process begins with practice sessions of very short duration with longer and longer durations as your goal. Time "away" is increased in increments as small as 10-seconds, if necessary. Step outdoors using your voice behind the door to let your dog know you are still near. Come back indoors. Later, walk to the mailbox on the street in front of your home. Come back home. Later, walk to the corner. Come back home. Slowly increase to 15 minutes, then, increase to one hour, then, increase to 1.5 hours of being alone two times a day, every day, for life. Progress may be slow at first, however the duration of stress-free alone time your dog can tolerate comfortably may increase quickly as learning progresses. Once your dog can manage your absence from 30–90 minutes, you dog will generally be sufficiently acclimated to being separated from you for a morning or afternoon.

- **Sleeping arrangements.** Customize your sleeping routines to meet the needs of your dog's level of anxiety being generous with comforting in every way. Be aware that sleeping in bed with you may have an effect on your dog's attachment to you particularly if your dog already suffers from separation anxiety. You may choose to snuggle together in bed but when it is time to sleep, consider having your dog sleep right next to you in a comfy bed on the floor or in a cloth crate on your bed. This is not always the optimal choice: puppies and rescued dogs and may need more hands-on comforting than the average dog.

Using Food in Treatment

Joseph Wolpe, the father of systematic desensitization, used food/eating in his anti-anxiety experiments. His findings revolutionized behavioral therapy (Wolpe, 1954b). His work demonstrated that there is compelling evidence for the value of food in incrementally decreasing anxiety. Most, but not all, independently validated research continues to point in this direction.

Wolpe (Wolpe, 1954a) suggests that facing one's fears does not always resolve them but the key to overcoming fear is accomplished "by degrees." This is especially true for dogs whose cognitive development is comparable to that of a 2- to 3-year-old child. We give a bottle to a baby who cries. Even if the baby is not hungry, the act of suckling may bring about relaxation (the first step in DS). Similarly, giving a dog an interactive food toy or a safe bone may have the same pacifying effect. One problem is that the absence of the reward may lead to frustration and result in a return to the maladaptive behavior.

Counterconditioning involves providing a stimulus of the *opposite valence*, meaning one that's seen as being "good" as opposed to "bad." Food provides a positive valence that offsets the negative valence of being left alone. The emotional state of anxiety is incompatible with relaxation and eating (Lindsay, 2008).

Eating acts as a form of displacement behavior and distraction: displacement behaviors and distraction are known to decrease anxiety. Displacement activities are well-documented coping mechanisms that discharge tension in the scientific literature on learning. Research indicates that food can play a powerful role in changing emotions, in this case anxiety about and the fear of being alone. Eating may have a therapeutic effect on anxiety and inhibit its resurfacing.

"Little Peter" is one of the earliest demonstrations of behavior modification illustrating how using high-value food can decrease anxiety and lower heart rate when used in separation anxiety protocols (Keller, 2020). This method was a precursor to the systematic desensitization therapies that followed. In classic psychology and learning literature, the "Little Peter" experiment (Jones, 1924) used counterconditioning to remove three-year-old Peter's fear of rabbits. A rabbit was placed in the room while Peter ate candy. The candy served as an appetitive food stimulus. The rabbit was moved closer and closer over the course of numerous sessions while Peter ate candy and Peter's fear of the rabbit gradually subsided. When done right, providing food through enrichment can help hasten a conditioned emotional response (CER).

Many dogs who suffer from SA are anorexic in the absence of the primary pet parent. It's imperative that the pet parent properly introduce food in a positive manner while at home. This helps set your dog up for success when you leave. There is a popular movement afoot encouraging non-dependence on food-inclusive therapies for SA. Although it may be more difficult to clearly interpret the body language of a dog engaged in a food-seeking activity, that does not necessarily justify eliminating food in SA treatment if it benefits the dog. As with any behavior modification retraining, a dog should be trained under the dog's *threshold of reactivity* in all stages of treatment.

Predeparture Desensitization and Counterconditioning Triggers

Change the emotional impact of the activities you typically perform before leaving the home. Desensitization and Counterconditioning begin with practice sessions where you perform the routines you have previously performed before you leave the house but you do not leave the house, turning the triggers that previously lead to your departure into *neutral events* for your dog. This technique changes the emotional meaning of the triggers which were past predictors of your departure.

Triggers. Track What You Typically Do Before Leaving the Home

Your dog has learned that a sequence of activities predict that you are preparing to leave the house. Observe your dog closely and list the possible triggers setting your dog's stress reaction in motion. Some examples of triggers are

- Buzzing of your alarm clock going off
- Rushing around the house
- Applying make-up or perfume (scent trigger)
- Shaving and applying aftershave (scent trigger)
- Putting on your shoes
- Putting on your coat
- Jangling your keys
- Picking up a purse and/or briefcase
- Approaching the door
- Closing the door
- Driving away in your car

Your dog cannot produce a continual stream of adrenaline for a long period of time. If you leaving the home is not always preceded by the jangling of keys, the jangling of keys will no longer be a signal you are leaving. Your dog will eventually hear the jangling of keys as "background noise" and stop associating the sound of jangling keys with being left alone. If you sit down and watch television while jangling your keys for example, the trigger will in time lose the power to generate fear and anxiety. The same learning principal applies to other triggers. Set the alarm clock for different times during the day but don't go out.

Follow the Steps in This Example

1. Pick up your keys, go to the door, but do not leave. Repeat again and again.
2. Open and close the door but do not leave. Repeat again and again.

3. Step outside, close the door, and come back inside after 3 seconds. Increase your away time in small increments.
4. Add walking to your car. Go back indoors.
5. Add starting the ignition of the car. Go back indoors.

Now, start adding more distance and duration as long as your dog is staying under threshold. Be certain your dog is successful at being left alone at one level before adding the next level of difficulty in terms of duration and distance.

Changing Your Routines—Arrivals and Departures

A well-structured change in routine may break the cycle of anxiety if practiced carefully and consistently. The goal is to decrease the emotional gap between your presence and your absence. Make your arrival home less emotionally filled with glee and make your departure less emotionally filled with regret. Get your dog off the adrenaline roller-coaster and refrain from immediate enthusiastic greetings and sad goodbyes. This is often difficult for pet parents; however, try to keep your dog's best long-term interest in mind as your priority.

- **Make your arrivals home somewhat boring.** Try delivering your most enthusiastic greeting after your dog has calmed down. Your dog is thrilled that you are home. Do not add kindling to an already raging emotional fire. For example, when you arrive home, get into the habit of smiling, saying "Hi" with a short pet, then check your email while your dog calms down.
- **Make your departures from home calmly upbeat.** If you are sad as you leave home, your dog will not understand why you are sad but will get the message that "Something's wrong with Mommy," from the tone of your voice. It may serve to trigger or increase the panic already set in motion. Alternatively, use an upbeat tone of voice when you leave home.

Getting Professional Help

If you continue to have difficulty or if your dog still has more than one of the symptoms of separation anxiety, work with a force-free behavioral consultant or consider consulting with an integrative veterinarian or a veterinary behaviorist.

Medication

Severe cases of separation anxiety that do not respond to a professionally and consistently applied emotional and behavioral modification program may warrant the use of medication. If your dog's response to separation does not improve or worsens, consider the advisability of adding anti-anxiety or panic medication to the treatment plan (Overall, 2013, p. 684). It is ill-advised to employ pharmaceutical treatment without implementing an emotional and behavioral modification protocol. Some researchers support the use of behavioral therapy alone because no improvement was found when comparing medication to a placebo, although pharmacological interventions along with behavioral therapy may be helpful.

When medicating, remember medication AND an emotional and behavioral modification program such as the one outlined above should always go hand-in-glove. Remember, your dog cannot self-report on the effects of medication, and in some dogs, there are undesirable side-effects such as paradoxical (opposite) side-effects. Please consult your veterinary behaviorist for medication options.

THE END

REFERENCES

Adams, G. J., & Johnson, K. G. (1993). Sleep-wake cycles and other night-time behaviors of the domestic dog Canis familiaris. *Applied Behavior Science, 36*(2–3), 223–248. https://doi.org/10.1016/0168–591(93)90013-F

Ainsworth, M. D., & Bell, S. M. (1970). Attachment, exploration, and separation: Illustrated by the behavior of one-year-olds in a strange situation. *Child Development, 41*, 49–67. https://doi10.2307/1127388

Air Quality Index. (n.d.). Retrieved Sept 7, 2020, from https://www.airnow.gov/

Aldis, O. (1975). *Playfighting*. Academic Press.

American Animal Hospital Association (AAHA). (2015). *Canine and feline behavior management guidelines*. https://www.aaha.org/professional/resources/behavior_management_guidelines.aspx

American Animal Hospital Association–American Veterinary Medical Association Preventive Healthcare Guidelines Task Force. (2011.) Development of new canine and feline preventive healthcare guidelines designed to improve pet health. *Journal of the American Animal Hospital Association, 47*(5), 306–311. https://doi.org/10.5326/JAAHA-MS-4007

American College of Veterinary Behavior (ACVB). (n.d.). *What is a board certified veterinary behaviorist?* https://www.dacvb.org/page/AnimalOwners

American Holistic Veterinary Medical Association (AHVMA). (2016). *What is holistic veterinary medicine?* http://www.ahvma.org/what-is-holistic-veterinary-medicine/

American Medical Association (AMA). (2019). First, do no harm. *AMA Journal of Ethics, 13*(9). https://journalofethics.ama-assn.org/issue/first-do-no-harm

American Medical Association (AMA). (1995–2021). AMA *Principles of medical ethics.* http://www.ama-assn.org/ama/pub/physician-resources/medical-ethics/about-ethics-group/ethics-resource-center/educational-resources/pocket-principles.page

American Psychological Association (APA). (2017). *Ethical principles of psychologists and code of ethics.* http://www.apa.org/ethics/code/

American Society for the Prevention of Cruelty of Animals (ASPCA). (2019). *Animal poison control: Poisonous household products.* http://www.aspca.org/pet-care/animal-poison-control/poisonous-household-products

American Society for the Prevention of Cruelty of Animals (ASPCA). (2016). *Venom reactions and treatment options.* http:/www.aspcapro.org/resource/shelter-health-poison-control/venom-reactions-and-treatment-options

American Society for the Prevention of Cruelty of Animals (ASPCA). (2015). *Ten most common pet toxins of 2014.* http:/www.aspca.org/news/ten-most-common-pet-toxins-2014

American Veterinary Dental College (AVDC). (2016). *Information for owners.* http://www.avdc.org/ownersinfo.html

American Veterinary Medical Association (AVMA). (2019, September 6). *Raw or undercooked animal-source protein in cat and dog diets.* https://www.avma.org/policies/raw-or-undercooked-animal-source-protein-cat-and-dog-diets

American Veterinary Medical Association (AVMA). (2019). *Principles of veterinary medical ethics of the AVMA.* https://www.avma.org/KB/Policies/Pages/Principles-of-Veterinary-Medical-Ethics-of-the-AVMA.aspx

American Veterinary Medical Association (AVMA). (2016). *Model veterinary practice act.* https://www.avma.org/KB/Policies/Pages/Model-Veterinary-Practice-Act.aspx#definitions

American Veterinary Medical Association (AVMA). (2015). *Market research statistics: U. S. veterinarians 2015.* https://www.avma.org/KB/Resources/Statistics/Pages/Market-research-statistics-US-veterinarians.aspx

American Veterinary Medical Association. (n.d.). *Dog bite prevention.* https://www.avma.org/resources-tools/pet-owners/dog-bite-prevention

American Veterinary Society of Animal Behavior (AVSAB). (2021a). *Position statement on humane dog training: How should a veterinarian decide who to refer to for training?* https://avsab.org/resources/position-statements/

American Veterinary Society of Animal Behavior (AVSAB). (2021b). *Position statement on humane dog training: What techniques should be avoided in training?* https://avsab.org/resources/position-statements/

American Veterinary Society of Animal Behavior (AVSAB). (2021c). *Position statement on humane dog training: Are aversive training techniques appropriate for animals who exhibit aggression?* https://avsab.org/resources/position-statements/

American Veterinary Society of Animal Behavior (AVSAB). (2008). *AVSAB position statement on puppy socialization.* https://avsab.org/wpcontent/uploads/2016/08/Puppy_Socialization_Position_Statement_Download_-_10-3-14.pdf

Anderson, E. (2017, August 10). *Why prong collars hurt.* https://eileenanddogs.com/blog/2017/08/10/why-prong-collars-hurt/

Anderson, R. K. (2004). *Puppy vaccination and early socialization should go together.* http://www.diamondsintheruff.com/rkanderson

Animal Legal and Historical Center. (2014). Michigan State University, College of Law. *Table of state dog tether laws.* https://www.animallaw.info/topic/table-state-dog-tether-laws

Animal Medical Center of Southern California (2016). *Fractures of the tibia are relatively common in the dog and cat, with tibial diaphyseal fractures the most commonly encountered injury of this bone.* http://www.animalmedcenter.com/faqs/category/management-of-tibial-shaft-fractures

Arnold, C. (2017). Why are dogs so friendly? Science finally has an answer. *National Geographic News.* http://www.nationalgeographic.com/news/2017/7/dog-breeds-pets-wolves-evolution

Balance IT®, Davis Veterinary Medical Consulting. (2004–2020). https://secure.balanceit.com/info/aboutus.php?fbclid=IwAR2ypHBGEULoncdRQCsLlQJdqcApqX2ZZQXtLSm-gRNqYCSLK-pIGX_MFvg

Bandura, A. (1965). Vicarious processes: A case of no-trial learning. In L. Berkowitz (Ed.). *Advances in experiential social psychology,* (2nd ed., pp. 1–55). Academic Press.

Ban Shock Collars. (2007). https://banshockcollars.ca/index.php

Barragán-Mejía, G., Broadway, J., Brooks, D., Calderón-Garcidueñas, L., Chapman, S., & Engle, R. W. (2008). Air pollution, cognitive deficits and brain abnormalities: A pilot study with children and dogs. *Brain and Cognition, 68*(2), 117–127. http://dx.doi.org.sci-hub.bz/10.1016/j.bandc.2008.04.008

Barrows, E. M. (2011). *Animal behavior desk reference: A dictionary of animal behavior, ecology, and evolution* (3rd ed.). CRC Press.

Beck, A. (2003, September). Future directions in human-animal bond research. *American Behavioural Scientist.* https://doi.org/10.1177/0002764203255214

Becker, K. S. (1997–2020). Biologically appropriate nutrition is the first building block of good health. *Healthy Pets.* https://healthypets.mercola.com/sites/healthypets/archive/2018/01/26/biologically-appropriate-pet-food.aspx

Becker, K. S. (2019). *Healthy Pets.* http://healthypets.mercola.com/sites/healthypets/dr-karen-becker.aspx

Bekoff, M. (2018). What and who dogs want and need: Love, not shocks. *Psychology Today.* https://www.psychologytoday.com/us/blog/animal-emotions/201801/what-and-who-dogs-want-and-need-love-not-shocks

Bekoff, M. (2017). A hierarchy of dog needs*: Abraham Maslow meets the mutts. *Psychology Today.* https://psychologytoday.com/blog/animal-emotions/201705/hierarchy-dog-needs-abraham-maslow-meets-the-mutts

Bekoff, M. (2013). Dogs are people, too: They love us and miss us fMRI's say. *Psychology Today.* https://www.psychologytoday.com/us/blog/animal-emotions/201310/dogs-are-people-too-they-love-us-and-miss-us-fmris-say

Bekoff, M. (2008). *Animals at play.* Temple University Press.

Bekoff, M. (2007). *The emotional lives of animals: A leading scientist explains animal joy, sorrow and empathy—and why they matter.* New World Library.

Bekoff, M. (2004, September-October). The great divide. *American Scientist, 92*(5). https://go.gale.com/ps/ anonymous?id=GALE%7CA121498346&sid=googleScholar&v=2.1&it=r&linkaccess=abs&issn=00030996&p=AONE&sw=w&u=googlescholar&asid=7b788ab0a22c2e637f368b0b59fed1d5&mg=true&fbclid=IwAR3apax36YRfbix2G5Jom0T8oi7alLXn9phr6MHQbSELpr1xs304W3A4jHQ

Bellows, J., Berg, M. L., Dennis, S., Harvey, R., Lobprise, H. B., Snyder, C. J., Stone, A. E., & Van de Wetering, A. G. (2019). AAHA dental care guidelines for dogs and cats. *Journal of the American Animal Hospital Association, 55*(2), 49–69.

Bellows, J., Colmery, B., Conway, M. L., Holmstrom, S. E., Knutson, K., & Vitoux, J. (2005). AAHA dental care guidelines for dogs and cats. *Journal of the American Animal Hospital Association, 41*(5), 277–283.

Belyaev, D., Rvinsky, A., & Trut, L. (1981). Inherited activation-inactivation of the star gene in foxes. *Journal of Heredity, 72*(4), 264–274. https://doi 10.1093/oxfordjournals.jhered.a109494

Bentivogliio, M., & Grassi-Zucconi, G. (1997). The pioneering experimental studies on sleep deprivation. *Sleep, 20*(7), 570–576. https://doi 10.1093/sleep/20.7.570

Berns, G. S. (2017). *What it's like to be a dog.* Hachette Book Group.

Berns, G. S. (2013). *How dogs love us: A neuroscientist and his dog decode the canine brain.* Houghton Mifflin Harcourt Publishing Company.

Berns, G. S. (2012–2016). *The Dog Project.* http://gregoryberns.com/dog-project.html

Berns, G. S., Brooks, A. M., & Spivak, M. (2015). Scent of the familiar: An fMRI study of canine brain responses to familiar and unfamiliar human and dog odors. *Behavioural Processes, 110*, 37–46. https://doi 10.1016/j.beproc.2014.02.011

Birmingham, E. N., Thomas, D. G., Cave, N. J., Morris, P. J., Butterwick, R. F., & German, A. J. (2014). Energy requirements of adult dogs: A meta-analysis. *National Library of Medicine*. PubMed.gov. PLOS One. https://doi.org/10.1371/journal.pone.0109681

Boecker, H., Sprenger, T., Spilker, M. E., Henriksen, G., Koppenhoefer, M., Wagner, K. J., Valet, M., Berthele, A., & Tolle, T. R. (2008). The runner's high: Opioidergic mechanisms in the human brain. *Cerebral Cortex, 18*(11), 2523–2531. https://doi.org/10.1093/cercor/bhn013

Bove-Rothwell, A. (2016, July). Adapted with permission from, "Living in a human world." *BARKS from the Guild*. https://issuu.com/petprofessionalguild/docs/bftg_july_2016_opt

Bradshaw, J. (2011). *Dog sense*. Basic Books.

Brendin, S. D., Nicol, C. W., & Warburton, D. (2006). Health benefits of physical activity: The evidence. *Canadian Medical Association Journal, 174*(6), 801–809.

Bronson, G. W. (1968). The fear of novelty. *Psychological Bulletin, 69*(5), 350–358.

Brown, R. E., Basheer, R., McKenna, J. T., Strecker, R. E., & McCarley, R. W. (2012). Control of sleep and wakefulness. *Physiological Reviews, 42* (3), 1087–1187. https://www.ncbi.nlm.nih.gov/pubmed/22811426

Brown, S. (Producer). (2008). *Play is more than just fun*. [Video]. TED Conferences. https://www.ted.com/talks/stuart_brown_says_play_is_more_than_fun_it_s_vital/transcript?language=en

Browne, C., Stafford, K., & Fordham. R. (2006). The use of scent-detection dogs. *Irish Veterinary Journal, 59*(2).

Buff, P., Carter, R., Bauer, J., & Kersey, J. (2014). Natural pet food: A review of natural diets and their impact on canine and feline physiology. *Journal of Animal Science. 92*(9), 3781–3791.

Burch, M. R., & Bailey, J. S. (1999). *How dogs learn*. Wiley.

Burn, C. C., Hendricks, A., & Packer, R. M. (2015). *Impact of facial conformation on canine health: Corneal ulceration*. PLOS ONE. http://journals.plos.org/plosone/article?id=10.1371/journal.pone.0123827

Burn, C. C., Hendricks, A., & Packer, R. M. (2012). Do dog owners perceive the clinical signs related to conformational inherited disorders as 'normal' for the breed? A potential constraint to improving canine welfare. *Animal Welfare, 21*(1), 81–93. http://www.ingentaconnect.com.sci-hub.bz/content/ufaw/aw/2012/0000 0021/A00101s1/art00010?token=004d17927e323bf6720297d7634737b 554a605f316a762c206d3f6a4b4b6e6e42576b642738e2

California Legislative Information Civil Code. (2020). https://leginfo.legislature.ca.gov/faces/codes_displaySection.xhtml?sectionNum=3342.&lawCode=CIV

Calpin, J. P., Clark, J. D., & Rager, D. R. (1997). Animal well-being II: Stress and distress. *Comparative Medicine, 47*(6), 571–579.

Canine Research Studies. (2017). [Facebook® group]. Founder, Rebekah Hudson. https://www.facebook.com/groups/1961822777391593

Case, L. P. (2014). *Dog food logic.* Dogwise.

Chance, P. (2014). *Learning and behavior* (7th ed.). Wadsworth.

Cho, C. (2017). The effects of perceived controllability on decision making and affective processing. [Doctoral dissertation, Rutgers University]. Rutgers University Libraries. https://doi.org/doi:10.7282/T3GF0XFX

Collard, L., Ancel, J., Benet, J. J., Paragon, B. M., & Blanchard, G. (2006). Risk factors for obesity in dogs in France. *The Journal of Nutrition, 136*(7), 1951–54S. https://doi:10.1093/jn/136.71951S

College of Veterinary Medicine, Washington State University. (n.d.). *Pet health topics web. Clipping your dog's claws.* https://www.vetmed.wsu.edu/outreach/Pet-Health-Topics/categories/procedures/dogs/clipping-your-dog's-claws

Collins, S. (2007). *Tail talk: Understanding the secret language of dogs.* Chronicle Books.

Colman, S. (2019). Keep your dog safe around the pool this summer. *Whole Dog Journal.* https://www.whole-dog-journal.com/care/keep-your-dog-safe-around-the-pool-this-summer/

Coren, S. (2010). Do dogs sweat? Dogs do not sweat in the same way humans do. *Psychology Today.* https://www.psychologytoday.com/blog/canine-corner/201011/do-dogs-sweat

Creevy, K. E., Grady, J., Little, S. E., Moore, G. E., Groetzinger Strickler, B., Thompson, S., & Webb, J. A. (2019). AAHA canine life stage guidelines. *Journal of the American Animal Hospital Association, 55*(6), 267–290. https://www.aaha.org/globalassets/02-guidelines/canine-life-stage-2019/2019-aaha-canine-life-stage-guidelines-final.pdf

Cummings Veterinary Medical Center, Tufts, Clinical Nutrition Service. (2017). What every pet owner should know about food allergies. https://vetnutrition.tufts.edu/2017/01/food-allergies/

Custance, D., & Mayer, J. (2012). Empathic-like responding by domestic dogs (*Canis familiaris*) to distress in humans: An exploratory study. *Animal Cognition, 15,* 851–859. https://doi.org/10.1007/s10071–012–0510–1

Darwin, C. (1871). *The descent of man and selection in relation to sex in two volumes.* John Murray.

DeBowes, L. J., Harvey, C. E., Logan, E., & Mosier, D. (1996). Association of periodontal disease and histologic lesions in multiple organs from 45 dogs. *Journal of Veterinary Dentistry, 13*(2).

Deng, P., & Swanson, K. S. (2015). Companion animal symposium: Future aspects and perceptions of companion animal nutrition and sustainability. *Journal of Animal Science. 93*(3), 823–834. https://doi:10.2527/jas.2014–8520

Department for Environment Food and Rural Affairs (DEFRA). (2010). Studies to assess the effect of pet training aids, specifically remote static pulse systems on the welfare of domestic dogs; field study of dogs in training—AW1402A. Research Project Final Report. http://randd.defra.gov.uk/Default.aspx?Module=More&Location=None&ProjectID=17568

Dickomeit, M. J., Grohmann, K., Kramer, M., & Schmidt, M. J. (2013). Severe brain damage after punitive training technique with a choke chain collar in a German shepherd dog. *Journal of Veterinary Behavior, 8*(3), 180–184.

Diez, M., Picavet, P., Dequenne, M., Renard, M., Bongartz, A., & Farnir, F. (2015). Health screening to identify opportunities to improve preventive medicine in cats and dogs. *Journal of Small Animal Practice, 56*(7). https://doi.org/10.1111/jsap.12365

Donaldson, J. (2002). *Mine: A practical guide to resource guarding in dogs.* The Academy for Dog Trainers.

Doggone Safe. (2018). [Home page]. https://doggonesafe.com/

Do No Harm Dog Training®. (2017). [Facebook group]. Founder, Linda Michaels. https://www.facebook.com/groups/664027960470508/

Dreschel, N. A. (2010). The effects of fear and anxiety on health and lifespan in pet dogs. *Applied Animal Behaviour Science, 125*(3–4), 157–162. https://doi: 10.1016/j.applanim.2010.04.003

Dunbar, I. (2007–2020). *The Dog Bite Scale: An assessment of the severity of bites based on evaluation of wound pathology.* http://www.dogstardaily.com/training/bite-scale

Dunbar, I. (2012). *The SIRIUS puppy raising initiative for dog professionals: Breeders, veterinarians, pet stores, trainers and shelters.* https://www.dogstardaily.com/training/sirius-puppy-raising-initiative-dog-professionals-breeders-veterinarians-pet-stores-trainer

Dunbar, I. (2007). *Lure reward training.* https://www.dogstardaily.com/training/lure-reward-training

Dunbar, I. (2004). *Before and after getting your puppy: The positive approach to raising a happy, healthy and well-behaved dog.* New World Library.

Easey, M. (2014). *Horse charming. Science based force-free education and training for people and horses.* https://horse-charming.com/

Edgar, R. S., Green, E. W., Zhao, Y., van Ooijen, G., Olmedo, M., Qin, X., Xu, Y., Pan, M., & Valekunja, U. K. (2012). Peroxiredoxins are conserved markers of circadian rhythms. *Nature, 485*(7399), 459–464. Bibcode: 2012Natur.485..459E. https://doi:10.1038/nature11088.ISSN 0028–0836. PMC 3398137. PMID 2262256

Ercumen, A., Colford, J. M., Jr., & Gruber, J. (2014). Distribution system deficiencies and gastrointestinal illness: A systematic review and meta-analysis. *Environmental Health Perspectives, 122*(7). http://dx.doi.org/10.1289/ehp.1306912

Fear Free® (2020a). *Certification: Fear free certification.* https://fearfreepets.com/fear-free-certification-overview/#1532109384264–705c8ce5–2632

Fear Free* (2020b). *About fear free: What is fear free?* https://fearfreepets.com/about/what-is-fear-free/

Ferdowsian, H. (2016). *The meaning and importance of consent for people and animals.* http://www.hopeferdowsian.com/the-meaning-and-importance-of-consent-for-people-and-animals/

Flaim, D. (2016). The importance of clipping dogs' nails. *The Whole Dog Journal.* http://www.whole-dog-journal.com/issues/19_4/features/Nail-Clipping_21430–1.html

Flournoy, W. S., Macintire, D. K., & Wohl, J. S. (2003). Heatstroke in dogs: Clinical signs, treatment, prognosis and prevention. *Compendium on Continuing Education for the Practicing Veterinarian, 25*(6), 422–431.

Fragkaki, I., Stins, J., Roelofs, K., Jongedijk, R., & Hagenaars, M. (2016). Tonic immobility differentiates stress responses in PTSD. *Brain and Behavior, 6*(11). https://doi 10.1002/brb3.546

Fuguzza, C. (2014*). Do as I do: Using social learning to train dogs.* Dogwise.

Fuoco, L. W. (2011). Pet tales: Heroes in the spotlight. *Pittsburgh Post-Gazette.* https://tinyurl.com/syh2bzh

Garrod, D. (2021). *Stress release for dogs: The canine emotional detox.* Dogwise.

Garvey, M., Stella, J., & Croney, C. (2016). *Implementing environmental enrichment for dogs.* Purdue Extension. College of Veterinary Medicine. https://extension.purdue.edu/extmedia/VA/VA-13-W.pdf

HABRI Human Animal Bond Research Institute. (n.d.) *Research.* https://habri.org/research/?gclid=CjwKCAjwr7X4BRA4EiwAUXjbt3oazCL0M_rcHPgp7aXc1q88I5dTNk4WQG3yYt2zVqABN8I-16p-8hoCjacQAvD_BwE

Hale, A. (2021, March 28). Stepping off the operant merry-go-round. The Virtual Dog Conference: The Marathon. Facebook. https://www.facebook.com/groups/1336863253341818/permalink/1360352394326237

Hale, F. A. (1998). Dental caries in the dog. *Journal of Veterinary Dentistry, 15*(2), 79–83.

Hammerle, M., Horst, C., Levine, E., Overall, K., Rodasta, L., Rafter-Richie, M., & Yin, S. (2015). 2015 AHAA canine and feline behavior management guidelines. *Journal of the American Animal Hospital Association, 51*(4) 205–221. doi:10.5326/jaaha-ms-6527

Hare, B. (2020). *The Dognition assessment: Get beyond "woof."* https://www.dognition.com/#:~:text=You'll%20play%20science%2Dbased,cunning%2C%20memory%2C%20and%20reasoning.

Hare, B., & Tomasello, M. (2005). Human-like social skills in dogs? *Trends in Cognitive Science 9*(9), 439–444. https://doi.org/10.1016/j.tics.2005.07.003

Hare, B., & Woods, V. (2013). *The genius of dogs: How dogs are smarter than you think.* Dutton.

Harrison, J. (2016). *Pedigree dogs exposed: The blog. Help this little chap get a decent night's sleep.* http://pedigreedogsexposed.blogspot.com/2016/08/help-this-little-chap-get-decent-nights.html

Haubrich, J., Crestani, A. P., Cassini, L. F., Santana, F., Sierra, R. O., Alvares, L. de O., & Quillfeldt, J. A. (2014). *Reconsolidation Allows Fear Memory to Be Updated to a Less Aversive Level Through the Incorporation of Appetitive Information. Neuropsychopharmacology, 40*(2), 315–326. doi:10.1038/npp.2014.174

Hens, K. (2009). Ethical responsibilities towards dogs: An inquiry into the dog-human relationship. *Journal of Agricultural and Environmental Ethics, 22*(1), 3–14. http://sci-hub.io/10.1007/s10806–008–9120-yHorn, L., Huber, L., & Range, F. (2013). The importance of the secure base effect for domestic dogs: Evidence from a manipulative problem-solving task. *PLOS ONE.* https://doi10.1371/journal.pone.0065296

Horowitz, A. (2015). *How do dogs "see" with their noses?* [Video]. YouTube. https://www.youtube.com/watch?v=p7fXa2Occ_U&feature=youtu.be&fbclid=IwAR04IhwszhCgyz_mfuNi2Knq0txificuLb9QxxHk17SYIMRw39aXoJ4cJ-I

Horowitz, A. (2009). *Inside of a dog: What dogs see, smell and know.* Scribner.

Horowitz, D.F. (2021). *Dog behavior problems: Coprophagia.* VCA. https://vcahospitals.com/know-your-pet/dog-behavior-problems-coprophagia?fbclid=IwAR23HB3ncWKOQLDmSJGmaGnQLss8zZdfU_Y12zmMc-oelfD7yhTC1IM_9gc

Horowitz, D. F., Ciribassi, J., & Dale, S. (Eds.). (2014). *Decoding your dog.* Houghton Mifflin Harcourt.

Hudson, R. (2019a). *Where dogs and science meet: Taking dogs to the back of the veterinary clinic. Why?* https://wherescienceanddogsmeet.wordpress.com/2018/07/06/taking-dogs-to-the-back-of-the-veterinary-clinic-why/

Hudson, R. (2019b). *Where dogs and science meet: Lunging, barking, biting, oh my.* https://wherescienceanddogsmeet.wordpress.com/2019/07/22/lunging-barking-biting-oh-my/

Humane Society of the United States. (2016). *Coyotes, pets and community cats.* https://www.humanesociety.org/resources/coyotes-pets-and-community-cats#:~:text=Dogs%20(especially%20small%20dogs)%20should,attracting%20coyotes%20to%20your%20yard.

Jagoe, A., & Serpell, J. (1996). Owner characteristics and interactions and the prevalence of canine behaviour problems. *Applied Animal Behaviour Science, 47*(1–2), 31–42. doi:10.1016/0168-1591(95)01008-4

Jones, Mary, C. (1924). A Laboratory Study of Fear: The Case of Peter. *The Pedagogical Seminary and Journal of Genetic Psychology, 31*(4), 308–315 DOI:10.1080/08856559.1924.9944851

Kahn-Greene, E. T., Lipizzi, E. L., Conrad, A. K., Haminori, G. H., & Kilgore, W. D. (2006). Sleep deprivation adversely affects interpersonal responses to frustration. *Personality and Individual Differences, 41*(8), 1433–1443.

Kaminski, J., Call, J., & Fischer, J. (2004). Word learning in a domestic dog: Evidence for "fast mapping." *Science, 304*(5677), 1682–1683.

Käufer, M. (2013). *Canine play behavior*. Dogwise.

Kaulfub, P., & Mills, D. S. (2008). Neophilia in domestic dogs (*Canis familiaris*) and its implication for studies of dog cognition. *Animal Cognition, 11*(3), 553–556.

Keller, N., Hennings, A., & Dunsmoor, J. (2020). Behavioral and neural processes in counterconditioning: Past and future directions. *Behavior Research and Therapy*. doi: 10.1016/j.brat.2019.103532

Kelly, S. (2019). *Canine enrichment*.

Kerasote, T. (2014). *Pukka's promise: The quest for longer-lived dogs*. First Mariner Books.

Kerns, N. (2012). Not for you? Don't take me to the dog park. *Whole Dog Journal*. https://www.whole-dog-journal.com/editorial/not-for-you/

Kirkham, L. (2014). Baby sounds for pets, dogs, cats and other animals. [CD]. Little Creatures Publishing.

Kis, A., Bence, M., Lakatos, G., Pergel, E., Turcsán, B., Pluijmakers, J., Vas, J., Elek, Z., Fruder, I., Foldi, L., Sasvari-Szekely, M., Miklosi, A., Ronai, Z., & Kubinyi, E. (2014). Oxytocin receptor gene polymorphisms are associated with human directed social behavior in dogs (*Canis familiaris*). *PLOS ONE, 9*(1). https://doi: 10.1371/journal.pone.0083993. eCollection 2014.

Klinck, M. (2014). Your dog needs a job. In D. F. Horowitz, J. Ciribassi, & S. Dale (Eds.). *Decoding your dog: The ultimate experts explain common dog behaviors and reveal how to prevent or change unwanted ones* (pp. 178–179). Houghton Mifflin Harcourt.

Knueven, D. (2008). *The holistic health guide: Natural care for the whole dog*. T. F. H. Publications.

Kolb, B., Gibb, R., & Robinson, T. E. (2003). Brain plasticity and behavior. *Current Directions in Psychological Science*. Canadian Centre for Behavioral Neuroscience, University of Lethridge and Department of Psychology, University of Michigan.

Kunkel-Jones, J. (2019.) *Puppy mills: The horrific truth*. http://www.dogpsychologistoncall.com/puppy-mills-the-horrific-truth/

Kuruvillaa, A. (2003). Heart rate of pet dogs: Effects of overweight and exercise. *Asia Pacific Journal of Clinical Nutrition, 12* (Suppl):S51.

Landsberg, G. (2020). Social behavior of dogs. *Merck Manual*. https://www.merckvetmanual.com/behavior/normal-social-behavior-and-behavioral-problems-of-domestic-animals/social-behavior-of-dogs

Leahey, T. H. (2001). *A history of modern psychology* (3rd ed.). Prentice Hall.

LeBlanc, C. (2015). Are "free-shape'" dogs better problem solvers? *BARKS Blog*. http://ppgworldservices.com/2015/03/16/are-free-shaped-dogs-better-problem-solvers/

LeDoux, J. (2011, Feb. 2). *What fearful rats can tell us about treating psychiatric disorders*. [Stockholm Psychiatry Lecture]. Karolinska Institute, Stockholm. New York University. [Video]. YouTube. https://www.youtube.com/watch?v=9_IIgXWdF-w

Lewis, H. (2016). *Fear-free veterinary clinics aim to soothe the beasts.* http://www.pressherald.com/2016/01/13/fear-free-veterinary-clinics-aim-to-soothe-the-beasts/

Lindsay, S. (2008). *Handbook of Applied Dog Behavior and Training, Volume 3: Procedures and Protocols.* Wiley-Blackwell.

Liu, N., Sargan, D. R., Adams, V., & Ladlow, J. (2015). Characterisation of brachycephalic obstructive airway syndrome in French bulldogs using whole-body barometric plethysmography. *PLOS ONE 10*(6): e0130741. http://journals.plos.org/plosone/article?id=10.1371/journal.pone.0130741

London, K. (2015). "Do as I do" dog training. *The Bark.* https://thebark.com/content/do-i-do-dog-training

Lucas, E. A., Powell, E. W., Murphree, O. D. (1977). Baseline sleep-wake patterns in the pointer dog. *Physiology & Behavior, 19*(2), 285–291. http://sci-hub.io/10.1016/0031–9384(77)90340–7

MacLean, E. L., Snyder-Mackler, N., vonHoldt, B. M., & Serpell, J. A. (2019). Highly heritable and functionally relevant breed differences in dog behavior. *Proceedings from the National Academy of Sciences.* Royal Society Publishing. https://royalsocietypublishing.org/doi/10.1098/rspb.2019.0716

MacLellan, L. (2016, Nov. 4). *The dog training strategies that work on kids.* Quartz. https://qz.com/807702/the-dog-training-strategies-that-work-on-kids/

Mahaney, P. (2012, July 3). *Flea prevention and treatment for cats and dogs.* PetMD. https://www.petmd.com/blogs/thedailyvet/pmahaney/2012/july/flea_prvention_and_treatments_for_cats_and_dogs-26376

Manning, S. (2016, January 13). *"Fear-free" veterinarians aim to reduce stress for pets.* Sun Herald. https://www.sunherald.com/latest-news/article54775130.html

Marcellin-Little, D., Levine, D., & Taylor, R. (2005). Rehabilitation and conditioning of sporting dogs. *Veterinary Clinics Small Animal Practice, 35,* 1427–1439.

Martiya, M. (2016, July). Grooming restraints. *BARKS from the Guild.* 38–39. https://issuu.com/petprofessionalguild/docs/bftg_july_2016_opt/54

Maslow, A. H. (1954). *Motivation and personality.* Harper.

Maslow, A. H. (1943). A theory of human motivation. *Psychological Review, 50*(4), 370–396.

Mayo Clinic. (2020a). *Nutrition and healthy eating: Functions of water in the body.* http://www.mayoclinic.org/healthy-lifestyle/nutrition-and-healthy-eating/multimedia/functions-of-water-in-the-body/img-20005799

Mayo Clinic (2020b). *Diseases and conditions: Hypothermia.* http://www.mayoclinic.org/diseases-conditions/hypothermia/basics/definition/con-20020453

McGreevy, P. (2010). *A modern dog's life: How to do the best for your dog.* The Experiment.

McMillan, F. D., Duffy, D. L., & Serpell, J. A. (2011). Mental health of dogs formerly used as "breeding stock" in commercial breeding establishments.

Applied Animal Behaviour Science, 135(1–2), 86–94. https://doi.org/10.1016/j.applanim.2011.09.006

Meola, S. D. (2013). Brachycephalic airway syndrome. *Topics in Companion Animal Medicine, 28*(3), 91–96. http://sci-hub.bz/10.1053/j.tcam.2013.06.004

Merrill, J. (2020). *Heatstroke in dogs.* Urban Search and Rescue Veterinary Group. http://usarveterinarygroup.org/usarvet/heatstroke-in-dogs/

Michaels, L. J. (Creator). (2020). *Hierarchy of Dog Needs* [Pyramid Infographic]. (Original work published 2015). http://www.dogpsychologistoncall.com/hierarchy-of-dog-needs-tm/

Michaels, L. J. (2017a). Grazing games. *UT Pet School.* http://www.dogpsychologistoncall.com/ut-pet-school-grazing-game-can-change-behavior/

Michaels, L. J. (2017b). The top 10 do's and don'ts of successful housetraining. *Del Mar Village Voice.*

Michaels, L. J. (2015a). Understanding Research: Making the Case for Force-Free Training. [Film, educational DVD]. Tawzer Dog.

Michaels, L. J. (2015b). *How to train your wolfdog, Wolfdog Radio interview with Linda Michaels, M.A., Psychology.* [Video]. YouTube. Gumroad. http://www.dogpsychologistoncall.com/how-to-train-your-wolfdog-with-linda-michaels-m-a-wolfdog-radio/

Michaels, L. J. (2015c). *Wolfdog "Come!" Good boy, Smokey!* [Video]. YouTube. https://www.youtube.com/watch?v=Htcca-q8g0w

Michaels, L. J. (2015d, May). Open letter to research scientists. *BARKS from the Guild.* https://barksfromtheguild.com/2015/05/29/an-open-letter-to-canine-research-scientists/

Michaels, L. J. (2012). Puppy socialization and vaccinations belong together. Pet Professional Guild. *BARKS from the Guild.* https://petprofessionalguild.com/resources/Pet%20Owner%20Handouts/Puppy%20Socialization%20and%20%20Vaccinations%20Go%20Together.pdf

Miklósi, Á., & Kubinyi, E. (2016). Current trends in canine problem-solving and cognition. *Current Directions in Psychological Science, 25*(5), 300–306.

Miller, P. (2020). Dogs fighting in your household. *Whole Dog Journal,* https://www.whole-dog-journal.com/issues/13_4/features/Dog-Fighting-Behavior-Aggression_16214-1.html. (Original work published 2010)

Miller, P. (2019). Winter warnings for your dog. *Whole Dog Journal.* https://www.whole-dog-journal.com/health/winter-warnings-for-your-dog/

Miller, P. (2017a). *Beware of the dog: Positive solutions for aggressive behavior in dogs.* Dogwise.

Miller, P. (2017b). How to manage a multi-dog household. *Whole Dog Journal.* https://www.whole-dog-journal.com/issues/5_7/features/Multi-Dog-Household-Management_5466-1.html (Original work published 2002)

Miller, P. (2004). *Positive perspectives: Love your dog. Train your dog.* Dogwise.

Miller, P. (2001). The great, awful outdoors. *Your Dog.* Tufts University.

Modell, H., Cliff, W., Michael, J., McFarland, J., Wenderoth, M. P., & Wright, A. (2015). A physiologist's view of homeostasis. *Advances in Physiology Education, 39*(4), 259–266.

Montag, C., & Panksepp, J. (2017). Primary emotional systems and personality: An evolutionary perspective. *Frontiers in Psychology, 2017*(8), 464.

Morgan, J. (2020). Why holistic? *Naturally Healthy Pets.* https://drjudymorgan.com/pages/why-holistic

National Institute of Health: National Institute on Aging. (2016). *Hot weather safety for older adults: Who is at risk.* https://www.nia.nih.gov/health/hot-weather-safety-older-adults#risk

National Resource Defense Council. (2003). *Study finds safety of drinking water in U. S. cities at risk.* http://www.nrdc.org/water/drinking/uscities.asp

National Sleep Foundation. (2016). *Healthy sleep tips.* https://sleepfoundation.org/

Nijenhuis, E. R., Vanderlinden, J., & Spinhoven, P. (1998). Animal defensive reactions as a model for trauma induced dissociative reactions. *Journal of Traumatic Stress,* 11, 243–260.

North Shore Animal League. (2015). *Grooming tips.* http://www.animalleague.org/expert-advice/health/articles/everyday-health/pet-grooming-tips.html

Oechtering, G. (2010). Brachycephalic syndrome: New information on an old congenital disease. *Veterinary Focus, 20*(2), 2–9. https://issuu.com/corecph/docs/2010__20.2

O'Neill, D. G., Jackson, C., Guy, J. H., Church, D. B., McGreevy, P. D., Thompson, P. C., & Brodbelt, D. C. (2015). Epidemiological associations between brachycephaly and upper respiratory tract disorders in dogs attending veterinary practices in England. *Canine Genetics and Epidemiology 2*(10), 1–10. https://cgejournal.biomedcentral.com/articles/10.1186/s40575–015–0023–8

Overall, K. L. (2013). *Manual of clinical and behavioral medicine for cats and dogs.* Elsevier.

Overall, K. L. (2011). *Dr. Karen Overall, DVM, PhD, Interview Part 2.* [Video]. YouTube. https://www.youtube.com/watch?v=VKNNbQjTjco

Overall, K., Seksel, K., Brammeier, S., Brennan, J., Brown, S., Bryant, D., Calnon, D., Stenson, T. C., Colwin, G., Dale, S., Dominguez, C., Dougherty, C., Dudzic, E., Gaugan, K., Jung, U., Kendell, K., Lem, M., Michelle, G., Olson, R., … Williams, S. A. (2006). From "Good trainers: How to identify one and why this is important to your practice of veterinary medicine." *Journal of Veterinary Behavior, 1*(1), 47–52. https://doi:10.1016/j.jveb.2006.05.001

Packer, R. M., Hendricks, A., Tivers, M. S., & Burn, C.C. (2015). Impact of facial conformation on canine health: Brachycephalic obstructive airway syndrome. *PLOS ONE, 10*(10), eoi37496. doi:10.1371/journal.pone.0137496

Palmer, R., & Custance, D. (2008). A counterbalanced version of Ainsworth's Strange Situation Procedure reveals secure-base effects in dog-human relationships. *Applied Animal Behaviour Science 109*(2–4), 306–319 https://doi.org/10.1016/j.applanim.2007.04.002.

Pam, N. (2013). *Differential reinforcement.* http://psychologicaldictionary.org/differential-reinforcement-of-other-behavior-dro

Panksepp, J. (2010). Affective neuroscience of the emotional BrainMind: Evolutionary perspectives and implications for understanding depression. *Dialogues Clinical Neuroscience, 12*(4), 533–545. https://www.ncbi.nlm.nih.gov/pmc/articles/PMC3181986/

Patel, C. (2015). *The bucket game introduction, part 1.* [Video]. YouTube. https://www.youtube.com/watch?v=GJSs9eqi2r8

Patel, C. (2010). *Teaching a dog to wear a muzzle (Muzzle training).* [Video]. YouTube. https://www.youtube.com/watch?v=1FABgZTFvHo

Pavlov, I. P. (1927). Conditioned reflexes: An investigation of the physiological activity of the cerebral cortex. *Annals of Neurosciences, 17*(3), 136–141. https://doi:10.5214/ans.0972–7531.1017309 https://www.ncbi.nlm.nih.gov/pmc/articles/PMC4116985/

Pelar, C. (2012). *Living with kids and dogs . . . without losing your mind: A parent's guide to controlling the chaos* (2nd ed.). Dream Dog Productions.

Personne, C. (2015). *Be safe—Dog bite safety and education.* Pet Professional Guild. https://petprofessionalguild.com/Resources/Documents/Advocacy%20Handouts/Handout%202%20Myth%20of%20Tail%20Waggin.pdf

Petfinder.com. (2020). *Dog adoption.* https://www.petfinder.com/pet-adoption/dog-adoption/

PetMD. (2016). *Electric cord bite injury in dogs.* http://www.petmd.com/dog/conditions/cardiovascular/c_dg_electric_cord_bite?page=show

PetMD. (2010). *Hypothermia in dogs.* https://www.petmd.com/dog/emergency/common emergencies/e__dg__hypothermia

Pet Poison Helpline. (2020). *Essential oil and dogs.* https://tinyurl.com/sllrood

Pet Professional Guild. (2020a). *Find an expert. Need help searching for a professional?* http://www.petprofessionalguild.com/Zip-Code-Search

Pet Professional Guild. (2020b). *Guiding principles.* https://www.petprofessionalguild.com/resources/PPG%20Logos/Guiding%20Principles.pdf

Pet Professional Guild. (2020c). *The PPG ethics committee roles and responsibilities.* http://www.petprofessionalguild.com/ThePPGEthicsCommittee

Pet Professional Guild. (2020d). *Puppy education: Important puppy training information.* https://www.petprofessionalguild.com/PuppyTrainingResources

Pet Professional Guild. (2012). *Your puppy socialization checklist.* https://petprofessionalguild.com/Resources/Documents/Puppy%20Socialization%20Check%20List.pdf

Phillips, K. M. (2020). *Dog bite law.* https://dogbitelaw.com/

Piaget, J. (1954). *The construction of reality in the child* (M. Cook, Trans.). Basic Books. https://doi.org/10.1037/11168–000

Pierson, M. H. (2015). *The secret history of kindness: Learning from how dogs learn.* W. W. Norton.

Pilley, J. (2013). *Chaser: Unlocking the genius of the dog who knows a thousand words.* [Video]. YouTube. https://www.youtube.com/watch?v=J982KYWohT8

Pires, N. P., Tufik, S., & Andersen, M. L. (2012). *Relationship between sleep deprivation and anxiety-experimental research perspective.* Einstein (Sao Paulo), *10*(4).

Polsky, R. P., (2000). Can aggression in dogs be elicited through the use of electronic pet containment systems. *Journal of Applied Animal Welfare Science, 3*(4), 345–357.

Premack, D. (1965). Reinforcement theory. In D. Levine (Ed.), *Nebraska Symposium on Motivation, 13,* 189–282. Lincoln: University of Nebraska Press.

Premack, D. (1959). Toward empirical behavior laws: I. Positive reinforcement. *Psychological Review, 66,* 219–233. http://dx.doi.org/10.1037/h0040891

Provet Healthcare Information. (2013). *Epiphyseal plate closure in dogs.* http://www.provet.co.uk/health/diagnostics/growthplatedogs.htm

Range, F., & Viranyi, Z. (2015, January 15). Tracking the evolutionary origins of dog-human cooperation: The "canine cooperation hypothesis." *Frontiers in Psychology, 5,* 1582. https://doi: 10.3389/fpsyg.2014.01582.

Ray, M., & Harding, J. (2005). *Dog tricks: Fun and games for your clever canine.* Thunder Bay.

Rehn, T. (2014). I like my dog, does my dog like me? *Applied Animal Behaviour Science, 150,* 65–73. https://doi.org/10.1016/j.applanim.2013.10.008

Rehn, T. (2013). *Best of friends? Investigating the dog-human relationship.* [Doctoral thesis, Swedish University of Agricultural Sciences]. https://pub.epsilon.slu.se/10793/1/rehn_t_130913.pdf

Richmond, M. (2019). Adding a new dog to a multi-dog household: Plan ahead! *Whole Dog Journal.* https://www.whole-dog-journal.com/issues/7_3/features/Multi-Dog-Households_5613–1.html (Original work published 2004).

Royal Society for the Prevention of Cruelty to Animals (RSPCA). (2021). *Flystrike in pets.* https://www.rspca.org.uk/adviceandwelfare/pets/general/flystrike

Reid, A. (2019). Novel problem-solving, exploration, and socialization with regards to sensory behaviors in the family *canidae. EC Veterinary Science 4*(3), 187–201.

Safina, C. (2015). *Beyond words: What animals think and feel.* Picador.

Sala, R. G. (2014, January 26). Incorrectly used collars, leashes can do harm. *New York Post.* http://nypost.com/2014/01/26/incorrectly-used-collars-leashes-can-do-harm/

San Diego Humane Society (2020). *Co-existing with wildlife: Raccoons.* https://www.sdhumane.org/about-us/news-center/stories/raccoon.html

San Diego Natural History Museum. (2020). *Herpetology.* https://www.sdnhm.org/science/herpetology/

Sargisson, R. (2014a,b,c,d). Canine separation anxiety: strategies for treatment and management. *Veterinary Medicine: Research and Reports, 143.* doi:10.2147/vmrr. s60424

Schultz, D. P., & Schultz, E. S. (2008). *A history of modern psychology* (9th ed.). Wadsworth.

Seligman, M. E. (2020). *Authentic happiness.* Penn University of Pennsylvania. https://www.authentichappiness.sas.upenn.edu/faculty-profile/profile-dr-martin-seligman

Seligman, M. E. (1972). Learned helplessness. *Annual Review of Medicine. 23*(1), 407–412. https://doi:10.1146/annurev.me.23.020172.002203

Selye, H. (1936). A syndrome produced by diverse nocuous agents. *Nature, 138,* 32. https://doi:10.1038/138032a0 https://www.nature.com/articles/138032a0

Serpell, J. A. (2020). *Canine behavioral assessment & research questionnaire (C-BARQ).* University of Pennsylvania.

Serpell, J. A. (Ed.). (2007). *The domestic dog.* Cambridge University Press.

Service, S. K. (2012). A genome-wide meta-analysis of association studies of Cloninger's Temperament Scales. *Translational Psychiatry, 2*(5). https://doi:10.1038/ tp.2012.37, https://www.ncbi.nlm.nih.gov/pmc/articles/PMC3365256/

Shannon, C. (2020). *Bad to the bone: Analyzing & assessing dog bites.* [Webinar]. Raising Canine. http://raisingcanine.com/education/bad-to-the-bone-analyzing-assessin g-dog-bites/

Shippen, G. (2016, September). *Sensory gardens: Another great pet environmental enrichment idea.* http://www.vetanswers.com.au/blog/post/sensory-gardens-another-great-pet-environmental-enrichment-idea/514

Shryock, J. (2018). *Family paws parent education: Dogs & storks—Dogs & toddlers.* https://www.familypaws.com/

Skinner, B. F. (1953). *Science and human behavior.* Free Press.

Skinner, B. F. (1938). *The behavior of organisms.* Copley.

Stewart, G. (2016). *Behavior adjustment training 2.0: New practical techniques for fear, frustration, and aggression in dogs.* Dogwise.

Stilwell, V. (2020). *Flooding.* Positively: The Future of Dog Training. https://positively. com/dog-training/positive-training/victoria-stilwell-articles/flooding/

Straus, M., & Kerns, N. (2019, October). Diet, dogs and DCM. *Whole Dog Journal.* https:// www.whole-dog-journal.com/food/diet-dogs-and-dcm/#:~:text=Study%20 found%20that%2023%20of,supplemented%20as%20well%20as%20taurine.

Tali, M. (2019). *Terevision|Koerte sunnivaba koolatamine|ETV|ERR.* [Television Broadcast]. Estonian National Morning Show. Estonia. https://etv.err.ee/999473/ koerte-sunnivaba-koolitamine

Taylor, S. (2019, March). Original influences. How the ideals of America were shaped by Native Americans. *Psychology Today.* https://www.psychologytoday.com/us/ blog/out-the-darkness/201903/original-influences

Tiira, K., & Lohi, H. (2015). Early life experiences and exercise associate with canine anxiety. *PLOS ONE, 10*(11), e0141907. https://doi.org/10.1371/journal.pone.0141907

Thompson, K. & Smith, B. (2014). Should we let sleeping dog lie…with us? Synthesizing the literature and setting the agenda for research on human-animal co-sleeping practices. *Humanimalia: A Journal of Human/Animal Interface Studies, 6*(1). 114–127.

Tinbergen, N. (1963). On aims and methods of ethology. *Zeitschrift* für *Tierpsychologie, 20*, 410–433.

Tobler, I., & Sigg, H. (1985, November). *Institute of Pharmacology*. University of Zurich, Switzerland.

Tong, A. (2020). Reducing leash reactivity: The engage-disengage game. https://www.clickertraining.com/reducing-leash-reactivity-the-engage-disengage-game

Topál, J., Miklosi, A., Csayni, V., & Doka, A. (1998). Attachment behavior in dogs (*Canis familiaris*): A new application of Ainsworth's (1969) Strange Situation Test. *Journal of Comparative Psychology, 112*(3), 219–229.

Topál, J., Miklosi, A., & Csányi, V. (1997). Dog-human relationship affects problem-solving behavior in the dog. *Anthrozoos: A Multidisciplinary Journal of The Interactions of People & Animals, 10*(4), 214–224. https://doi: 10.2752/089279397787000987

Tracy, J., & Randles, D. (2011). Four models of basic emotions: A review of Ekman and Cordaro, Izard, Levenson, and Panksepp and Watt. *Emotion Review, 3*(4), 397–405.

Trut, L., Kharlomova, A., Kekekova, A., Acland, G., Carreier, D., Chaes, K., & Lark, K. (2002). Morphology and behavior: Are they coupled at the genome level? In E. Ostramder, U. Giger, & K. Lindblad-Toh (Eds.), *The dog and its genome* (pp 515–538). Cold Harbor Springs Laboratory Press.

Tudge, N. (2015). *People training skills for pet professionals*. Lulu Publishing.

Tyson, P. (2001). *The Hippocratic oath today*. NOVA Body and Brain. http://www.pbs.org/wgbh/nova/body/hippocratic-oath-today.html

Verstraete, F. J. (2016). Veterinary dentistry: Dental care for pets. *Healthymouth: Dental care that dogs, cats and horses drink*. https://www.healthymouth.com/Articles.asp?ID=250

Veterinary Institute of Integrative Medicine. (2019). *Transforming animal health through education*. http://viim.org/

Viranyi, Z., Topal, J., Miklosi, A., & Csanyi, V. (2006). A nonverbal test of knowledge attribution: A comparative study on dogs and children. *Animal Cognition, 9*(1), 13–26.

Volk, J. O., Felsted, K. E., Thomas, J. G., & Siren, C. W. (2011). Executive summary of the Bayer veterinary usage study. *Journal of the American Veterinary Medical Association, 238*(10). http://avmajournals.avma.org/doi/pdf/10.2460/javma.238.10.1275

vonHoldt, B., Shuldiner, E., Janowitz Koch, I., Kartizinel, R., Hogan, A., Brubaker, L., Wasner, S., Shahler, D., Wynne, C., Ostander, E., Sinsheimer, J., & Udell, M. (2017). Structural variants in genes associated with human Williams-Beuren syndrome underlie stereotypical hypersociability in domestic dogs. *Science Advances 3*(7), e1700398.

Watson, J., & Rayner, R. (1920). Conditioned emotional reactions. *Journal of Experimental Psychology, 3*(1): 1–14.

Weigle, K. (2019). *Things you should know before you buy a shock collar.* https://ultimatebarkcontrol.com/blogs/news/things-you-should-know-before-you-buy-a-shock-collar

Wilde, N. (2018). *Keeping the peace: A guide to solving dog-dog aggression in the home.* Phantom.

Wilde, N. (2010). *Don't leave me! Step-by-step help for your dog's separation anxiety.* Phantom.

Witmer, M. (2014). *Using the Pet Tudor to trim nails.* [Video]. YouTube. https://www.youtube.com/watch?v=sJdbiWEjzRA

Wolpe, J. (1954). Reciprocal inhibition as the main basis of psychotherapeutic effects. *A.M.A. Archives of Neurology and Psychiatry, 72,* 205–226.

Wu, K. (2017). *Love, actually: The science behind lust, attraction, and companionship.* Science in the News (SITN). Harvard University. http://sitn.hms.harvard.edu/flash/2017/love-actually-science-behind-lust-attraction-companionship/

Wynne, C. (2019). *Dog is love: Why and how your dog loves you.* Houghton Mifflin Harcourt.

Yin, S. (Director). (2014a). *Handling, moving and restraining dogs in stressful environments, part 1.* [Film, educational DVD]. CattleDog Publishing.

Yin, S. (Director). (2014b). *Handling moving and restraining small and medium-sized dogs with skill and ease, Part 2 .*[Film. educational DVD]. CattleDog Publishing.

Yin, S. (2012a). *Which types of collars and harnesses are safe for your dog?* https://drsophiayin.com/blog/entry/which-types-of-collars-and-harnesses-are-safe-for-your-dog/

Yin, S. (2012b). *Low stress handling of dogs and cats: Creating the pet-friendly hospital, animal shelter or petcare business.* [Film, educational DVD]. Cattledog Publishing.

Yin, S. (2011). *How to greet a dog.* http://info.drsophiayin.com/how-to-greet-a-dog-ebook

Yin, S. (2009). *Low stress handling, restraint and behavior modification of dogs and cats.* CattleDog Publishing.

Zentall, T. R. (1996). An analysis of imitative learning in animals. In C. M. Heyes & B. G. Galef, Jr. (Eds.), *Social learning in animals: The roots of culture* (pp. 221–243). Academic Press. https://doi.org/10.1016/B978–012273965–1/50012–1

Zimlich, R. (2014). *A farewell to Dr. Sophia Yin: Reeling from the loss, friends and colleagues work to further her legacy in wake of suicide.* DVM360. http://veterinarynews.dvm360.com/farewell-dr-sophia-yin

ONLINE RESOURCES

Do No Harm Dog Training
(2017). Linda Michaels, MA., founder and lead administrator. Join our group to ask dog training and behavior questions and to discuss the material in this book. https://www.facebook.com/groups/664027960470508/

DoNoHarmDogTraining.com
Archive of No Shock, No Prong, No Choke and other memes, articles, blogs, and hand-outs for *Do No Harm Dog Training*® trainers and pet parents. http://www.dogpsychologistoncall.com/resources/

HierarchyOfDogNeeds.com
An easy to understand and use wellness and force-free behavior modification guide tailored for use by all dog professionals and dog lovers. Downloads are FREE. The Hierarchy of Dog Needs® is available in 11 different languages to date: English, French, Spanish, Portuguese, Chinese, Danish, German, Estonian, Korean, Greek, and Arabic. http://www.dogpsychologistoncall.com/hierarchy-of-dog-needs-tm/

PsychologyToday.com
Linda Michaels interview with scientist Dr. Marc Bekoff, *Maslow Meets the Mutts*. [Web post blog]. https://www.psychologytoday.com/us/blog/animal-emotions/201705/hierarchy-dog-needs-abraham-maslow-meets-the-mutts

PetProfessionalGuild.com
Archive of ethics and position statements, online educational webinars, articles, blogs, and hand-outs for force-free trainers and pet parents and a *Find a Force-free trainer by zip code* search function. https://www.petprofessionalguild.com/

Canine Research Studies

A group for sharing and discussing scientific research studies that relate to dogs. Rebekah Hudson, MPH., CVT, founder and lead administrator. https://www.facebook.com/groups/1961822777391593

Dogwise.com

Humane dog training, dog nutrition and dog competition books, DVDs, eBooks. https://www.dogwise.com/?aff=260

TawzerDog.com

Subscribe to access hundreds of +R training videos. https://www.tawzerdog.com/

PHOTO CREDITS

Chapter 9.
39. Eric Isselee

Chapter 10.
40. alexei_tm
41. Eric Isselee

Chapter 11.
42. Cynoclub
43. adogslifephoto

Part 3.
44. adogslifephoto

Chapter 12.
45. Khaneeros
46. Justyna

Chapter 13.
47. Evgeny
48. Eric Isselee
49. Irina K.

Chapter 14.
50. Grigory Bruev
51. CallallooAlexis

Chapter 15.
52. Eric Isselee
53. Sonja Calovini

Chapter 16.
54. Cynoclub
55. CallallooAlexis
56. Cynoclub
57. Cynoclub
58. cynoclub
59. Mikkel Bigandt
60. Steve Mann
61. cynoclub

Part 4.
62. CALLALLOO CANDCY

Chapter 17.
63. Dogs
64. cynoclub
65. wip-studio
66. Dimid
67. dmussman
68. Eric Isselee
69. Mat Hayward
70. ThamKC

Chapter 18.
71. New Africa

Chapter 19.
72. cynoclub

Chapter 20.
73. Capifrutta
74. Marco Antonio Fdez

Chapter 21.
75. cynoclub

Chapter 22.
76. DoraZett
77. Vell
78. Life in Pixels
79. Elles Rijsdijk
80. Willee Cole

References.
81. Africa Studio

INDEX

A

abandonment and attachment, 64–65
adoption
    personality of dog for, 107
    preparing you home for, 113
    selecting a breeder and puppy for, 109–111
adult dogs
    elimination opportunities for, 153
    exercise for, 27
    home exercise techniques for, 29
    play with puppies, 134
    self-handicapping in play, 134
    sleep patterns in, 34
    techniques for mouthing, 157
Affective Neuroscience Model, 9, 62–64
aggression, *See also* Chapter 17, 195-236
    assessment,199, 202-213
    barking with, 242
    causes of, 8, 116, 144, 187
    context specificity of, 223–224
    dog-dog aggression treatment, 225
    dog fight breaking up, 227
    DO NOT list, 224
    human aggression treatment, 223
    no jealousy game in treatment, 231
    open bar/closed bar technique in treatment, 231–232
    prevention, assessment, and treatment of, 195–202, 230
    professional consultation for, 202–211
    Rage (emotion) (Panksepp), 64
    red flags, 200
    "Red Zone" dog myth, 224
    resource guarding, 232

sibling rivalry, 229
sleep deprivation effects on, 33
socialization and, 120, 132
tethered outdoor time and, 37
from veterinary/grooming visits, 119–120
vocalizations with, 201
aging/senior dogs
    cognitive deficit barking in, 242
    dog park and beach safety for, 136
    exercise requirements for, 28
    overgrown nails in, 49
    sanctuary space needs of, 35
    scent work for, 80
agreeableness (personality), 253
air (oxygen) needs, 29–32
air muzzle, 51, 122, 130
air-snap, 199
airway, 30–31, 135, 188. *See also* aversive collar
  devices
alarm barks, 242–243
allergies, 237-240
    creation by diet, 21
    diet management for treatment, 239
    preventing infection with, 240
    symptoms and care for, 237–238
alpha roll, 123
alternate behavior reinforcement (DRA), 96–97
alternate reward reinforcement, 171
American Animal Hospital Association (AAHA)
    Canine and Feline Behavior Management Guidelines, 54–55
    "Changing Behavior, Behavior Modification, Aversive Techniques" (AAHA), 6
    guidance on aversive training, 6, 55–56

position on raw feeding, 23

American Holistic Veterinary Medical Association (AHVMA), 57–58

American Humane Association Hero Dog Awards, 223

American Kennel Club (AKC), 112

American Medical Association (AMA), "AMA Code of Medical Ethics", 6–7

American Society for the Prevention of Cruelty to Animals (ASPCA)
Animal Poison Control Center hotline, 41
"Venom Reactions and Treatment Options", 38

American Veterinary Dental College (AVDC), signs of dental/oral disease, 59–60

American Veterinary Dental Society, 59

American Veterinary Medical Association (AVMA)
"Dog Bite Prevention", 250
position on raw feeding, 23
"Principles of Veterinary Medical Ethics", 6

American Veterinary Society of Animal Behavior (AVSAB)
behavior management guidelines, 54
equipment/techniques to avoid in training, 115
"Position Statement on Humane Dog Training", 54, 115, 224
"Position Statement on Puppy Socialization", 121, 195
puppy socialization statement, 121
treating challenging behavior, 224

anal examination desensitization, 123

Anderson, Eileen ("Why Prong Collars Hurt"), 30

Anderson R. K., "Puppy Vaccination and Early Socialization Should Go Together", 121

Animal Legal and Historical Center, outdoor chaining or tethering, 37

"Animal Well-being II: Stress and Distress", 69

Animals at Play (Bekoff), 77–78

anorexia with separation anxiety, 261, 264, 267

antecedent modification methods
decreasing barking, 242
techniques for, 93–94

anti-anxiety medications
Composure TM, 124, 130
with habituation, 132
for separation anxiety management, 269

for veterinary care, 122

anxiety
aversive emotional systems, 64
fence-barrier stress and aggression with, 37
with flooding, 144
personality, 253
recognition by veterinary professional, 122
sensory garden for, 141
separation anxiety/housetraining, 140
sleep deprivation association with, 34
from veterinary/grooming visits, 119

anxious-preoccupied attachment style, 65

Appetitive Emotional System, 63

appetitive value of rewards, 149

approach/retreat, dog-dog aggression treatment, 227

"Are 'Free-Shaped' Dogs Better Problem Solvers?" (LeBlanc), 164

arousal
aversive collar devices and, 17, 90
decreasing, 158–159
with fear, 254
fun stops method for decreasing, 159
with greetings, 231
growling with, 143
mouthing/biting and level of, 158
punishment effects on, 116
from threatening/dominant person, 224
vocalizations with, 143

arthritis, 28–29, 242

ask (vs. command), 149

associative learning, 98–99

Atopic Disease (AD) management, 238–239

attachment
indications of problems in, 144
separation anxiety disorder and, 255-258
styles of, 64–65

automatic behavior/default behavior, 181

aversive collar devices
cause of aggression, 224
effects of use in training, 17
health issues from, 30–31
injuries from, 116
mechanism and effects of, 30–31
misuse in training, 114, 224
See also shock (No Shock)

Aversive Emotional Systems (Panksepp), 64

aversive training
AAHA guidance/policy on, 55–56

misapplication of, 39
See also punishment

B

babies/children
dogs and babies, 245-249
introducing dog and baby, 250
safety precautions for baby/small children
with dog, 247
"Baby Sounds for Pets, Dogs, Cats and Other
Animals", 249
baby steps in training, 133, 149, 163, 232, 266
Balance IT, 22, 239
"balanced trainer", 88
barking, 241-244
with aggression, 242
changes with injury, 116
context for meaning of, 143–144
with play, 242
recurrent laryngeal nerve injury and, 116
redirecting behavior for, 140
training to decrease, 242–243
types of barking, 242
basic skills training, 175-189
come training, 183–187
down and settle down, 179–182
greetings and jumping, 175–178
leash-walking, 187–191
sit training, 178–179
wait/stay training, 182–183
See also specific behaviors
basket muzzle, 130
bathing/shampooing
for allergy care, 238
desensitization to, 128
Beck, Alan (HABRI), 73
Becker, Karen
appropriate diet, 21
integrative wellness, 57
Becker, Marty, Fear Free® initiative and
certification program, 56–57
bee stings, 38
Before and After You Get Your Puppy (Dunbar),
108, 151
behavior
aggressive, 200
cause of relinquishing to shelter, 121
with dog-dog aggression, 225–226
with fear, 252

goals for training, 222–223
hyperactive, 222
as real-life reinforcement, 167
Behavior Adjustment Training 2.0 (Stewart), 81
behavior modification techniques
antecedent modification in, 93
change effects on brain chemistry, 58
differential reinforcement in, 96–97
for force-free education/training, 88
management of undesired behavior, 92, 97
positive reinforcement, 94
behavioral diagnostics. *See* functional analysis
Behavioral Model, 8–9
behavioral models
Affective Neuroscience Model, 8–9
Behavioral Model/Behavioral Analysis, 8–9
Biological Model, 10
Ethological Model, 9
Medical Model, 9
Bekoff, Marc
Foreword, xix
affective neuroscience, 62–63
American Scientist (book review), 80
animal emotions, 66, 68
dogs' needs, 66, 68
The Emotional Lives of Animals, 62–63
fair play rules for play, 77–78
b-endorphin, 73
benevolent leadership, 70–71
Bentivogliio, M., sleep deprivation effects, 33
Berns, Gregory
brain area regulating self-control, 70
Dog Project mapping, 66
How Dogs Love Us, 66
Bessler, David, 30–31
"Best of Friends? Investigating the Dog-Human
Relationship" (Rehn), 74
biddability, 75
Big Five dimensions of personality, 253
Biological Model, 10
biological needs, 19-60
exercise, 25–29
grooming care, 47–51
indoor shelter, 36–37
nutrition, 20–24
safety, 40–43
sleep, 32–36
sufficient air, 29–32
temperature control, 44–47

veterinary care, 51–61
water, 24–25
bite inhibition learning from other dogs, 76
biting
to another dog, 229
assessment of, 199, 202
body language warning of, 143, 199
inhibition of, 75
public safety issue, 17
redirect in dog fight (onto handler), 227
triggers for, 224–225
from use of shock, xxviii, 17
bladder control, age for full control, 153–154
bleach, 41
blocking for trigger management, 226
bloody diarrhea, 135
boarded dogs, 258–259
body language
aggressive warnings, 200
in assessing triggers, 100–101
communication with, 86, 137, 143
displays of stress with veterinary care, 120
of dog with baby, 247
with fear, 145, 252, 254
"freezing" in, 143
hyperactive active body language, 222
in play situations, 133–134
posture as emotion indicator, 143
reading of, 142–145, 247
sleeping position, 36
tonic immobility in, 144
warning of biting, 143
bonding, 72-77
brain chemistry in, 65
dog-dog bonding, 75
dog-human bonding, 65, 73–74
oxytocin role in, 68
with professional staff in clinic/groomer, 125
secure attachments and sociality, 84
bone growth plates, 27
Bordetella transmucosal vaccine, 124
boredom
activities for relief of, 80, 83
barking with, 242
environmental enhancement/enrichment for, 138
idiopathic obsessive behaviors with, 37
mistaken for separation anxiety, 256

Bove-Rothwell, April, "Living in a Human World", 138–139
brachycephalic morphology
choke/prong collar use in, 30–32
heatstroke risk in, 45
sleep deprivation in, 32
use of collar with, 188
brachycephalic obstructive airway syndrome (BOAS), 30–31
Bradshaw, John
biddability, 75
love vs. attachment, 65
brain chemistry
dog-human bonding and, 65
with pleasurable experience, 66
brain injury/lesions
from air pollution, 32
choke collar use and, 31
Brassi-Zucconi, G., sleep deprivation effects, 33
breathing impairment, 30, 116
breeders
best practices for, 111–112
extreme conformation standards for, 31
breed-related tendencies/disorders
bone growth plates closure in, 27
breathing disorders, 31–32
heatstroke/hyperthermia, 135
hypothermia, 47
long spinal column effects, 29, 35
loose facial skin care, 128
lure/chase toy for prey-driven, 28
morphology exaggerations in, 31
obesity risks for, 24
predisposition to separation anxiety, 258
swimming ability, 43
upstairs fetch for natural retrievers, 29
Brown, Stuart, 76
brushing
coat for allergy care, 238
training for grooming, 128
See also oral/dental care
The Bucket Game (Patel), 82
butt dragging, causes for, 123

C
Canine and Feline Behavior Management Guidelines (AAHA), 54–55
Canine Behavioral Assessment and Research Questionnaire (C-BARQ) database, 18

Canine Enrichment: The Book Your Dog Needs You to Read (Kelly), 84

"The Canine Life Stages Guidelines" (AAHA), 55

Canine Play Behavior (Kaufer), 77

cannabinoids (endogenous), 63

capturing behaviors
positive reinforcement for, 94, 116
reward use for, 144
for settle down, 181–182
for sit training, 178
spontaneous behavior in, 164–165

Care (emotion) (Panksepp), 63

carpet, rugs, and upholstery cleaning, 155

carriers. *See* crates

C-BARQ database, 253

cervical spinal injury, 116

"Changing Behavior, Behavior Modification, Aversive Techniques" (AAHA), 6

chewing behavior
appropriate chew items, 159–161
benefits of, 80
environmental enhancement/enrichment for, 83, 138
functions of, 160
hazards from, 42
See also mouthing, training for control

chocolate, 41

choice, self-rewarding nature of, 81–82

choke chains/collars. *See* aversive collar devices

circadian rhythms, 34

classical conditioning
bonding of two stimuli for, 98
learning new associations, 99
mechanism and effects of, 8
See also separation anxiety

clicker training
behavior marking with, 144
rules and tips for, 173–174
as secondary reinforcement, 172
sequence of events in, 173–174

clothing (for dogs) for allergy management, 239

cognition
5 Cognitive Dimensions, 80
brain changes with pleasurable experience, 66
components of, 80
emotion influence on, 69
mental processes in, 80
for recognition of threat, 69

cognitive ability
of child to understand dog, 246
deficits from air pollution, 32
of dogs, 135
level of dogs, 70, 266
problem-solving, 84–85
resource guarding and, 232

cognitive deficit barks, 242

cognitive needs, 79–86

collars. *See* flat collars

"Come" long distance. *See* lightening recall

"Come" training, 184–186

"command" term in training, 149

communication
barking, types and functions of, 242
cognitive dimensions, 80
dog-dog communication, 76
by dogs, 143
emotions in, 62
modes of, 143
patterns of, 80

companionship and bonding, 74, 84

Composure TM, 124, 130

Conditioned Emotional Response (CER), 98, 232

conscientiousness (personality), 253

consent (asking for)
consent test for play, 133–134
in grooming practice, 128
in stressful conditions, 81–82

consequence learning. *See* operant learning

consistency, need for, 70, 83, 183

conspecific learning. *See* **social learning**

Construction of Reality of the Child (Piaget), 246

contagion. *See* social learning

containment
in housetraining, 152
for large dogs in car, 123, 128
as management technique, 92
for new puppy, 113
for newborn puppies, 35
in separation anxiety treatment/management, 262–263
treat association with, 128
See also Doggy Enrichment Land™

contingency learning. *See* operant learning

continuity and stability, 70

correction. *See* punishment

cortisol levels, 67, 73, 77

counterconditioning, 99, 266. *See also*
  desensitization and counterconditioning
  (D&CC)
    See also separation anxiety
coyotes, 38
crates
  for bed, 34
  desensitization/training for, 127–128
  desensitize to carrier, 123
  introducing dog to home, 113
  for riding in car, 123
  as safe space or security blanket, 263
  as sanctuary (dog zone) from children, 248
  for sleeping, 266
  use for housetraining, 152
  using food with training, 140
critical periods
  aggression with stranger-dogs, 132
  fear-acquiring developmental period, 133
  for learning, 75
  for preventing aggression, 196
  for socialization, 132, 253–254
crying. *See* whining/crying
cues/cueing, 149
  in **"kiss-kiss"** training, 159
  for marking behavior, 164
  pairing hand signals and verbal cues, 163
  safety cue in separation anxiety, 265
  in training, 82
culture (in animals), 80
cunning (cognitive dimension), 80

D
decision-making
  brain structures in, 66
  in cognitive events, 80
  expression of assent and dissent, 82
defecation. *See* elimination needs
deficiency need, 29
Delaney, Sean, 22
Department for Environment, Food & Rural
  Affairs (DEFRA), 91
desensitization and counterconditioning
  (D&CC)
  emotional and behavioral changes with, 221
  in fear treatment, 254
  in force-free training/education, 102
  noise phobia treatment, 252
  for resource guarding from humans, 232

rules/principles for, 221
  systematic graduated exposure for, 100
  techniques for, 219–220
  trigger identification, 220
  use of food for, 139
developmental stages. *See* critical periods
diarrhea
  with allergy, 237
  with heatstroke, 46, 135
  from water or food, 25
diet/nutrition
  biological appropriate and balanced, 20–21
  causes of allergic reactions in, 239
  choosing foods for, 21–23
  enrichment methods for, 84
  feeding raw diet, 23–24
  for homeostasis, 21
  protein sources for, 22
  as "treats" in training, 118
  See also food as reward
differential reinforcement (DR) of DRI,
DRA, DRO, DRL, 96
  changing behavior with, 96–97
  differential reinforcement in, 96–97
  for modification of barking, 242–243
differential reinforcement of alternate behavior
  (DRA), 96–97
differential reinforcement of incompatible
  behavior (DRI), 91, 96–97
differential reinforcement of low frequency
  behavior (DRL), 91, 96–97
differential reinforcement of other behavior
  (DRO), 97
digging pit, 29
dilated cardiomyopathy (DCM) and diet, 24
disappearing
  in sit/wait training, 182
  See also Three Ds (plus one)
dismissive-avoidant attachment style, 65
displacement behavior as distraction, 267. *See*
  also Three Ds (plus one)
distance. *See* Three Ds (plus one)
distraction. *See* Three Ds (plus one)
distraction/getting dog's attention. *See* name
  response
distress
  frustration reactivity, 222
  from punishment, 88
  with threat to homeostasis, 69

vocalizations with, 247
withholding urination and, 257
See also separation anxiety
Do As I Do technique (Fugazza), 104
Do No Harm. *See* force-free education/training
Do No Harm Training and Behavior Manual
  behavioral models for, 8–10
  ethical codes of, 5–8, 16–18
  force-free education/training definition, 88
  Maslow's Hierarchy of Needs in, 10–11
  use in practice and business, 12–16
DO NOT list. *See also* Aggression, Chapter 17,
  195-235
    avoiding bite triggering, 224–225
    for separation anxiety management, 262
Dog Bite Law (Phillips), 135
The Dog Bite Scale (Dunbar), 199–200
dog fights, management of, 227–228
Dog Food Advisor, 23–24
Dog is Love (Wynne), 67
dog park and beaches
  choosing, 135
  monitoring body language at, 134
  safety tips for, 134–136
  snake safety for, 39
Dog Project (Berns), 66
dog walkers, for exercise needs, 28
dog zone
  digging pit in, 29
  enrichment area, 264
  for practice being independent, 263
  sanctuary/enrichment area, 161, 238
  separate from baby zone, 248
  sleeping requirements, 35–36
  See also Doggy Enrichment Land™
dog-child interaction, training for, 109
dog-dog aggression, 225-231
  assessment of, 210–214
  dangers of, 225–226
  how to break up a dog fight, 227
  in grooming facilities, 50, 219
  treatment/training for, 225–227
Dog-dog Bite Hierarchy (Shannon), 200
Doggy Enrichment Land™
  for containment, 262–270
  for dogs and babies, 248
  for environmental allergy management, 238
  for housetraining, 152, 156

items for, 113
use as sanctuary and training, 161, 248
for separation anxiety, 262-265
See also dog zone
dog-human aggression, 223. *See also* aggression
Dognition (Citizen Science enterprise, Hare),
  80, 86
dogs and babies, 245-250
  aggressive behavior with, 250
  bringing baby home, 249–250
  Dogs and Babies seminar, 250
  dog's body language with, 247
  management of child, 246
  preparing dog during pregnancy, 247–249
  relationship to baby, 245–246
  training requirements for dog, 246–247
domestication, 66, 80
dominance training methods
  effects on behavior, 224
  unsafe training method, 114
Donaldson, Jean
  Mine, 102
  *Mine! A Practical Guide to Resource Guarding
    in Dogs,* 102, 233
  on use of food as reward, 117–118
dopamine
  in Appetitive Emotional System, 63
  association with well-being, 73
  positive reinforcement association with, 95
  with social deficits, 74, 77
Down training
  position for, 181
  shaping behavior for, 179
  sphinx position, 181
drop training
  with lure-chase toys, 29
  in resource guarding management, 235
  training for, 29
  See also trade up and drop
Duke University Canine Cognition Center, 80
Dunbar, Ian
  Before and After You Get Your Puppy, 151
  The Dog Bite Scale, 199–200
  on lure training, 165
  occupational therapy, 160
  treats in elimination training, 153
  urgency of early socialization, 132
  Before You Get Your Puppy, 108

duration
    in separation anxiety treatment/management, 265–266, 269
    in sit and wait training, 182–183
    See also Three Ds (plus one)

E

ears
    in body language/communication, 143
    examination in home exercises, 128
Easey, Max (consent training), 82
electric cord burns/electrocution, 42
elimination needs
    in allergy management, 238
    ammonia as trigger for, 155
    behavior warning signals for, 156
    choice of area for, 154
    cleaning soiled area, 155
    confinement use for accidents, 153
    in Doggy Enrichment Land™, 113, 156
    feeding schedule opportunities for, 153–154, 257
    in separation anxiety, 260
    sod tray for training, 152
    voice cues with, 154
    See also **housetraining**
Elizabethan collar
    desensitization to wearing, 123, 128
    for grooming, 50
emotional contagion learning, 104
The Emotional Lives of Animals (Bekoff), 62–63
emotional needs, 62–71
    associated with biddability, 75
    benevolent leadership, 70
    consistency, 70
    love, 62
    primary emotional systems, 63–64
    security, 62
    trust, 68
    unsupervised risks outdoors, 37–41
Emotional Systems Model (Panksepp), 63–64
emotions
    associative learning modification of, 98
    body language in communication of, 143–144, 195
    involuntary behavior (with classical conditioning), 98
    neuromodulators of, 63–64

emotions and behavior, scavenging for change of, 139
empathy
    cognition, 80
    cognition and, 80
    cognitive dimensions, 80
    comfort-offering behavior, 67
    play teaching of, 77
empowerment-based training, 81
emulation learning, 104. *See also* **social learning**
Engage-Disengage Game, teaching self-interruption, 221
enrichment/enhancement (of environment), 137-141
    for boredom, 138
    elements of, 84
    grazing games, 140
    novelty in, 83
    nutritional enrichment methods, 84
    occupational enrichment, 137
    paradigm for dogs, 84
    predictability in environment, 69
    types of, 83–84
    in veterinary offices, 52
environmental allergens, 238–239
Environmental Protection Agency (EPA), 25
epinephrine, 64
escape avoidance behavior, 119
esophageal damage, 116
essential oils, 41
establishing operation, adding and removing, 93
estrogen, 63
ethical codes/position statements
    American Medical Association, 6–7
    American Psychological Association, 7
    American Veterinary Medical Association, 6
    American Veterinary Society of Animal Behavior, 54–55
    Do No Harm ethical codes, 5–8
    of *Do No Harm Training and Behavior Manual*, 5–8, 16–18
    of professional organizations, 5–8
    standards of care and force-free practices, 3–5
    See also specific organizations
Ethological Model, 9
exercise, 25-28
    factors determining need for exercise, 26
    gastric torsion with, 135
    lure/chase toy for exercise, 28

moods and behavior with, 26
for developmental stages of life, 26–28
upstairs fetch for, 29
See also heatstroke
extinction, 97, 261
extraversion (personality), 253
eye contact
automatic check-ins, 227
in veterinary care, 124
eye-contact, in dog-dog aggression management, 227

F
fabric softener sheets, 42
facial skin cleaning, 128
fair play rules, 77–78
Family Paws Parent Education (Shryock), 250
fast-mapping and exclusion learning, 84–85
fawn. *See* Fight-flight Syndrome
fear, 251-254
from aversive collar devices, 30
aversive emotional systems (Panksepp), 64
body language in communication of, 143
developmental period for acquiring, 133
from incompetent training, 114
genetics, 253
indications of, 252
learned fear, 91, 100
one-trial learning with, 99–100
in separation anxiety, 255
from shock use, 39
socialization effects on, 254
tail and ear display with, 143
triggering events, 254
from veterinary/grooming visits, 119
See also flooding (exposure); tonic immobility
Fear Free® visits, for veterinary care, 122
Fear/Anxiety (emotion) (Panksepp), 64
fearful-avoidant attachment style, 65
feeding/food
feeding raw diet, 23–24
routine schedule for tracking elimination needs, 154
scatter breakfast and/or dinner, 139
use to change emotions, 139
in separation anxiety treatment, 266
feelings. *See* emotional needs
fence-barrier stress, 37
Ferdowsian, Hope, 82

50:50 Rule in play, 133
Fight-Flight Syndrome, 39–40, 64. *See also* Rage (emotion) (Panksepp)
"The Five Elements of Canine Enrichment" (Kelly), 84
flat collars
for identification, 116
misuse of "training collars", 144–145
flea allergy dermatitis (FAD), 239
flea and tick remedies, 41
flexible/retractable leash, 115
flooding (exposure), 102
and tonic immobility, 144
use in training, 115
See also fear; tonic immobility
fly strike, 37
fly-snapping, 37
food allergies, 239–240
food as reward, 117-118, 163
with elimination, 152
foraging/scavenging, 84
in house training after accident, 155
in management/treatment of fear, 254
use in separation anxiety, 266
food bowls in resource guarding, 234–235
footpad examinations
desensitization to, 128
home practice for, 123
force-free training needs, 87-104
antecedent modification in, 91
best practices for, 86, 91
consent (asking permission) in, 82
desensitization and counterconditioning, 102
differential reinforcement use in, 96
ethical codes/position statements, 5–8
exclusions from, 89
future directions for, 16–18
hand pairing, 234
from **Hierarchy of Dog Needs**, 87–104
leadership for, 70–71
operational definition of, 88
the Premack Principle in, 91, 164
scientific support for, 17–18
standards of, 88–89
terms used in, 149
in veterinary care, 122
foreleg nerve damage, 116
foul breath, 123
four on the floor, redirection for jumping, 177

fractures in puppies, 26–27
"freezing", in body language/communication, 143
frustration reactivity distress, 222
fun stops method (biting/mouthiness), 157, 159–160
functional analysis, 214–216
functional Magnetic Resonance Imaging (fMRI), 65–66

G

GABA, 64
Garrod, Diane (*Stress Release For Dogs: The Canine Emotional Detox*), 33
genetics
  aggression and trainability traits, 253
  domestication and affection for people, 66–67
  in fear, 253
  hyper-social behavior and, 74
  isolation and anxiety effects, 37
  obesity risks at risk for, 24
  separation anxiety predisposition, 256
The Genius of Dogs (Hare), 67, 80, 86
glutamate, 63–64
good manners training, 147-190
  changing emotional responses, 148
  force-free principles for, 148
  reasons for difficulty learning a behavior, 149
  reward effects on behavior, 148
  reward use for, 148
  techniques for undesirable behavior, 149
"Good trainers: How to identify one" (Overall), 17, 115
grazing
  for sensory enrichment, 84
  in treatment/management of separation anxiety, 264
  use for training, 139–140
Grazing Games™, 137-141
  behavior change with, 139–140
  with desensitization, 261
  for enrichment, 137–138, 264
"The Great Awful Outdoors" (Miller), 37
greetings, 195
  alternate behavior to jumping, 96
  basic training needs for, xxx
  contain to calm for guests, 175-176
  how to protocol, 197

redirecting doorbell barking, 140
  in separation anxiety, 269
  you and family members, 176
Grief (emotion) (Panksepp), 64. *See also* separation anxiety
grooming, 47, 125-130
  best practices and standards for grooming, 50–51
  choice in, 82
  choosing a groomer and salon, 119, 126–127
  dangerous equipment and practices in, 49–50
  desensitization steps for, 127–128
  first appointment, 129–130
  nail trimming, 48–49
  selecting a professional for, 125–126
  tonic immobility with, 51
  See also muzzles
growling
  aggressive warnings, 201, 224, 244, 250
  with arousal and discomfort, 143
  meaning of (warning), 143
guarding home, 240
guarding stations, 218–219
gum disease, 59

H

habituation
  learning types, 4
  muzzle wearing video, 128
  in socialization, 131–132, 253
Hale, Andrew (*UK Dog Behaviour and Training Charter*), 97
hand signals
  adding verbal cues with, 163
  come, 184, 186
  down, 180
  hand-luring movement, 165–166
  sit, 179
  teaching, 171
  wait, 182
hand targeting, 190–191
handfeeding, 234
hard surface cleaning, 155
Hare, Brian
  cognitive skills and style in dogs, 80
  effects of petting, 66–67
  The Genius of Dogs: How Dogs are Smarter Than You Think, 67, 80, 86

harm avoidance (temperament dimension), 253
harnesses
 for car use, 123
 for exercise, 27
 for leash-walking training, 188
 recommended types of, 116
 use for training, 115
Harris, Lee, careful, selective socialization plan, 121
Harrison, Jemima (*Pedigree Dogs Exposed*), 32
heartworm, 38
heatstroke. *See* hyperthermia
Hierarchy of Dog Needs (HDN) pyramid, 2
Hierarchy of Dog Needs (HDN), 1-104
 best force-free practices, 87–104
 biological needs, 19–61
 bloggers and TV interviews, examples for, 14–15
 breeders, use by, 16
 emotional and behavioral methods endorsed by, 89–90
 force-free model and standards for, xxvii–xxviii
 groomers, 16
 holistic care system, xxi–xxiii
 infographic for, 2
 private consultations, examples for, 15
 purposes and goals of, 3–5
 rescues and shelters, 16, 109-110
 speakers, examples for, 14
 teaching, examples for classes, 15
 veterinary care, 15–16
Hierarchy of Needs (Maslow), 10–11
high value food/reward/reinforcement/treat
 in aggression treatment, 163, 232
 alarm barking control, 243
 capturing spontaneous behavior with, 164
 clicker training, 173
 in come and recall training, 183, 186
 as comfort item, 263
 in counterconditioning, 100
 creating digging pits, 141
 decreasing anxiety with, 267
 desensitization and counterconditioning, 139, 222
 in Doggy Enrichment Land™, 113
 drop training, 235
 food as reward, 118
 for food enrichment, 84

greeting training, 176, 197
 for grooming, 129
 hand pairing training, 159, 234
 for housetraining accidents, 140, 153, 155
 introducing new dog to home, 198
 jumping training, 177
 in leash-walking, 188
 in lure-chase toys, 29
 open bar/closed bar technique, 227
 scatter feeding of, 264
 with separation anxiety, 264
 settle down training, 182
 sit training, 179
 stuffed chew toys, 161
 as treats/reinforcement, 148
 use for containment training, 123, 128
 in veterinary care setting, 124
 See also Premack Principle
A History of Modern Psychology, 98–99
holiday decorations/lights, 42
The Holistic Health Guide (Knueven), 239
home, preparing for dog
 Doggy Enrichment Land™, 113
 items needed, 113
home anchor, in walking, 226
home practice, exercises for grooming, 127
home-cooked meals, 20, 22, 239
homeostasis
 factors which may threaten, 69
 nutritionally balanced diet for, 21
 physiological need for oxygen, 29
 temperature control, 44
 threats to maintenance of, 69
homing, transition to forever home, 253
Honeckman, Lynn
 on body language, 143
 socialization opportunities, 121
hormones
 in classical conditioning, 98
 in stress and anger, 86
Horowitz, Alexandra
 "How Do Dogs "See" with Their Noses?", 85–86
 Inside of a Dog, 35
 sleep cycles in adult dogs, 34
household hazards, poisons, and toxins, 41–42
housetraining, 151-156
 positive interrupt sound in, 154
 locations for partially trained puppy, 156

regression in behavior problems, 144
techniques for, 152
urine marking management, 156
using food with accidents in, 140
water access during, 25
"How Do Dogs "See" with Their Noses?"
(Horowitz), 85–86
How Dogs Learn, functional analysis defined, 214
How Dogs Love Us (Berns), 66
How to Greet a Dog (Yin), 250
Hudson, Rebekah
good veterinary care, 120
"Lunging, Barking, Biting, Oh My", 219
human directed aggression, types of, 223–224
human foods to avoid, 41
Humane Society of the United States, leaving
outdoors unattended, 37
hyperactive active body language, 222
hyperactivity reactivity. *See* frustration reactivity
distress
hyperthermia
causes of, 44
emergency care with, 135
prevention of, 45–46
rectal temperatures with, 44
risks factors for, 135
symptoms of, 46
in unsupervised animal, 36
hypothermia
causes and prevention of, 46–47
rectal temperatures with, 44

I

I Like My Dog, Does My Dog Like Me? (Rehn),
74
idiopathic obsessive behaviors, 37
idiopathic separation anxiety, 256
ignoring behavior (for extinction), 97
imitative learning, 103. *See also* social learning
immune dysfunction, 69
impulse control (personality), 253
incompatible behavior reinforcement (DRI), 96,
158–159
indoor shelter
emotional and behavioral risks outdoors,
37–40
outdoor risks and dangers, 36–37
in-home (mobile) care, grooming, 125, 127,
219

in-home (mobile) care, veterinary, 120, 122,
219
insects, hazards, 38
instrumental learning. *See* **operant learning**
integrative medicine. *See* **veterinary care**
intelligence
defined/examples of, 86
types of, 80
See also cognitive ability
intent in training methods, 88
International Association of Better Business
Bureaus (IABBB)
check on grooming professionals, 127
complaints against veterinarian/clinic, 122
locating groomers, 127
interrupt redirection in housetraining, 154
intimidation, techniques misused for, 115
intimidation misuse in training, 114
intraspecific communication, 76
It's Me or the Dog (Animal Planet), 144
introductions dogs and babies, 250. *See also*
greetings

J

Journal of Brain and Cognition, 32
jumping, redirecting for, 176–178

K

Kaufer, Mechtild (*Canine Play Behavior*), 77
Kearns, Nancy, 136
Kelly, Shay
*Canine Enrichment: The Book Your Dog Needs
You to Read*, 84
"The Five Elements of Canine Enrichment",
84
kibble
feeding by scattering, 139
nutrition of, 20–23
in stuffed chew toys, 161
use in resource guarding training, 234
use as reward, 148
"kiss-kiss" teaching, 158–159
Klinck, Mary (factors determining need for
exercise), 25–26
Knueven, Doug
choosing food, 22
The Holistic Health Guide, 239
Kunkel-Jones, Jeanine ("Puppy Mills: The
Horrific Truth"), 110–111

L

Landsberg, Gary ("Social Behavior of Dogs"), 75

laryngeal collapse/injury, 32, 116

learned helplessness (Seligman), 11, 79

learning

  acceleration with consistency, 70

  classical and operant conditioning in, 9

  critical periods during development, 75–77

  critical periods for, 75

  difficulty in, 149, 163, 166

  intelligence and, 86

  novelty association with, 83

  novelty-seeking behavior and, 83

  social rules with play, 63

  types of, 4

  See also specific types of learning

leashes

  flexible/retractable leash, 115

  for leash-walking training, 188

  recommendations for, 117

  use in training, 115

leash-walking, 187–190

  automatic eye contact, 190

  equipment for, 116

  equipment/techniques for, 188–189

  following walking, 227

  hand targeting heel, 190

  location to avoid trigger stacking, 219

  parallel walking, 227

  response to pulling, 189

  re-training techniques and protocols for, 226–227

  slow walking, 190

  for snake safety, 39

  working below reactivity threshold, 226–227

LeDoux, Joseph (fear conditioning), 90–91

"let's go" redirection, 227

liability contract template for consultants, 216–217

lifestyle and family in choice of dog, 107–108

lightning recall

  proactive use in fight prevention, 227

  proactive/prevention of resource guarding, 233

  See also "come" long distance

linking behaviors, 171

"Little Albert" Experiment, 99–100

"Little Peter" Experiment, 267

"Living in a Human World" (Bove-Rothwell), 138–139

Living with Kids and Dogs (Pelar), 250

Locus of Control, 81

loneliness/isolation barks, 242

long response time reinforcement (DRL), 97

longevity

  in choice of dog, 108, 112

  factors affecting, 69

  Pukka's Promise: The Quest for Longer-Lived Dogs (Kerasote), 112

  in puppy selection, 111

loose facial skin, care of, 128

love, 62, 65–67. *See also* attachment

"Love, Actually", 65

love hormone. *See* oxytocin

Low Stress Handling of Dogs and Cats DVD (Yin), 61

Low Stress Handling, Restraint and Behavior Modification for Dogs & Cats (Yin), 61

lower frequency behavior reinforcement (DRL), 97

lunging

  in aggressive behavior, 200, 206, 219–220, 224

  inadequate early socialization and, 132

  "Lunging, Barking, Biting, Oh My", 219

"Lunging, Barking, Biting, Oh My" (Hudson), 219

lure-chase toys

  for exercise, 28, 223

  rules for use, 29

luring behavior

  "Are Free Shaped Dog Better Problem Solvers?" (LeBlanc), 164

  for down training, 180

  positive reinforcement with, 94, 116, 144

  removing the lure, 171, 179

  for sit training, 178–179

  use for training, 165–166

Lust (emotion) (Panksepp), 63

"lying in wait". *See* guarding stations

M

magnetic resonance imaging (MRI)

  brain lesions from air pollution, 32

  Dog Project mapping, 66

Mahaney, Patrick (PetMD), flea allergy management, 239

maintain behavior, 174
management, 92
manners training, 147-189
Manual of Clinical Behavioral Medicine
(Overall), 28
marking, using food for elimination of, 140
marking behavior (for training)
for capturing, 164
with clicker, 144, 173
of eye contact, 189–190
hand targeting in leash-walking, 190
reward use for, 144
for shaping, 179
in sit training, 179
teeth-touching skin, 159
Martiya, Michelle (best practices and standards
for grooming), 50
Maslow, A. H.
Motivation and Personality, 11
A Theory of Human Motivation, 29
Maslow's Hierarchy of Needs, 10–11
mat/throw rug, 113
medical injury/illness
barks with, 242
exercise for prevention of, 25–26
housetraining regression and, 152
sleep deprivation effects, 33
from training, 114
from withholding urination, 257
Medical Model, 9
medications
hazards from, 41
for separation anxiety management, 269–270
treatment of behavior problems, 58
memory
in cognitive events, 80
stress effects on, 69
mental events, 11–12, 79–86. *See also* **cognition**
Merck Veterinary Manual, 75
Merrill, Janet (risk factors for heatstroke), 44–45
Michaels, Linda
About the Author, iii
Grazing Games, 139
Hierarchy of Dog Needs [Pyramid
Graphic], 2
Hierarchy of Dog Needs—Standards
of Care and Best Force-Free Practices:
Management, 92; Antecedent Modification,
93-94; Positive Reinforcement, 94-95;

Differential Reinforcement, 96-97;
Classical and Counterconditioning, 98-
100; Desensitization, 100-102; Premack
Principle, 102-103; Social Learning, 103-104
Hierarchy of Dog Needs [tiers]: Biological
Needs, 19-60; Emotional Needs, 62-71;
Social Needs, 72-77; Cognitive Needs, 79-
86; Force-Free Training Needs, 87-103
"How to Train Your Wolfdog, Wolfdog
Radio interview
Liability Contract Template for Behavior
Consultations, 216-217
"Open Letter to Research Scientists", *BARKS
from the Guild*
"Puppy Socialization and Vaccinations
Belong Together", 76
"Top Ten Do's and Don'ts for Successful
Housetraining", 152-155
"Understanding Research: Making the Case
for Force Free Training", iii
Miklosi, Adam ("Do As I Do" technique), 104
Miller, Pat
dog park and beach safety tips, 134–135
"The Great Awful Outdoors", 37
mobile grooming and veterinary care, 120-
127, 219
Modal Action Patterns (MAP), 9
model rival (teacher-dog as), 104
modeling (with positive reinforcement), 94
Morgan, Judy (*Naturally Healthy Pets*), 57–58
Motivation and Personality (Maslow), 11
motivation in cognitive events, 80
mouth examination
with heatstroke symptoms, 135
techniques used for, 128
mouthing, alternate behavior for, 158
multi-dog household, aggression treatment in,
229
muzzles
air muzzle, 51, 122, 130
basket muzzle, 130
desensitization to wearing, 123, 128
training for grooming, 51
used by groomers, 49

N
nail trimming
effects of overgrown nails, 49
need for, 123

name response
for distraction from trigger, 227
for reactivity control, 197
for redirecting behavior, 189
training before baby comes, 249
training for, 184–185
See also come training
nares, stenotic, 32
natural behaviors (enrichment), 84
Naturally Healthy Pets (Morgan), 57–58
neck stress, injuries from, 116
neophobia, 254. *See also* **desensitization and counterconditioning**
neuromodulators, 63–64
neuroticism (personality), 253
nicotine and marijuana, 41
noise phobia, 252
non-food enrichment, 84
norepinephrine/noradrenaline, 64, 77
nose-games, 223
No Shock. *See* shock
novelty-seeking behavior
expression of temperament, 253
function of, 83
nutrition, 20-24

O
obedience training, methods for, 81
obesity
breathing disorders and, 31
causes and risk factors for, 24
early veterinary care for prevention, 53
exercise and, 25
heatstroke association, 45
monitoring during exercise, 26
simple carbohydrate link to, 22
sleep deprivation association of, 33
observational learning. *See* **social learning**
occupational enrichment, 83, 137
odor profiles, processing of, 86
odor removal, 155
Oechtering, Gerhard, 32
off-leash responsibility, recall for, 136
omission training (DRO), 97
one-trial learning. *See* fear
online resources, 289–290
open bar/closed bar technique
in dog-dog aggression treatment, 226–227
sibling rivalry management/training, 231–232

openness to experience (personality), 253
operant conditioning/learning
mechanism and effects of, 8–9
reinforcement as tool for, 96–97
successive approximation (shaping) in, 96
See also differential reinforcement (DR)
operant learning, in shaping behavior, 96
operational definition of force-free training, 88
opioids (endogenous), 63–64
oral/**dental care**
brushing and professional cleaning, 60
chewing kibble, 23
foul breath with decayed teeth, 123
periodontal disease, 59
orthopedic bed, 113
other behavior reinforcement (DRO), 97
outdoor emotional and behavioral risks, 36–38.
See also indoor shelter
outdoor tethering (unsupervised), 37–40
Overall, Karen, 63–64
behavior education of veterinarians, 53–54
"Good trainers: How to identify one", 17, 115
"Protocol for Understanding and Helping Geriatric Animals", 28
"Relaxation Protocol", 101
on Sophia Yin, 6
veterinarian training in behavior, 121
"Why Shock is Not Behavior Modification", xxviii
over-enthusiasm. *See* **frustration reactivity** distress
oxygen (deficiency need), 24, 29, 31
oxytocin
with animal-human interactions, 73–74
in bonding, 68
in emotions, 63–64
mediation of social behavior, 65–66
petting effects on, 77
with positive reinforcement, 95

P
pain misuse for training, 114
Panksepp, Jaak, Emotional Systems Model, 62–64
panting
in frustration reactivity, 222
muzzle use and, 45
sign of heatstroke, 135

for temperature control, 44

parallel walking, 198, 227

pass-bys, 265. *See also* separation anxiety

Patel, Chirag

  The Bucket Game, 82

  muzzle desensitization steps, 128

  "Teaching a Dog to Wear a Muzzle (Muzzle Training)" video, 123, 128

Pavlovian/respondent conditioning. *See* **classical conditioning**

Pedigree Dogs Exposed (Harrison), 32

Pelar, Colleen (*Living with Kids and Dogs*), 250

perception

  in cognitive events, 80

  Dog Project mapping, 66

  of threat by dog and human, 69

periodontal disease, 59

persistence (temperament), 253

personality

  brain chemistry and hormonal factors in, 67–68

  determinants of, 253–254

  dimensions of, 83

  emotional stability, 253

  exercise needs and, 26

  in interaction with baby, 248

  match to family and lifestyle, 107

  openness to experience (personality), 253

  socialization and environment effects on, 111–112

  temperament relative to personality, 111

pet parenting

  first veterinary visit, 124

  handling your frustration, 149

  inappropriate behavior in dog parents, 134–135

  initiating grooming, 125

  legal problems at parks and beaches, 135

  off-leash responsibility, 136

  park and beach tips, 135

  responsibilities of, 69

  during veterinary care, 120

Pet Professional Guild (PPG)

  force-free education/training, 88

  principles of, 18

  "Puppy Socialization and Vaccinations Belong Together", 76

  socialization guide to, 121

  training certification organization, 5

veterinary care search through, 122

pet professional practice and business

  categories of, 14

  developing training plans, 12

  increasing work flow, 12

  research, law, and role of celebrities, 16–18

  using the Hierarchy of Dog Needs, 13–16

Petfinder.com, 109

PetMD, electric cord burns/electrocution, 42

Phillips, Kenneth M. (*Dog Bite Law*), 135

physical correction avoidance techniques, 115

physical enrichment, 83

physical force definition, 88

physical injury from punishment, 116

Piaget, Jean (*Construction of Reality of the Child*), 246

pick of the litter, 112

Pierson, Melissa Holbrook (*The Secret History of Kindness: Learning from How Dogs Learn*), 117

Pilley, John P. (YouTube video), 80

play

  50:50 Rule for, 133

  appetitive emotional system, 63

  assessment and supervision of, 133–134

  barks with, 242

  benefits of, 76–77

  fair play rules, 77–78

  gear worn during, 136

  sniffing activities as break in, 134

  as social need, 76–77

Play (emotion)(Panksepp), 63

play bow, 78

playpen

  use in housetraining, 152

  using food for training in, 140

pleasure chemical. *See* dopamine

poisonous plants, 41

poisons/toxins/household hazards list, 41–42

Positive Psychology (Seligman), 10

positive reinforcement (+R)

  defined and characteristics of, 95

  dopamine and, 95

  increasing frequency of behavior, 94

  use in training, 118

  See also rewards

positive training (Overall), 116

praise, use for training, 115

predictability

  routines for, 70

for trust, 69
See also **consistency**, need for
Premack, David, behavior as reinforcement, 102, 167
Premack Principle, 102–103
    in force-free training/education, 166–168
    See also reinforcement
problem-solving, 84-86
    in cognitive events, 80
    enriched environment effects on, 86
    skills in dogs, 84–85
professional consultations
    annoyance problems, 213
    bite incidents, 207–210
    contents of veterinary behavioral report for, 218
    dog-dog aggression treatment, 210–212
    functional analysis, 214–216
    human aggression treatment, 206–207
    intake questionnaire for aggression cases, 202–214
    liability contract template for consultants, 216–217
    separation anxiety and fearfulness, 212–213, 259, 269
    training goals, 214
prong collars. *See* aversive collar devices
property laws (of dogs), 235
"Protocol for Understanding and Helping Geriatric Animals" (Overall), 28
psychological injury, 116
    from training, 114
Pukka's Promise: The Quest for Longer-Lived Dogs (Kerasote), 112
punishment
    arousal effects of, 116
    effect on barking, 244
    effects in training, 116
    emotional disturbance from, 17
    injuries and behavioral effects of, 31, 90, 244
    movement away from use of, 16–18
    physical and psychological injury from, 116
    reward mix in "balanced trainer", 88
puppies
    brachycephalic airway syndrome in, 31
    critical/sensitive period for socialization, 120–121, 253
    critical/sensitive periods, 75, 132, 253–254
    dog-dog socialization for, 120–121

dream states in, 35
elimination opportunities for, 153
exercise requirements for, 26
fractures in, 26–27
human bonding in, 65
interaction with adult dogs, 134
learning bite inhibition, 76
partially housetrained, 156
play and communication in, 74
redirecting biting, 158
safety in house, yard, and pool, 40
selecting for adoption, 111–112
separation anxiety prevention in, 111, 113, 256
sleep needs of, 33, 35
socialization in home, 132
socialization in unvaccinated, 120–121
tips for selection, 112
urination training in, 152
puppy mills, avoiding, 110–112
"Puppy Mills: The Horrific Truth" (Kunkel-Jones), 110–111
puppy pad, urination training with, 152
"Puppy Socialization and Vaccinations Belong Together" (Michaels), 76

R
rabies, 38
"rag wipe" technique, 198
Rage (emotion) (Panksepp), 64
random reward reinforcement, 171–172
rapid eye movement (REM) sleep, 35
rawhide dog chews, 42
reactivity threshold
    in aggression with humans, 206
    alternative behaviors with, 197
    in desensitization and counterconditioning, 220–222
    developmental exposure and, 56, 131
    in dog-dog aggression, 206, 219
    dog-dog distance for, 232–233
    establishing with reinforcement, 222
    factors contributing to, 219
    in flooding/fear, 254
    introducing new dog to home, 198
    with noise phobia, 252
    retraining for dog-dog aggression, 226–227
    in separation anxiety treatment/management, 252, 265–266

in **sibling rivalry**, 230
socialization effects on, 131
in stressful conditions, 230
teaching alternative behaviors to, 197
threshold for walks, 226
trigger management, 218
for walks, 226–227
working below for walks, 226
See also **frustration reactivity** distress
realistic expectations, 222
real-life reward rewards
behavior as reinforcement, 169–170
food reward replacement by, 118
for linking behaviors, 171
reasoning (cognition), **cognition**, 80
recall. *See* come training
recurrent laryngeal nerve injury, 116
redirecting behavior
for barking, 140, 243–244
for biting, 158–159
to chew toys, 160–161
in fighting, 227
for jumping, 176–178
name response for, 189
preventing undesirable behavior, 92–93, 96,
102–103, 144
scavenging for, 139–140
reflexes in classical conditioning, 98
Rehn, Therese
"Best of Friends? Investigating the Dog-
Human Relationship", 74
I Like My Dog, Does My Dog Like Me?, 74
rehoming
after dog-dog aggression, 232
cause of relinquishing to shelter, 121
failed aggression treatment and, 236
of rescued dogs, 258
for serious fighting, 232
reinforcement
alternate reward reinforcement, 171
for barking modification, 242
clicker as secondary, 172–173
consistency in use, 70
differential reinforcement, 96
identifying items and activities for, 170
intermittent vs. continuous schedules for,
169
low value food vs. high value food, 234–235
preferred behavior as, 102–103

random reward reinforcement, 171–172
rate of with dog-dog aggression training, 227
rate of, 174, 222, 227, 232
real-life reward reinforcement, 118, 167, 171
secondary, 172–173
for successive shaping behavior, 96
types of, 148
See also differential reinforcement (DR);
    positive reinforcement (+R); rewards; treats
reinforcement of lower frequency/long response
time (DRL), 97
"Relax" Down, 181
"Relaxation Protocol" (Overall), 101
relief-seeking (Hale), 97
request/attention barks
to ask for something, 242
response to, 244
resource guarding, 232-235
between dogs, 233
food bowls, 234
guarding from humans, 232
hand association in training for, 234
high value food/treat, 219
reactivity in, 218–219
unsupervised tethered outdoor time, 37
response learning. *See* **operant learning**
reward learning. *See* operant learning
rewards
alternate reward reinforcement, 171
appetitive value of, 149
behavior probability and, 167
behaviors to not reinforce, 148
defining/determining, 95
high-value treats for housetraining, 153
in housetraining, 152
intermittent use in grooming, 128
judicious use of, 148–149
random reward reinforcement, 171–172
"talking back" with, 144
See also positive reinforcement (+R)
lightning recall
proactive use in fight prevention, 227
proactive/prevention of resource guarding,
233
See also "come" long distance
R—S learning. *See* operant learning
rules and boundaries
consistent application of, 70
fair play rules, 77–78

S

sacral joint examination exercises, 123, 128
safe environment
    enrichment, 84
    in force-free training/education, 88
safety, 40-43
    dog park and beach safety tips, 134–136
    gear worn during play, 136
    household hazards, poisons, and toxins,
        41–42
    swimming practice and drowning, 42
    unsupervised outdoor time, 36–40
San Diego Humane Society, rabies in wildlife,
    38
sanctuary space, 230. *See also* **Doggy**
    Enrichment Land
scavenging
    emotion and behavior change with, 139
    nutritional enrichment with, 84
    use in training, 227, 243
    See also **grazing games**
scent work
    during aggression treatment, 223
    for aging/senior dogs, 80
    exercise for adult dogs, 27
    for exercise in aging/senior dogs, 28
scent-sensitivity (in dogs), 85
secondary reinforcement, 172–173
*The Secret History of Kindness: Learning from
    How Dogs Learn* (Pierson), 117
secure attachment style, 65
security, 64
    attachment and abandonment, 64–65
    cognitive benefits of, 65
    of yard, 38
Seek (emotion) (Panksepp), 63
self-handicapping in play, 134
self-imposing breaks in play, 133
self-interruption (coping skill), 221
self-mutilation
    outdoor tethering (unsupervised), 37
    with separation anxiety, 260, 263
Seligman, Martin E. (*Positive Psychology*), 10, 79
Sensitive/critical periods, 75–76. *See also* critical
    periods
sensory enrichment
    enriched environment, 84
    gardens for, 138
    sensory garden for, 141

sensory garden, 138, 141
separation anxiety, 265-269
    assessment of, 258
    barking with, 242
    changing routines to manage, 268–269
    desensitization and counterconditioning,
        267
    Doggy Enrichment Land™ in treatment,
        263–265
    exercise for distress in, 26
    Grief (emotion) (Panksepp) in, 64
    identifying and managing of triggers in,
        267–268
    medication for, 269–270
    mistaken for housetraining problem, 140
    pass-bys, 265
    prevention training, 111, 113, 257
    risk factors for, 258–259
    separation practice trials, 265–266
    symptoms of, 144, 259–261
    treatment/training for, 261–262
    using food in treatment of, 266–267
serotonin levels, 77
Settle Down training
    capturing for, 181–182
    in dog-dog aggression treatment/
        management, 227
shaping behavior
    differential reinforcement for, 96
    for down and settle down, 179–181
    positive reinforcement for, 94, 96
    steps in training, 166
shelter. *See* **indoor shelter**
shivering, 47. *See also* hypothermia
shock (No Shock)
    animal abuse masquerading as dog training,
        xxvii
    American Veterinary Society of Animal
        Behavior (AVSAB) tools to avoid, 115
    aggression association (Overall), 90; 202
    averting use of, 28
    aggression with, 17
    BanShockCollars.ca, 91
    bites with, xxviii, 17, 90
    DEFRA study, 91
    electric cord and holiday light burns with, 42
    fear with (LeDoux), 90-91
    future directions in research, law, celebrities,
        16-18

invisible shock fencing, 90
lack of trainer competency with, 40, 71, 114, 115
learned helplessness, 11
misuse for training, 114, 176, 187
no shock logos, 91
opposing the use of, (American Animal Hospital Association), 6, 56
pain with, 116
position on the use of (Pet Professional Guild), 5, 18, 89
snake aversion training misusing shock, 39
speaking for those who cannot speak for themselves, 17
"Things You Should Know Before You Buy a Shock Collar" (Weigle), 17
tonic immobility similarity, 145
unintended fear associations with, 99
veterinary referrals to, 56
euthanasia false claim for justification (Overall), xxviii
"What and Who Dogs Want and Need: Love, Not Shocks" (Bekoff), 68
"Why Shock is Not Behavior Modification" (Overall), xxviii
Shryock, Jennifer, Family Paws Parent Education, 250
shutdown, 144. *See also* **tonic immobility**
sibling rivalry
    prevention and management, 230
    treatment/training for, 229
signal, 149
SIRIUS Puppy training Initiative, 132
Sit training, capturing and luring for, 178–179
skin creams and ointments, 41
Skinner, B.F., *The Behavior of Organisms*, 95
Skinner, B.F. (*The Behavior of Organisms*), 95
sleep, 32-35
    arrangements with separation anxiety, 266
    bed placement and location for, 34–35
    in bed with pet parents, 258
    dog vs. human patterns of, 34
    dreaming and deep sleep, 35
    effects of deprivation, 33–34
    positions/postures for, 36
    requirements for dogs, 32–33
    unsupervised tethered outdoor time, 37
slick floors and stair hazards, 42

"slip lead". *See* aversive collar devices
snakes
    aversion training using shock, 39
    bites and venom vaccine, 39
    outdoor hazards, 38
"sniffaris", 28, 138
sniffing activities
    elimination signal, 156
    enrichment by, 80, 84
    for scent identification, 137
    sensory garden for, 141
    window to the world, 28, 138
"Social Behavior of Dogs" (Landsberg), 75
social enrichment
    in play, 77
    need for novelty, 83–84
social facilitation learning, 104
social interactions, enriched environment effects on, 86
social learning, 103–104
social needs, 72-78
    bonding with people, 73–74
    critical /sensitive periods of learning, 75–76
    dog-dog bonding, 75
    play, 76–77
socialization
    exposure to new stimuli in first 100 days, 131
    fear-acquiring developmental period, 133
    play rules and manners, 133
    sensitive/critical period for, 253
    trigger exposure in, 131–132
    vaccinations and veterinary care, 120–121
sod tray for housetraining, 152
sphinx Down position, 181
"spider walks", 226
squealing during play, 134
Stay training, 183. *See also* Wait/Stay training
stereotypies (idiopathic obsessive behaviors), 37
Stewart, Grisha (*Behavior Adjustment Training 2.0*), 81
Stilwell, Victoria (flooding explanation), 144
stomach examination, home practice for, 123
Stress Release For Dogs: The Canine Emotional Detox (Garrod), 33
stress/stressors
    assessing, 69–70
    conditions for, 230
    distress relation to trust, 68

dog's perception of, 69
eliminating, 230–231
noise phobia, 252
signs of, 254
tonic immobility with, 145
from veterinary/grooming visits, 53
Substance P, 64
successive approximation (shaping). *See* shaping
  behavior
sunburn, 36
sunscreen, 136
sweating, 44
Systematic Desensitization (Wolpe), 100–101

T
tail-chasing, 37
tails in body language/communication, 143
Tali, Maarja, xxviii, Estonian National Morning
  Show
tapeworm infestation, 38
target use, 190
"Teaching a Dog to Wear a Muzzle (Muzzle
  Training)" video (Patel), 123, 128
temperament
  for behavior with infants, 248
  dimensions of, 83, 253
  as expression of personality, 253
  genetic basis of, 111, 253
  training (luring) with food, 165
temperature control
  airway malformation effects on, 32
  heatstroke, 44–46
  hyperthermia and hypothermia, 37
  normal and abnormal guidelines, 44
testosterone, 63
The Human Animal Bond Research Institute
  (HABRI), 73
theory of mind (in animals), 80
Three Ds—Duration, Distance and Distraction
  criteria for increasing, 163
  in desensitization and counterconditioning,
    101
  "disappearing" in wait/stay training, 182–183
  dog-dog aggression management, 226
  in open bar/closed bar technique, 232
  separation anxiety treatment, 265–266, 269
  techniques used for, 163
  in training for good behavior, 163

threshold of reactivity. *See* reactivity threshold
throw downs (of treats)
  dog-dog aggression treatment, 227
  for ignoring triggers, 168
thyroidal damage, 116
tonic immobility
  as coping mechanism, 144–145
  mislabeling as good behavior, 251–252
  triggers for, 51, 119
  See also flooding (exposure)
tooth brushing, 60
toys
  hazards from, 42
  as reinforcement for working/sporting dogs,
    169
  stuffing food enrichment toys, 238
  use for training, 115
tracheal injury, 116
trade up and drop
  in aggression treatment, 225
  force-free education/training, 235–236
  with lure-chase toys, 29
  resource guarding management, 235–236
trainers, 114-118
  finding an ethical and competent
    professional, 114
  secrets of, 169–174
training techniques/goals, 162-172
  alternate reward reinforcement, 171
  clicker training option, 172
  concepts in, 163–164
  equipment/techniques to avoid in training,
    115
  food as reward, 117–118, 266-267
  linking behaviors, 171
  "opt out" option, 115
  positive training principles, 116
  random reward reinforcement, 171–172
  safe and effective tools for, 115
  trainer secrets for, 169–174
treat bag, 118, 188
treats
  in clicker training, 173–174
  in housetraining, 152–154
  graduated system for training, 118
  for leash-walking training, 188
  preventing dependence on, 169
  refusal to take, 222, 252

throw-downs of treats in treatment of
    aggression, 227
  use in training, 115
trick training, 163–164
triggers
  for barking, 242
  controlling reaction to, 168
  desensitization technique for, 100–101
  exposure during socialization, 131–132
  exposure to commonly known, 132–133
  generalization of. *See* fear
  identification of, 220
  management of, 218
  modifying antecedent stimuli, 93
  recognition by pet parent, 69
  in separation anxiety, 267–268
  stacking, 69, 230–231
  voice cues for housetraining, 154
trust
  caregiver as safe haven, 69–70
  hormonal basis of, 68
  re-establishing for aggression treatment, 224
  threat perception by dog, 69
"trust hormone". *See* oxytocin
Tudge, Niki (Pet Professional Guild founder)
  functional assessment/analysis process,
    215–216
  functional assessment steps, 215
  operant learning, 95
  respondent learning, 98

U
unintended associative learning, 99
United States National Institute of Play, 76
unsteadiness, 135
unsupervised tethered outdoor time, 37–40
urination. *See* elimination needs; housetraining
urine marking management, 140, 154, 156

V
vaccinations
  socialization with, 120–121
  use of oral, 124
vasopressin, 63
verbal and hand signal pairing, 163, 165, 179
veterinary care, 51-6-, 119-124
  allergy management and treatment, 237–240
  basic and specialty services, 53
  behavior problems and, 53–54

brachycephalic airway syndrome, 31-32
  choosing a professional, 119–124
  consent in husbandry, 82
  dental care, 59–60
  early disease detection by, 52–53
  environmentally enriched clinics, 52
  first appointment, 124
  guidance on aversive training, 55
  Hierarchy of Dog Needs use by, 15–16
  home practice exercises for, 122–123
  for incessant barking, 241
  integrative veterinary medicine, 56–58
  psychiatric medication and brain plasticity,
    58
  report for behavioral consultant, 218
  wellness exam for housetraining regression,
    152
veterinary dentistry. *See* oral/dental care
Veterinary Institute of Integrative Medicine
  (VIIM), 57–58
vocalizations
  with aggression, 201
  with fear, 252
  hyperactive, 222
  signaling with, 86
  snarling, 201
  types and meanings, 143
vomeronasal organ, 86, 138
vomiting
  with allergies, 237
  with heatstroke symptoms, 46, 135
  poison and toxins and, 42
von Holdt, Bridgett
  genetic basis for interest in people, 67–68
  genetic basis of social dog behavior, 75

W
Wait/Stay training
  preparing for baby, 249
  steps for, 181–183
walking. *See* leash-walking
Ward, Katrina, xxviii
water, 24
  at dog park/beaches, 135
  in heatstroke prevention, 45–46
  hydration for metabolic purposes, 24
  quality in the United States, 24–25
Weigle, Karen, use of aversive collars, 17–18
wheelbarrow technique (dog fight), 228

whining/crying
   aggressive warnings, 201
   in anxiety, 247, 259–260
   with baby, 247
   behavior modification for, 97
   hyperactive vocalization, 222
   indication of arousal, 143
   meaning of, 143
whistle training lightning recall, 187. *See also*
  lightning recall
Whole Dog Journal
   "Diets, Dogs, and DCM", 24
   food ratings by, 24
   problems in dog parks, 134, 136
   swimming ability myth, 43
"Why Prong Collars Hurt" (Anderson, Eileen), 30

"Why Shock is Not Behavior Modification"
  (Overall), xxviii
wildlife threats, 38
Williams-Bueren syndrome, 67–68
Wolpe, Joseph (**Systematic Desensitization**),
  100–101
Wynne, Clive (*Dog is Love*), 67

X
xylitol, 42

Y
Yin, Sophia
  on choke chains, 30
  How to Greet a Dog, 250
  publications, 60–61

Printed in the USA
CPSIA information can be obtained
at www.ICGtesting.com
LVHW052350050824
787461LV00041B/1744

9 781732 253704